HOW ETHIOPIA AND AL-SHABAAB CRIPPLED WESTERN EFFORTS IN SOMALIA

HOW ETHIOPIA AND AL-SHABAAB CRIPPLED WESTERN EFFORTS IN SOMALIA

A Senior Somali Commander's Perspective

MAJOR ABDIRAHMAN O. WARSAME "JEENIQAAR"

1446/2025
Leicester, England
Mogadishu, Somalia

LOOH PRESS LTD.
Copyright © Abdirahman O. Warsame "Jeeniqaar" 2025
First Edition, First Print April 2025

All rights reserved.
No part of this publication may be reproduced, stored in any retrieval system, or transmitted in any form or by any means, including photocopying, recording, or other electronic or mechanical methods, without the prior written permission of the publisher, except in the case of brief quotations embodied in critical reviews and certain other non-commercial uses permitted by copyright law.

For permission and requests, write to the publisher or the author, at the address below.

PRINTED & DISTRIBUTED BY
Looh Press Ltd.
Leicester, England. UK
Mogadishu, Somalia
www.LoohPress.com
LoohPress@gmail.com

CONTACT AUTHOR
Westrenefforts@gmail.com

A catalogue record for this book is available from the British Library.
British Library Cataloguing-in-Publication Data

COVER DESIGN & TYPESET
Cover design & typeset : Kusmin (Looh Press)
Editing   : John Jamesson (Looh Press)

ISBN
978-1-912411-53-5   (Hardback)
978-1-912411-54-2   (Paperback)

CONTENTS

Acronyms xi
Dedication xiii
Acknowledgments xv
Forward by by General Salah Jama Hassan "Salah Iiif" xvii
Forward by by Colonel Abdiwahid Mohamud Hassan xix
Forward by by Abdirizak Diriye xxi
Forward by Kamaal Marjaan Ali xxiii
Forward by Sh. Hassan Dhooye xxv
About the Author xxvii
   About My Life & Family xxvii
   Camel Herders xxix
   Education xxx
   About My Parents xxx
Preface xxxi

CHAPTER 1:
GOVERNMENT RELOCATION FROM MPAGATHI, KENYA TO MOGADISHU, SOMALIA 2004 3

   1.1. At the beginning of the Relocation. 7
   1.2. How did President Abdullahi Yusuf address such complex situation? 8
   1.3. The chosen path and the process. 10
   1.4. More TFG from Puntland defection 15
   1.5. Army battalions from Abudwak and Balanbal joined 22
   1.6. Infrastructure challenges 23
   1.7. Difference within TFG 23
   1.8. Relocating Within the Country 27
   1.9. Relocation from Bossaso to Mogadishu 34
   1.10. Ethiopia's sinister intention 35
   1.11. TFG Key Financial Resources in the Absence of Donor Fund 37

CHAPTER 2:
BAYDHABO SUICIDE ATTACK 41

   2.1. How the Attack Happened and What Was the Surrounding Mystery? ..42
   2.2. How the Terrorist Attack Happened 48

CHAPTER 3:
THE DEFEAT OF ISLAMIC COURT UNIONS BY TFG AND MILITARY STRATEGY 57

   3.1. TFG Strategy Deployed to Defeat ICU 58

3.2. ICU's Perspective on TFG Before Their Fight Against ARPCT 61
3.3. TFG Democratic Efforts Vilified by International Media and
     International Organizations..62
3.4. TFG Without the Ethiopian Intervention...62
3.5. TFG Commanders from USA and USSR Military Academies in Baidoa
     and Strategy They Developed 63
3.6. On the Offensive Strategy 65
3.7. On the Defensive Strategy..66

CHAPTER 4:
THE 5TH BRIGADE 73

4.1. Introduction...73
4.2. The 5th Brigade Defense of the Federal Government against ICU
     Forces..74
4.3. How Did the Ferocious War Between the Two Forces Happen?.............75
4.4. Misalignment Between TFG Leaders and ENDF Commanders Over
     How to Proceed to Mogadishu..81

CHAPTER 5:
VILLA SOMALIA... 85

5.1. Introduction...86
5.2. Untrue Diplomatic Picture Between TFG and ENDF Painted by
     Analysts..87
5.3. Ethiopia Denied Violations..87
5.4. From Mogadishu Airport to Villa Somalia 89
5.5. Warlords' Disarmament and Challenges Encountered.........................94

CHAPTER 6:
ASSASSINATION ATTEMPT AGAINST THE PRESIDENT BY
ETHIOPIA IN VILLA SOMALIA.. 101

6.1. Introduction... 101
6.2. Other Events in Villa Somalia, March 2, 2007. 105

CHAPTER 7:
HOW ETHIOPIA'S AGENDA CRIPPLED BOTH SOMALI AND
WESTERN EFFORTS IN STABILIZATION AND STRATEGIC
INTERESTS 109

7.1. Introduction... 110
7.2. Displacement... 113
7.3. The Purpose of Ethiopia's Invasion in Somalia 113
7.4. ICU Forces Melted 115
7.5. TFG Democratic Process Distorted and depicted as Weak
     Government... 116
7.6. The Truth About TFG 117

7.7. A Lost Opportunity 119
7.8. Different Tactics Deployed by Players 119
7.9. The Truth About the Tactics Employed by the TFG and the One Employed by ENDF 121
7.10. Why didn't TFG act this way over the past two years that it had been working in Baidoa and Jowhar? 122
7.11. Humanitarian Access 122
7.12. TFG Before Ethiopian Invasion (Feb, 2005-Dec, 2006) 124
7.13. TFG During Ethiopian Invasion (Dec, 2006-Aug, 2008) 125
7.14. TFG After Ethiopia's Withdrawal (2009 and Beyond) 125
7.15. USA Position in Ethiopia's Invasion of 2006-2009 regarding ENDF indiscriminate killings and bombardments. 127
7.16. Securitization Against TFG: Unexpected Tension between TFG and ENDF Emerged 128
7.17. Unilateral Decision by Ethiopian Forces 132
7.18. Other undermining 134
7.19. Civilian Securitization 134
7.20. Ethiopian Influence on Somalia's Federal Institutions and Broader Political Ecosystem 135
7.21. Salary of the National Army Payment 137
7.22. General Dahir Aden Elmi Indho-Qarsho 138
7.23. Office of the President hit by Katyusha by ENDF 139
7.24. Concealing Evidence of Villa Somalia Bombardment 140
7.25. The arrest of Mogadishu Mayor by Ethiopian Intelligence 140
7.26. SNA and Ethiopian Forces Confrontation Over Indiscriminate Bombardments in Mogadishu 142
7.27. The Confrontation Between SNA and Ethiopian Forces Over a Somali Girl in SYL Hotel 144
7.28. Ethiopia Withdrawal 145
7.29. Proof of How Ethiopia Crippled Both Western and Somali Interests: Performance Evaluation System 146
7.30. Gen Gordon's Strategy 146
7.31. About General Gabre Yohannes Abate: The Ethiopian Troop Commander in Somalia 147
7.32. About ONLF and the so called *"Jail Ogaden"* 151
7.33. General Abdi Qeybdiid Prevents Ethiopian Intelligence from Dismantling Somali Police Force, as done previously done with SNA 152
7.34. How Gen. Abdi Qeybdiid Prevented Ethiopia's Ambition to bring Somali Police Force under Ethiopian control 153
7.35. General Abdi Qeybdiid and President Yusuf 154
7.36. A call from Ethiopian commanders who withdrew from Mogadishu to terrorize TFG 156
7.37. Conclusion 157

7.38. On strategic issues, Ethiopia will be the China of Africa from the Western interests perspective 157

CHAPTER 8:
TRANSITIONING FROM RESISTANCE TO GOVERNMENT AND AL-SHABAAB 163

8.1. Sheikh Sharif Election as a President and the Task I Was Assigned 163
8.2. The TFG after Ethiopia's withdrawal in 2009 167
8.3. The Liberation of Mogadishu 168

CHAPTER 9:
HOW DID OTHER AMISOM FORCES PERFORM IN THE PEACEKEEPING OPERATIONS? 173

9.1. Uganda's Role 175
9.2. Burundi's Role 176
9.3. Djibouti's Role 177
9.4. Kenya's Role 178

CHAPTER 10:
HOW AL-SHABAAB CRIPPLED SOMALIA'S STATE BUILDING PROCESS 183

10.1. How Al-Shabaab Took Advantage of the 4.5 Power Sharing System in Somalia 185
10.2. Revenue Collection 186
10.3. Justice and Al-Shabaab 186
10.4. Al-Shabaab's Use of Direct Deals to Compromise Senior Commanders 187
10.5. How Al-Shabaab Threatens People to Achieve Its Objectives 187
10.6. How Al-Shabaab Crippled Somalia's Election Processes 188
10.7. Parallel Traditional Leaders 189
10.8. Empowering Pro-Al-Shabaab Traditional Leaders 190
10.9. Potential Cases Undertaken by Mr. Ereg 190
10.10. Factors Contributing to Weakening Government Plans Against AS but Enhancing Al-Shabaab Plans' Success: Job Security 190
10.11. Consequences of AS Intermingled with Government 191
10.12. How Al-Shabaab Treats Population Living in Territories Under Their Full Control 192
10.13. Foreign Fighters and Women Marriage 193
10.14. Al-Shabaab and Forestation Program 194
10.15. 14th October Zope Suicide Attack 194
10.16. Al-Shabaab and Ethiopian Collaborations 195
10.17. El Bur District 195
10.18. Moqokori, Another Crucial Town 197

10.19. Ethiopia's unilateral withdrawal and handover of the military bases has been a pattern repeated many times recently across Somalia. 199
10.20. Changing Fortunes 199
10.21. What Al-Shabaab Said About Ethiopia's Withdrawal 200
10.22. What Addis Ababa Said About Its Withdrawal from 10 Military Bases in Central Somalia 200
10.23. What AMISOM Said About Ethiopia's Withdrawal from Its Bases in Central Somalia 201
10.24. How al-Shabaab Blockades Exacerbates Humanaitarian Crisis in Somalia 202
10.25. Millions Facing Starvation as a result of Al Shabaab blockade 203
10.26. ETHIOPIA'S CONNECTION WITH AL-SHABAAB Hilton Hotel – Addis Ababa 205

CHAPTER 11:
EUTM SOMALIA 209

11.1. Misalignment 212

CHAPTER 12:
DANAB SPECIAL FORCES & U.S ROLE 217

12.1. Reestablishment of Danab Special Force: US Army Role 218
12.2. About Infrastructure Development 219
12.3. United States Increases Security Assistance through Construction of SNA Bases 220
12.4. Awdheegle District 222
12.5. Complaint Filed Unprecedented Scale of Rape and Extortion of Money Reported 223
12.6. Awdheegle Operation Meeting Convened 224
12.7. As the Danab Commander, I responded: 225
12.8. Awdheegle Operation Planning Meeting Held in Halane – Mogadishu: Halane Stakeholders Meeting 225
12.9. EU Presentation 226
12.10. AMISOM Sector One Presented 226
12.11. Danab Presented 227
12.12. Conclusion 228
12.13. El-Saliin Operation 229
12.14. One more perception for Danab 231
12.15. On my way to Balidoogle base 231
12.16. Operation Preparation Started (15/07/2019 to 02/08/2019) 232
12.17. 7 days later 232
12.18. Fully prepared to start operations: Awdheegle Operation Take Off . 233
12.19. Oppressed Civilians and Their Feelings After Liberation 234
12.20. Al-Shabaab Attacked Us on 06/08/2019 at 12:00 PM 234
12.21. Awdheegle Bridge Operation 234

12.22. Drawing Scenarios 235
12.23. Al-Shabaab Revenge Attack 235
12.24. Drawing Scenarios: Mission Accomplished 236
12.25. USA Efforts Devoted to the War Against Terrorism in Somalia 236
12.26. Danab: US-trained Somali Special Forces 237
12.27. US Military Expertise 238
12.28. About Danab Special Forces 238
12.29. Reinstitution of Danab Special Force 238
12.30. About the Name Danab "Lightning" 239
12.31. Decision Latitude 239
12.32. Danab Population is Very Limited 240
12.33. Combating Terrorists 240
12.34. Symmetric and Asymmetric Warfare 240
12.35. Joint Military Exercise (US and Danab) 240
12.36. The First Time Danab Was Badly Defeated in the Battlefield 241
12.37. Mission (Jowhar to Beledweyne) 242
12.38. Tuure's justification 243
12.39. Danab at Justified Accord 2024 243

CHAPTER 13: SOMALI NATIONAL ARMY 247

13.1. Gen Gordon strategy 249
13.2. Somali Soldier 249
13.3. General Salah Jama Hassan (Salah liif) SNA commander 2007 – 2008 252
13.4. Ethiopia's Unwillingness to See Effective SNA System and Performance 255

APPENDIX: ARTICLE
HIGHEST COMMENDATION TO DANAB BRIGADE THE SPECIAL FORCE OF SNA. 257

APPENDIX: PICTURES 259

BIBLIOGRAPHY 263

BOOKS: 263
WEBSITE: 263

INDEX 267

ACRONYMS

AMISOM	: African Union Mission in Somalia
ARPCT	: Alliance for the Restoration of Peace and Counter-Terrorism
AS	: Al-Shabaab
ATMIS	: African Union Transition Mission in Somalia
AU	: African Union
BMA	: Bali-Dogle Military Airport
CAS	: Comprehensive Approach to Security
CIED	: Counter Improvised Explosive Device
DANAB	: (Lightning) Somalia Special Forces
EDF	: Ethiopian Defence Force
ENDF	: Ethiopian National Defence Force
EU	: European Union
EUTM	: European Union Training Mission
FGS	: Federal Government of Somalia
FMS	: Federal Member States
HRM	: Human Resource Management
ICU	: Islamic Courts Union
IDPs	: Internally Displaced Persons
IED	: Improvised Explosive Device
IGAD	: Intergovernmental Authority on Development
ISIS	: Islamic State in Syria
KDF	: Kenya Defence Force
MI	: Military Intelligence
MOD	: Ministry of Defence
MSRs	: Main Supply Routes
ONLF	: Ogaden National Liberation Front
SNA	: Somali National Army
SSDF	: Somali Salvation Democratic Front
TFG	: Transitional Federal Government

UN	: United Nations
UNFAO	: United Nations Food and Agriculture Organization
UNSCR	: United Nations Security Council Resolution
UPDF	: Uganda People's Defence Force
USA	: United States of America
USSR	: Former Soviet Union
VBIED	: Vehicle-borne Improvised Explosive Device

DEDICATION

I dedicate this book to the fallen heroes loyal to the people of Somalia and the region during these horribe years.

DEDICATION *Major Abdirahman O. Warsame "Jeeniqaar"*

ACKNOWLEDGMENTS

I would like to thank all the people who have supported me in writing this book.

First and foremost, I acknowledge Mr. Abdirizak Diriye for the tremendous effort he devoted to writing this book. Without him, this book could not have been completed. I also thank Bashiir Suuley, Mohamed Maare, Kamaal Ahmed Ali (Kamaal Murjaan), Dr. Omar Abdi Bare (PhD), the late Major Mohamed Abdiwahid Farah, and the late Mohamed Abdiasiis Ispariije.

I acknowledge Kamaal A. Ali for his valuable advice and encouragement. Other key contributors include General Mohamed Ali Buh and the late Major Mohamed Abdiwahid Farah, who unfortunately passed away recently before the book's publication.

Finally, I acknowledge the support and encouragement extended to me by many friends and colleagues in writing this book.

ACKNOWLEDGMENTS *Major Abdirahman O. Warsame "Jeeniqaar"*

FORWARD

This is the right book at the right time. The author has put forth tremendous effort in collecting and preparing such valuable information about what happened over those years. He is a courageous major. I am particularly impressed by the extent to which the author was informed about what was happening in the Somali security sector during those years, when I was among the key leaders holding an SNA commander position. He provides details about challenges posed to us by Ethiopian National Defence Force commanders and their hidden agenda meant merely to undermine Somalia and its SNA. Despite being a victim of Ethiopia's influence on both the political and security sectors of the country and their naked securitization moves, which led to my resignation from the SNA commander position, the author effectively sheds light on how ENDF and Al-Shabaab interests converged and unified their efforts in destroying the SNA. This included, but was not limited to, the supply of unlimited ammunition and other materials to Al-Shabaab by Ethiopia.

The book will be helpful for both current and future generations in Somalia. It will also be useful for Western countries who have been relentlessly helping Somalia to stand on its own feet to better understand how their allies in the region behaved. This is the right book for everyone willing to have an in-depth understanding of Somalia and the region.

It will also be helpful for international and regional policy institutions, military experts, diplomats, as well as congressmen involved in foreign policies. It provides sufficient and powerful insights on security and politics in the region and strategic interests. I advise those I mentioned above to have their own copies on their desks for making better and more informed decisions.

General Salah Jama Hassan "Salah liif"
Somali National Army Commander 2007–2008

FORWARD

The author of the book really triggered my brain to recall both the horrible challenges and crucial success processes we underwent together during the Transitional Federal Government. He put forth immense effort to document exhaustively what happened over past decades both politically and militarily. He decided to take such responsibility to document crucial events including those Ethiopia and Al-Shabaab collectively and intentionally conducted to undermine both Western and Somalia's strategic interests. The collaboration they forged together was aimed at destroying the TFG. Among these include the indelible Katyusha bombardment on both the civilian highly populated areas and Villa Somalia where the president and his government had been operating.

He particularly mentioned in a clear way in his book how Ethiopia weakened the SNA and empowered Al-Shabaab, which still reverberates in our ears. The author wrote nearly all challenges that the TFG encountered in its time, primarily those posed by ENDF and Al-Shabaab, though many people perceived Ethiopia came to Somalia to help the TFG. The author and I had been working together in the office of the president, serving as Special Presidential Guard and Chief Protocol of the office of the president respectively, although I eventually accompanied the president to Yemen after his resignation and finally resorted to emigrating to the USA.

Colonel Abdiwahid Mohamud Hassan
Chief Protocol Office of the President

FORWARD

The author presents untold challenges in Somalia's state and peacebuilding processes posed by Ethiopia and the al-Qaida affiliated group called Al-Shabaab, providing valuable insights which will enable Western countries to reflect and rethink about the way they viewed the region in terms of their policies and strategic interests. The author exposes the truth of what happened in Somalia over the past decade, the great misalignment of Western interests and the interests of various players in the Horn of Africa. He reveals how the political and security landscape evolved over time and the different rules of the game being played. How different players acted and what options were taken in different circumstances.

He particularly focuses on how Ethiopia and Al-Shabaab's interests converged and undermined Western interests in Somalia and the desirable future state of Somalia. He explains how their collective efforts undermined and eventually destroyed the Somalia state and peace building processes and the SNA. The author states clearly the true competence and capabilities of the TFG, particularly how the powerful leadership of President Abdullahi Yusuf and democratic processes applied had been successful, but were vilified by international and regional media outlets, whether wittingly or unwittingly. The book exposes particularly how the divergent Ethiopian agenda and the Western agenda were operating within the same political and security ecosystem in Somalia and how Ethiopia undermined its Western ally.

It further states how Ethiopia will be a threat against Western interests in Somalia and the region now and in the future based on analysis spanning several decades, including how Ethiopia behaved over past decades through Western blind eyes. The insights presented will help Ethiopia's Western allies become enlightened about how different players behaved in the security and political landscape in Somalia, thus reviewing and reframing the way they view it. It demonstrates how crucial it is to rethink and realign future strategic interests and positions on the region.

Abdirizak Diriye
Former Somali Diplomat

FORWARD

A rare state collapse and national fragmentation of the scale witnessed in Somalia remains one of the most misunderstood crises in modern history—both locally and internationally. Whether through deliberate distortion or unintentional neglect, the Somali conflict and the long struggle for stability have often been misinterpreted due to misinformation, lack of access to authentic voices, and misguided perceptions. This book stands out as a bold and courageous attempt to uncover the untold truths, real forces, and hidden factors that have shaped Somalia's prolonged misfortune.

Written by **Abdirahman Jeeniqaar**, a former camel herder turned soldier—born amidst crossfire and displacement—this work is not only a personal journey but a historical document of national significance. Coming from a family uprooted by the civil wars that erupted after the collapse of Siad Barre's regime, Jeeniqaar joined the military at just 18 years old. He was among the first personnel involved in establishing the Puntland government and later rose to become a senior officer within Somalia's reemerging federal security apparatus. Through his vantage point as an insider, he presents an unfiltered, firsthand account of events that many stakeholders have chosen to obscure or forget.

FORWARD

This book is not simply a memoir or a security report—it is a raw, truthful, and deeply human narrative. It recounts pain, miracles, strategic decisions, betrayal, moments of awe, and historical turning points. Much of what is shared here has either been witnessed directly by the author or experienced in close proximity. His insights offer a crucial key to understanding why, after decades of international engagement, Somalia's search for stability remains unresolved. Jeeniqaar squarely identifies foreign interference and the exploitation of Somalia's vulnerability as the central barrier to recovery.

Having spent 20 years in journalism and writing—analyzing Somali political history and its evolving realities—I recall the oft-repeated phrase, "Somalis are an oral people." While perhaps romanticized by colonial perspectives, this notion was once accurate: our history was proudly preserved through poetry, oral literature, and cultural memory. But as these traditions faded and modern education was weakened by war, the spoken word alone proved insufficient to capture and preserve truth. In this vacuum, foreign analysts and external narratives became dominant—often relying on secondhand sources, sometimes distorted or even intentionally misleading.

What makes this book particularly important is that it does **not** rely on speculation. It is a direct witness account. This matters, especially for young Somalis, researchers, policy-makers, and anyone seeking to understand the hidden layers of Somalia's political and security story. Too often, the voices of those who saw the events with their own eyes have been lost—taking with them essential truths. This book defies that pattern. It opens a critical space for Somalis to reclaim authorship of their own narrative and dares others to do the same.

For decision-makers, scholars, researchers, and especially the new generation of Somalis who struggle to access reliable, firsthand documentation of their nation's recent past—this book is essential reading. Read it. Reflect on it. And let it inform your understanding of Somalia's complex history and its uncertain, yet hopeful, future.

Kamaal Marjaan Ali
Senior journalist, translator, and
writer of multiple published books

FORWARD

I had the privilege to read the unpublished manuscript **How Ethiopia & Al-Shabaab Crippled Western Efforts in Somalia.** by **Major Abdirahman O. Warsame "Jeeniqaar"** This book is nothing short of a landmark work. Authored by a living witness and senior Somali commander, it unveils the hidden agendas and enduring hostility Ethiopia has harbored toward Somali statehood. The author courageously documents how Ethiopia exploited the war on Al-Shabaab as a strategic cover to sabotage Somalia's progress and manipulate international support. Most striking is the book's compelling evidence suggesting covert collaboration between Ethiopia and Al-Shabaab—an alliance that devastated both Somali and Western aspirations for peace and stability.

This is not just a book; it is a national treasure and a historical testimony from one of Somalia's patriotic sons. I strongly recommend that Somali government institutions archive this work and consult it as a reference when formulating policies or negotiating with Ethiopia. It is a vital contribution to our national memory and strategic future.

Would you like a version in Somali as well?

Sh. Hassan Dhooye,
Respected Imam and well-known leader.

FORWARD *Major Abdirahman O. Warsame "Jeeniqaar"*

ABOUT THE AUTHOR

About My Life & Family

I was born in 1978 in Goldogob, a village west of Galkaio. The circumstances of my birth were fascinating: Somali special forces were conducting an operation against a group of Somali Salvation Democratic Front (SSDF) members, including my father, Omar Warsame Adde, who were recruiting new soldiers to topple Siad Barre's regime. The Somali Military Intelligence (MI) guided these operations. The MI was so powerful in that former president Abdulahi Yusuf, who was the SSDF commander, acknowledged their competence, as they influenced him to use an Ethiopian passport during his struggle—a decision that led to his arrest by the Ethiopian government for six years on claims he was an Ethiopian national.

Just before the special forces operation began, my father and two colleagues, Mohamed Somali and Abdi Ali Warsame (Wiile), left the recruitment venue that was under attack by Danab to visit me, a newborn baby boy. Decades later, I would become the commander of these very same Danab Special Forces that had once attacked my father and his companions. Fortunately, these two men became the only survivors of the special forces operation launched from Dhusamareeb district. My family escaped immediately from Goldogob to Wardheer village in the Somali region of Ethiopia, where SSDF maintained a military training camp with Ethiopian support.

Due to harsh conditions and severe lack of nutritious food in Wardheer, both my mother and I suffered extensively. I lived with prolonged illness and developed a stunted appearance. People believed I would not survive these conditions. My mother conceived again pregnance and gave birth to my sister, Ruqiyo Omar Warsame, 2 years later.

Wardheer was a war zone with frequent attacks by the Somali Army. SSDF built numerous military trenches for protection against heavy artillery shelling from the Somali army, which supported continuous infantry attacks. When war broke out between the attacking Somali army and SSDF fighters, artillery shelling would follow immediately and cause severe damages, death and destruction. As a result, Civilians had no choice but to seek shelter in the trenches to survive from the shelling One morning around 10 AM, fierce fighting unexpectedly erupted between the two sides, followed by immediate shelling that sent everyone, including my mother carrying my young sister, running toward the trenches. Once inside, my mother scanned the trenches and didn't see me anywhere. She immediately realized I had been left behind.

She yelled, "Where is my son?" Then she laid down my sister and ran out of the trenches, through crossfire, to grab me. The Somali army, which had dominated the battlefield, captured us. They treated us humanely and transferred us to their main base, where my mother Hawo Dirie Gehle encountered an extended family member serving as a commander. The commander immediately ordered that my mother and I be airlifted to Mogadishu along with wounded soldiers for treatment. Hours later, we received treatment at Martin Military Hospital, which then referred us to Ansaloti Public Hospital, managed and supported by the Finnish government. I saw President Siad Barre when he visited the injured soldiers at Martini Hospital.

The Finnish doctors devoted significant attention to us and provided extensive treatment for six months. Without them, I could never have achieved the numerous successes in my life nor become who I am today. I was discharged from the hospital six months later, which opened the door to educational opportunities. I began my basic education two years later and continued until 1991, when civil war broke out and Siad

Barre was ousted by SSDF and other armed opposition groups such as USC. The Finnish doctors and military commanders who airlifted us to Mogadishu played a pivotal role in ensuring my mother and I survived to receive treatment and education.

Camel Herders

Following the civil war that erupted in 1991 in Somalia and the subsequent collapse of the central government, my family fled from Mogadishu to Galkaio, where we resumed our ancestral occupation as camel herders. We joined other pastoralists who herded camels for their livelihood. Herding camels carried great responsibility as it was central to both livelihood and economic growth. We relied on camel production to survive and prosper. Disputes over camel management led me to protest and leave the business permanently. I instead decided to join the army and build a new career. In late 1996, i arrived to Galhamur, a village in the reserve area from a rural area in between Burtinle and Lascaanood where i used to herd our camels. Abdulahi Yusuf was recruiting a new army at Galhamur for Puntland. I enlisted and was brought to Galkaio, with other recruits. I was then included to a group sent to Balibusle, near Jariiban. I spent six months there receiving my first military training.

After completing my training, I was placed in the 54th division as a new cadet. I was then selected to join the presidential escort. I became part of the presidential guard's inner circle when Abdulahi Yusuf was Puntland's president. I rose to the hierarchy and become commander of presidential security. I was sent to several academies to improve my skills and competencies in presidential special guard duties within the country. I held different ranks within the presidential security guard, including special unit commander and special commander of the Office of the President. As I grew closer to the president, particularly during Ethiopia's invasion from December 2006 through late 2008, I witnessed the horrible and catastrophic way that Ethiopian Defence Forces treated to both the Somali people and the Somali government including indiscriminate shelling of artilaries and massive killing of civilians across the country. The unimaginable hostility within the historic enmity framework that Ethiopia used to treat the people and government of Somalia, and the fig leaf of claiming to help Somalia fight terrorists, but it aimed to weaken increasingly the SNA and empowering the the terrorist compelled me to write this book.

My other remarkable positions included I work SNA foreign relation department, and Control Centre leadership, Rapid Response Forces Commander, and ultimately Danab Special Force Commander. As Somali Special Force commander, I led several key operations to liberate territories from terrorists across large geographical areas in South Central Somalia, in coordination with U.S. Africom Command.

Education

I completed my basic education in Mogadishu before the central government's collapse in 1991. I later resumed my secondary education in Galkacyo before joining the Puntland Defense Force (PDF) army. While serving as a senior military soldier at Villa Somalia, I earned my first degree in public administration from Hope University in Mogadishu from 2016 to 2020. In subsequent years, I attended numerous military courses at various academies, including those in Uganda, Rwanda, and Turkey.

About My Parents

My mother's priority was ensuring my safety. She was a beautiful young woman who loved my life more than her own. The Somalia National Army acted ethically when they spotted her in the middle of crossfire, saving her life and providing wonderful assistance to both of us. While we often heard of the SNA's severe mistreatment of women in the battlefield, our experience showed the opposite. My father was a well-known figure in the region and beyond. He was both a pastoralist and businessman, highly respected for his impartiality in local communal conflicts and his ability to generate appropriate solutions to potential challenges. This brief summary of my personal background illuminates what drove me to write this book and my access to decision-making areas.

PREFACE

This book comprises thirteen chapters, arranged to help readers understand the sequence of events and trajectory of Somalia's security and political ecosystems and how different players undermined collective Western efforts in Somalia. With the support of the international community, a Somali National Reconciliation Conference was held in Kenya between October 2002 and 2004 to form a new government for Somalia to prevent terrorists from taking advantage of the existing vacuum.

Chapter One begins with the Somali Government's relocation from Mpagathi, Kenya, to Mogadishu, enabling readers to understand how events evolved and how Western efforts failed to achieve their anticipated results. In this chapter, we examine how the Transitional Federal Government (TFG) leadership managed to survive in the absence of all prerequisite mechanisms, infrastructures, and resources. The TFG leaders started from scratch, facing unprecedented political differences and lacking public infrastructure to operate and fulfill desperately needed services. This chapter details how the Somali government addressed the relocation process from 2004 to 2006, and how Ethiopia distorted this genuine relocation process when invited to help fight the Islamic Courts Union in December 2006. During this process, Ethiopia hijacked the transition, presenting itself as having enabled the TFG to reach Mogadishu, and used this as a cynical fig leaf to subsequently destroy both the TFG's efforts and the international community's commitment to stabilize the country.

Chapter Two examines the Baidoa suicide attack and assassination attempts against President Abdullahi Yusuf Ahmed.

Chapter Three analyzes how the Union of Islamic Courts was defeated and the military strategy deployed by Somalia National Army (SNA) leaders.

Chapter Four: 5th Brigade. This chapter examines the role of the 5th Army in the relocation process and its position as the cornerstone that enabled the TFG to relocate to Villa Somalia from Garowe between 2004 and 2006.

Chapter Five: Villa Somalia. This chapter covers the challenges TFG leaders faced in their efforts to recover Villa Somalia and convince people to peacefully hand over the compound.

Chapter Six: Assassination Attempt Against the President by Ethiopia in Villa Somalia.

Chapter Seven investigates how Ethiopia's agenda crippled Western and Somali interests.

Chapter Eight: Transitioning from Resistance to Government and Al-Shabaab. This chapter presents how part of the Islamic Courts Union evolved into Al-Shabaab terrorists affiliated with Al-Qaeda.

Chapters Seven and Ten particularly examine how Ethiopian government forces and Al-Shabaab terrorists collectively crippled Western efforts to stabilize the country. These chapters expose the truth about Al-Shabaab terrorists, their behavior, attitudes, culture, and mistreatment of people living in territories under their control. They further expose collaboration between the two to weaken Somalia and the SNA.

Chapter Nine: How Other AMISOM Forces Performed in Peacekeeping Operations. This chapter covers the role of other African Union Mission in Somalia (AMISOM) peacekeeping forces (Kenya, Uganda, Burundi, and Djibouti).

Chapters Eleven, Twelve, and Thirteen examine the EUTM role, the value created by the European Union Training Mission (EUTM) Somalia, while examining how Ethiopia undermined their efforts to make Somalia a peaceful, stable, prosperous democratic nation. They also cover the U.S. role, particularly the US-trained special force Danab, and finally the SNA, including the challenges they encountered in their efforts to protect citizens and maintain resilience against Ethiopia's sinister intentions.

CHAPTER 1

GOVERNMENT RELOCATION *from* MPAGATHI, KENYA *to* MOGADISHU, SOMALIA 2004

[MAP 1: Somalia.][1]

---

1. Human Rights Watch, "So Much to Fear: War Crimes and the Devastation of Somalia," December 8, 2008, https://www.hrw.org/report/2008/12/08/so-much-fear/war-crimes-and-devastation-somalia

CHAPTER 1

GOVERNMENT RELOCATION *from* MPAGATHI, KENYA *to* MOGADISHU, SOMALIA 2004

> Institutions built by bayonet will not last long, but those built on democratic values take root and become sustainable and productive.

Following a reconciliation process that lasted two years between 2002 and 2004, which brought together all Somali politicians, civil society organizations, and warlords, a new government was formed on October 14, 2004.

Colonel Abdullahi Yusuf was elected and sworn in as president of Somalia in October 2004 in Nairobi. The newly

[**Fig. 1:** Right: Colonel Abdullahi Yusuf being sworn in as president of Somalia in October 2004 in Nairobi.]

formed government, led by President Yusuf and his Prime Minister Ali Mohamed Ghedi, faced the formidable challenge of relocating from Nairobi to Mogadishu—one of the toughest situations the president had ever encountered in his life. The TFG came under pressure from Kenya's government and Western diplomats to move to Mogadishu. The new cabinet approved the deployment of 5,000 to 7,000 foreign troops to help restore law and order in the country. A team of MPs also arrived in Mogadishu to assess the situation.[2]

[**Fig. 2:** Left: President Abdullahi Yusuf arriving at Garowe airport for his first visit as president of Somalia, marking the first step of the relocation process.]

As reported by IRIN on February 9, 2005, the Transitional Federal Government set February 21, 2005, as its relocation date. The report stated that Somalia's transitional federal government planned to start relocating from Nairobi, Kenya, to Mogadishu on February 21. Prime Minister Ali Muhammad Gedi announced, "We will begin relocating on that date, depending on support from the donor community." This

---

2. IRIN News, "Somalia: TFG Preparing to Begin Operating from Jowhar," The New Humanitarian, accessed January 25, 2025, https://www.thenewhumanitarian.org/report/55029/somalia-tfg-preparing-begin-operating-jowhar.

statement was made in Nairobi during the signing of a declaration of principles for cooperation with the international community.[3]

Unfortunately, not a single soldier from the 7,000 foreign troops requested by the Transitional Federal Government arrived until December 2006, when Ethiopia intervened in Somalia for its own strategic interests. Leaders often face tremendous challenges in their lifetime and to solve mysterious situations and circumstances they find themselves in. However, the challenges that Abdullahi Yusuf experienced in the relocation process from Nairobi to Mogadishu were devastating and unique—a situation that no leader had ever faced in recent history. The TFG never received all the pledges made by regional and international communities during the relocation process.

Although not received as planned, "A budget for relocation has been drawn up and handed over to donors." The declaration of principles was signed by Somali Prime Minister Ali Mohamed Gedi and the acting representative of the UN Secretary-General for Somalia, Babafemi Badejo.[4]

In light of the international community's support gap in both financial and military assistance, the newly elected President Abdullahi Yusuf chose a democratic approach (inclusive and broader participation dialogue) and began seeking people's endorsement for the new government across the country, except in Somaliland regions. However, a group of Somaliland military officers and approximately 250 army personnel would later join the relocation process and be part of the reconstituted new SNA. During this period, he encountered numerous opportunities and challenges.

These challenges include the wrong assumption as if Kenya and Somalia were two equal countries. Although the formation of the new government in Mpagathi, Kenya took two years, Kenya was a developing country with relatively strong institutions in place and a law-abiding society. Somalia, in contrast, had no functioning public infrastructure

---

3. IRIN News, "Somalia: TFG Preparing to Begin Operating from Jowhar," The New Humanitarian, February 9, 2005, https://www.thenewhumanitarian.org/report/55029/somalia-tfg-preparing-begin-operating-jowhar.
4. IRIN News, "Somalia: TFG Preparing to Begin Operating from Jowhar," The New Humanitarian, February 9, 2005, https://www.thenewhumanitarian.org/report/55029/somalia-tfg-preparing-begin-operating-jowhar.

that could enable the government to function and implement its new plans to deliver crucial services.

In Somalia, civilians who had little knowledge of the newly formed government and were often opposed to it had been using former government offices as shelters and for other purposes for almost two decades. Finding unoccupied government buildings and convincing civilians to vacate them proved to be a formidable task—simple to propose but difficult to execute. All members of the international community—including the EU, USA, AU, Arab League, and others—pressured President Yusuf and his government to quickly relocate from Kenya to Mogadishu ignoring absence of infrastructure to use in order government start its operations. However, despite this international pressure, it was obvious that there were no public infrastructures in Mogadishu or other provinces for the government to operate from. No one was able to design a viable model that would enable the new President and his government to relocate to Mogadishu and begin functioning. Initially, even President Yusuf and his government teams had no clear strategy for the relocation, let alone the international community. No one could offer a practical solution for moving from Nairobi to Mogadishu, where there was no supporting infrastructure for the new government to operate. The agreement laid out the obligations of the transitional government and the international community in their dealings with each other. "This signing today represents an important development in which the TFG met a major requirement of donor community for support," Badejo told IRIN.[5]

"The intention of the declaration is to set goalposts by which the government's progress will be judged, and to assess the international community's fulfillment of its own obligations to the government," Bethuel Kiplagat, Kenya's special envoy for the Somali peace process, told IRIN.[6] The international community's conclusion was simple: having invested in the reconciliation process and formed a new government, they insisted the president must return to his country. However, they

---

5. IRIN News, "Somalia: TFG Preparing to Begin Operating from Jowhar," The New Humanitarian, February 9, 2005, https://www.thenewhumanitarian.org/report/55029/somalia-tfg-preparing-begin-operating-jowhar.
6. Ibid

offered neither a supporting road map from the UN nor the international community. No one considered that this government, formed outside the country, needed to win legitimacy from the people to operate in Somalia. This was among the key factors that TFG leaders considered prerequisite to forming an inclusive government that could develop informed reconstruction and development plans. Another significant challenge was the informed reports issued by various entities, including UN agencies and human rights organizations, blaming the government for failing to deliver services. These reports continuously vilified the TFG democratic process as weak, noting it only controlled Jowhar and Baidoa. They never viewed the situation from different angles or deployed multifaceted lenses to carry out a proper diagnostic of the environment and landscape in which the TFG operated. While these reports were partly useful, they wrongly criticized the TFG's democratic process, which could have resulted in sustainable democratic institutions.

Abdullahi Yusuf was shocked, having no idea how to proceed with the relocation process. If you find yourself in such a scenario, what would you do to relocate your government from Nairobi to Mogadishu and make it function? Key aspects and characteristics that distinguish a leader from a manager are their personalities, leadership skills, and attributes that enable them to overcome situations with reduced risks.

1.1. At the beginning of the Relocation.

Unlike what international partners had anticipated, President Abdullahi Yusuf traveled to Garowe, headquarters of Puntland state, instead of Mogadishu. Garowe was his constituency, where people offered him unwavering financial and logistical support.

His plane landed at Garowe Airport at around 7 pm, shockingly the airport had no light and visibility to enable the pilot to land the plane safely. However, a group of vehicles were brought to the airport runway to shed light to the runway and eventually after several attempts the pilot managed the safely land the airplane and Meanwhile, he sent his prime minister to Mogadishu, where the prime minister's clan predominantly controlled everything, including government infrastructure. Despite the prime minister's move to Mogadishu along with some cabinet ministers and legislators, the problems extended beyond the absence of required infrastructure that would enable them to function properly and deliver services. They encountered a tepid welcome from the public. The major issue was legitimacy, as this government was not only formed outside the country but also had not been elected by the people. As such, the government first needed to win public trust and support. They lacked a well-thought-out plan about the way forward, and their actions were merely motivated by the president's decision to relocate the government back to Mogadishu.

This is because it not only lacks critical infrastructure but also suffers from negative public perception regarding the newly formed government. Due to lack of inclusivity and broader participation, people had difficulty figuring out how they could offer their support and why they should trust the government. Only a few people understood the importance of the new government and the value it might create for greater Somalia. Abdullahi Yusuf's main tasks included bringing together different players on the ground—those who supported him, those who opposed him, and those who were apathetic about the newly formed government—in order to form an inclusive government that could engender people's trust. Other players with conflicting interests whom the TFG was supposed to engage included regional countries. In such a context, the position of the international community was merely to instruct the TFG to relocate back to Mogadishu, function properly, and deliver pressing basic services.

1.2. How did President Abdullahi Yusuf address such complex situation?

He has chosen a democratic path. The president traveled to Garowe from Nairobi and, together with his team, began gathering information about potential players—whether military officers, prominent persons, former civil servants, or politicians across Somalia—to engage with and convince them to participate in and support the government relocation process, including the reconstitution of the SNA and the state-building process. From Garowe to Mogadishu, the president planned with his prime minister and cabinet members to engage senior military officers, intellectuals, business people, and traditional leaders for consultation, inviting them to join the government and support its relocation to Mogadishu to function properly. The goal was for the government to relocate and operate in Villa Somalia, the main premises of the Somali presidency in Mogadishu.

The objective was to govern the nation from the Somalia presidency and reinstall government institutions, delivering on promises made including education, water, health, justice, and other key infrastructure building such as airports and ports to meet people's pressing issues in the complex and rapidly changing environment. This meant that everything had to start from scratch in the absence of crucial support from the people that the government would serve. It was not easy to achieve such goals while there was no clarity of the process, including the priorities and sequence of key steps, and without shared meaning and purpose among all key stakeholders. This was accompanied by an extreme shortage of resources to implement any given set of plans. However, in the light of democratic processes to gain legitimacy through broadened inclusive and participative processes by TFG leaders and through working in under-resourced circumstances, there had been many vilified reports against the TFG issued by well-trusted institutions, for instance:

- The timing of the ICU's attacks on Baidoa in late 2006 suggests that the action was intended to wipe out the TFG before the arrival of the international peacekeeping force authorized by UNSCR 1725. From the perspective of the ICU, the AMISOM force was an attempt by the international community to legitimize and bolster the faltering TFG. The ICU was the de facto authority in Somalia while the TFG, incapable of exerting control beyond Baidoa, appeared to enjoy broad support internationally.[7]

This was an uninformed narrative, which deliberately vilified the powerful democratic process applied by the TFG since February 2005, in which it gained more support and legitimacy from all regions in Puntland and south central Somalia. The proof is that between February 2005 and December 2006, the TFG reconstituted 11,500 SNA forces from across Somalia, and there was no hostility by the people who contributed SNA forces. There was no hostility against the TFG in all those regions. So anyone labeling the TFG as faltering and weak, controlling only Baidoa and not all of Somalia, must have considered that *"Institutions built by*

---

7. Ethiopia (Ethiopia's intervention in Somalia) 2006-2009, page 137

bayonet will not last long, but those built on democratic values take root and become sustainable and productive."

The proof emerged when ENDF withdrew from Mogadishu by the end of 2009, and the country was just as it was in December 2006, everywhere under the control of ICU and other insurgents. TFG forces were recognized as the only reliable and effective forces who could fight with ICU and other insurgents, and eventually the TFG had been used to liberate Mogadishu without the support of ENDF. This shows that even in December 2006 when Ethiopia invaded Somalia, it was an unnecessary intervention, as the TFG, despite being vilified by international and regional actors, was sufficient to defeat ICU alone without inflicting shelling, displacement, and death on the people in Mogadishu. Ethiopia's most critical strategic mistake during the conflict was its unilateral support of the TFG and its attempt to supplant the ICU with an ineffectual regime. Fragmented, corrupt, and unpopular with the local populace, the TFG, ushered into power by force with the aid of a nation considered by many Somalis to be the enemy, had no long-term viability as a governing power (Ethiopia's intervention in Somalia). President Abdullahi Yusuf set out from Garoowe for Mogadishu bearing the responsibility for relocating the government to the capital city of Somalia, Mogadishu.[8]

1.3. The chosen path and the process.

It was 2005, the place is called **Abqale**, a military training camp in Puntland, Somalia. At sunset, the first destination was Galkaio. About 5,000 trained forces, initially planned for Puntland under the name of Puntland Defense Forces, were now ready to be deployed to Mogadishu to facilitate the relocation process. The president led the relocation process, accompanied by his Prime Minister Ali Mohamed Ghedi, the then Puntland President General Ado Muse, and a number of cabinet ministers and legislators. From Garowe to Galkaio, which is in the Mudug region of Somalia. Immediately upon our arrival at Gaalkacyo, my presidential gua0rds were instructed to step down and join the 5th brigade, which was from Ari-adeye and Abesaley of the Sool region. Before we continued our journey, the president addressed the army and

---

8. Ethiopia (Ethiopia's intervention in Somalia) 2006-2009, page 137

made a historic speech in Galkaio. He emphasized in his speech that the brigade was the foundation of a new Somali National Army that would be created to defend the country and the nation from domestic and foreign enemies. The president said that they didn't represent the whole of Somalia and there was a need to create an army comprising people from across Somalia.

To show empathy to us, the president disbanded his own presidential guard, informing us that we would go to Mogadishu on foot, while the next destination would be Wardheer, then Shilabo, and then Fadhiyare, where small army units led by Colonel Mohamed Adan Bidaar and Colonel Abdirizak Muse Hirsi had been awaiting us and were tasked to work as intelligence units in contact and collaboration with Ethiopian counterparts. In his speech, the president provided us details of our journey and the objectives and reasons why we were being deployed to Mogadishu. He further emphasized the unique characteristics and behavior we must exhibit during the course of our journey to Mogadishu. He also instructed high-ranking officers about their roles and responsibilities, including allowing very limited units of the army to access weapons to provide security for the wider army until they joined other army units mobilized from other districts such as Jowhar, Beledweyne, Abduwak, Balanbale, and Dhusomareeb. His intention was to equip the whole army at once to show them equal access to weapons and logistics to create trust. Only a few units from the 5th brigade and 54th were allowed to get access to weapons and ammunition to protect the remaining army in case of an attack as they moved toward different destinations.

Although it was a very tough democratic journey in which the president personally engaged with all stakeholders in collaboration with his prime minister and cabinet members, no one considered this an important process that could pave the way for a sustainable and inclusive government that would enjoy a degree of legitimacy rather than coercing people and forcing them to accept a government they never voted for. The international community and international agencies never view this process as valuable, and they kept labeling the TFG as weak, claiming it didn't control the country except for Jowhar and Baidoa. However, the army perceived the president's speech in different ways, including:

1. Some understood the speech, given the complex environment ahead from Puntland to Mogadishu or Banaadir, as a path from which there was no return.
2. The second group was shocked as to why only a few units were allowed to access weapons while the risks moving from Puntland were notorious and very high.
3. The third group was my team, who were trained as presidential guards and now instructed to go along with the other army, while we thought we would accompany the president and other government officials and use vehicles instead of traveling on foot.

Puntland's President Ade Muse also addressed the army and explained the reward and punishment policy, stating that each and every soldier should adhere to orders and exhibit appropriate behavior. He warned that any attempt to defect from the army with weapons, ammunition, or vehicles would result in being brought before a military court and facing severe punishment.

Hearing such warning, close to 50 soldiers announced they were not willing to go to Mogadishu, which resulted in President Ade Muse issuing an arrest order. They were immediately taken to Garowe detention cells for prosecution. As a presidential guard commander, I proposed to President Ade Muse, the then Puntland President, that at least two vehicles and a group from my team remain and keep the security of the president and other officials until they took off from the airport. This group and the two vehicles would later rejoin the army in Wardheer. However, President Ade Muse accepted my proposal but demanded the following:
1. From this point to Galkaio, Puntland President's security guards would escort President Abdullahi Yusuf.
2. They were required to commit to the president's security escort as their primary responsibility.

We agreed to ensure the safety and security of the president and not to abandon him as such. However, the prime minister, Mr. Ali Mohamed Ghedi, came up with a similar proposal that there should also be some presidential guards to travel with the president and himself.

Senior military officers who were accompanying the president in his travel to Jowhar included the following officers:

1. General Osman Hassan Ali (Afdalow)
2. Late Col. Abdirizak Mohamed Hersi (Garcad)
3. Col. Abdiwahid Mohamud Hassan Lugey
4. Late Col. Ali Abdi Guled (Ali Duguf)
5. Col. Dahir Mohamed Hersi (Dahir Faruur)
6. Late Mahad Abdullahi Farah Urdan (Mahad Doorshe)
7. Late Captain Abdirashid Hersi Mohamed
8. Abdulkadir Ali Yusuf Lugey
9. Harawe Ali Jiriban
10. Lt. Abdisaid Farah Gure
11. Abdirizak Mohamud Gaylan
12. Mohamed Bashir Bidaar
13. Abdikarim Khaliif Abdi Dhala
14. Abdishakur Ali Jariiban
15. Farah Abdikadir Diriye Warfaa (Farey Geesood)
16. Iro Gaagaab Aw-Jaamac
17. Abdilahi Gees-Dheer
18. Cpt. Said Hassan Osman (Gururub)
19. Lt. Abdi Asis Jinni Irale
20. Late Maj. Farah Ahmed Dari (Farah Caan)
21. Asiya Mohamud Hassan
22. Said Mohamed Aden
23. Gaydho Hassan Hashi
24. Fanah Isse Aley

These were the first senior military team who arrived in Jowhar, and they were composed of senior-ranking military officers, file soldiers, and the president's protocol unit. There was also another notable diaspora group who traveled to Jowhar from Nairobi to contribute to the relocation process, including:

1. Hussein Ali Saylaan
2. Mohamed-Deek Abdul Ahmed
3. Abdirizak Durqun
4. Hussein Huub Sireed
5. Sanwayne Ali Hashi Geele
6. Amino Deeble
7. Madahey Abdulahi Omar Bootaan
8. Diraa Hussein Fagaase

9. Daahir Mire Jibriil
10. Aadan Isse Hadde Aadan Dhagah
11. Sureer Abdi Firin
12. Ahmed Bow Bowle
13. Abdullahi Farabadane (Abdullahi Dheere)
14. Dr. Mohamud Yusuf Wayrah former Minister of Finance of Somali Republic
15. Abdiqafaar Yaasiin Farah Yaaquub (Gacamey), who would lose his hand in a suicide attack that would take place in Baydhabo on September 18, 2006.

Following a long journey between Abqaale and Wardheer, we finally arrived at the Qurac Gafow area, an area appropriate for a military base. We then continued our journey from Wardheer to Shilaabo.

We arrived at Wardheer early in the morning, and several hours later we came to Garlogubey. Garlogubey is 38 km south of Wardheer. We continued our journey for the day and finally arrived at **Shilaabo** in the evening, camping north of Shilaabo. The environment was favorable as it was spring time and puddles full of water were everywhere. We camped there for two nights waiting for some vehicles from Boosaaso. As often happens whenever an army is making a shift from one location to another, the timing should be known to only a few top commanders. As such, we set out at midnight from Shilabo through Labibaar and Dhanbacaad roads toward the south. As we traveled through these roads for hours, we encountered unknown vehicles full of armed men at the junction of Dhanbacaad and Higlooley roads. However, we were instructed not to engage with all unknown armed convoys we might encounter as we moved toward Jowhar. The reason being, we were merely Puntland Defense Force and about 250 soldiers from Somaliland regions and not National Army, and we could only engage with threats when we achieved an army comprised of forces from all regions of Somalia. This was among the goals and paths that TFG leader President Abdullahi Yusuf was pursuing. This has never been mentioned in any report from media

We were already informed about a potential threat before we reached Danbacaad. As such, some commanders believed the threat was higher and few armed units would not be enough to protect the majority of unarmed soldiers. They demanded every soldier be armed with the available guns and given access to ammunition. It was night, very dark, and we remained in our positions until morning. Early in the morning, we realized that these were a convoy of 30 vehicles full of Ethiopian armed forces. There was no immediate confrontation, and we sent two soldiers, one of them speaking an Ethiopian language, to provide details of our journey toward Jowhar, and we continued our relocation process peacefully. We were traveling within the Somali region of Ethiopia. On our way to Labibaar, most of the vehicles became stuck in the sandy road, forcing us to remain there for one night. As a result, we were unable to reach Feer-feer, which was just a few hours away. This resulted in a decision to equip at least two more units with rifles for more protection of the wider unarmed soldiers.

About 35 of the newly equipped soldiers defected that night after securing weapons, because they didn't want to be part of the relocation process and its tough situation. Only 9 of them were arrested in the effort to arrest all of them. However, we continued our journey and finally arrived at Feer-feer, where at least two intelligence units led by Col. Mohamed Adan Bidaar and Abdirizak Muse Hersi had been camping for one month. Feer-feer is a border town on the Somalia side of the Hiiraan region. As Feer-feer falls under the Hiiraan region, Abdikari Farah, aka Laqanyo, the then Hiiraan governor, paid a visit to the army. However, following his consultation with the commanders, a new decision taking us back to Fadhiyare was made. Our commanders decided to deploy the army back to Fadhiyare, which is not a favorable environment. However, due to the nature of military training, we were able to survive in that environment unlike civilians who are not trained for harsh life. It was a dusty environment, notorious for deadly poisonous snakes. We survived with water fetched from the river, which required a purification process.

1.4. More TFG from Puntland defection

While we were in Fadhiyare, we experienced the largest number of defections, over 210 soldiers, 70 of them armed, who defected for fear of more challenges ahead. When you are in both Fadhiyare and Feer-feer and you used to live in Boosaso, Lasanod, Galkaio, and Garoowe, you feel a horrible life and choose to defect rather than serving the nation by defending against both domestic and foreign threats in such circumstances. Other times, you may find yourself at night dreaming of enjoying time with your family, while sleeping in a horrible place.

Anyway, although we used to have comfortable lifestyles in those cities, we convinced ourselves to stay in the new situation we found ourselves in and preferred to serve the nation. The next move was to Beledweyne district, which was 330 km north of Mogadishu, where there is a military base known as Lamagalaay. However, there had been challenges among segments of the community in Beledweyne, including traditional leaders, over our arrival and use of the Lamagalaay military base. Nonetheless, a team led by the Hiiraan governor, who were in contact with President Abdullahi Yusuf, had been working on the matter to find a solution. The situation kept us there for some days. Fortunately, a few days later, we received a positive outcome that the problem was resolved, and we continued to move to Beledweyne to station in the Lamagalaay military base.

We also realized that the Hawadle traditional leader and the state defense minister of the transitional federal government who recently arrived in Beledweyne district agreed to the deployment of the army and were ready to receive us there. Although TFG leaders put forth collective efforts to relocate the government back to Mogadishu, the chairman of the Somali National Reconciliation Conference, Ambassador Bethwel Kiplagat, expressed his view of the relocation and, expressing optimism about the future of Somalia, said: *"Problems can and will happen, but as long as the Somali government puts down firm roots, it will be able to weather these problems"*[9] However, there had been unfulfilled pledges and commitments made by AU and IGAD in relation to the relocation process. Knowing all unfulfilled promises by regional and continental bodies as well as the international community, the TFG's unilateral relocation efforts over 2005 and 2006 had been regarded as meaningless by the very same international bodies who failed to meet their commitments.

For example, at an African Union (AU) summit in Abuja, Nigeria, in late January, the Intergovernmental Authority on Development (IGAD) and the AU both pledged to deploy peace support missions to Somalia to facilitate the peaceful relocation of the government. Djibouti, Ethiopia, Sudan, and Uganda committed themselves to supporting a peace mission for Somalia by providing troops or equipment to an IGAD force. Gedi also confirmed that Mogadishu would continue to

---

9. IRIN News

be the Somali capital and seat of government once the relocation was complete. Somalia's transitional federal parliament elected Abdullahi Yusuf Ahmed as president on October 10, 2004, bringing to an end a two-year reconciliation process sponsored by IGAD.[10]

The relocation process was bigger and much more profound than Western countries and AU Mission thought. The aim was for the government to be relocated to Villa Somalia when it was more inclusive and participative and breathing with the support of not only military officers or national army but with the support of civil society and the larger Somali people. This was not something that the international community facilitated or even paid attention to. This is the reason why media misreported the relocation process as if it started from Baidoa and Ethiopian National Defense Force made it possible for the TFG to be relocated to Mogadishu. Contrary to this, Ethiopian National Defense Force joined a healthy and constructive relocation process overlaid by democratic values and eventually turned it into a genocide by indiscriminately bombarding across Mogadishu and south central Somalia. Should the process have continued as planned by TFG leaders instead of the 2006 invasion by Ethiopian forces and its untold securitization move, Somalia could never have experienced such massive civilian killings and displacement of the people in Mogadishu and South Central Somalia. Instead, a very inclusive, participative government with strong democratic institutions would have been relocated and a stable, peaceful, and prosperous democratic nation would have been achieved.

Ignoring all democratic processes adopted by TFG leaders from Garowe to Baidoa, international media depicted such efforts as irrelevant, repeatedly writing the following narrative: Ethiopia's ally, the TFG, was corrupt and feeble, and it welcomed the Ethiopian military support. In 2006 it had a physical presence in only two towns, provided no useful services to Somalis, and with the ICU's ascendancy was becoming increasingly irrelevant.[11] The United States, which denounced ICU leaders for **harboring wanted terrorists**, supported Ethiopia's actions

---

10. IRIN https://www.thenewhumanitarian.org/report/55029/somalia-tfg-preparing-begin-operating-jowhar
11. https://www.thenewhumanitarian.org/report/55029/somalia-tfg-preparing-begin-operating-jowhar

with political backing and military assistance.[12] On our way to Beledweyne, through Kalabayr area, 4 water trucking vehicles and 3 vehicles mounted with mortars and 30 soldiers led by General Awil Ahmed Yusuf (Dhiig-sokeeye) and Abdirizak Afguduud were sent and tasked to fetch water from Elgal water borehole. However, as they moved toward Beledweyne, they were intercepted and encircled by 300 militias armed with heavy weapons including RPG-7 and PKM, who disarmed the 30 soldiers and captured vehicles including water tracking vehicles. Nonetheless, one soldier named Abgalow resisted dropping his gun. Abgaalow ran into the bush and focused on defending himself from potential attack from the militia that disarmed his colleagues.

We faced a different situation instead of a relevant amicable situation in line with the agreement reached in Beledweyne. However, the militia commander ordered his militia not to open fire on the soldier who resisted his order, for the reason that such a person isn't easy to capture. He said the risk is greater, as such, he might cause massive loss of lives. Fortunately, they were busy with vehicles and other military hardware, and the commander left the two commanders with their pistols. Luckily, commanders managed to communicate with us and with the President who was in Jowhar and briefed him about the new situation they encountered. General Abdirizak Afguduud reported the situation and said 7 vehicles including water tanks had been captured by clan militia in the area. President Abdullahi Yusuf asked, "What are you planning?" And he responded, "We need to go back to Fadhiyare base." The president concurred with General Abdirizak Afguduud.

He then requested to speak with General Dhiig-sokeeye. Knowing that he might take a different decision, the president told General Dhiig-sokeeye to consider the interest of the nation and the objectives of the mission, thus he advised to avoid any confrontation occurring in Hiiraan or Beledweyne. They all agreed in consensus to avoid confrontation within Hiiraan territory. The President told them that he would communicate with Puntland President Ade Muse, and in the meantime suggested they communicate with Col Hiif Ali Taar to facilitate new water tanks for them to secure access to water. The final decision lay with Major Commander General Saed Dhere who had no information about what happened due

---

12. Ibid

to the inadequacy of communication tools we were using. We had only an international satellite phone to communicate with the president and Saed Dhere, but he had to stop the convoys and find an antenna.

However, the militia freed the 30 soldiers and two commanders, and they returned to reunite with their army who was not far away. Unfortunately, the decision adopted by the president and two commanders was challenged by the large army who became stressed and refused to condone it. The reason being, they had never been defeated in many fronts they were involved in since they were created. On the opposite side, the militia perceived that this territory was their own and no one could make an attempt to dominate them.

Immediately our troops rejoined the larger army on journey, the situation changed and everyone could feel tension as something went wrong. Commanders entered an urgent meeting with army commanders and new instructions were being given to each soldier, particularly to take defense positions. Logistics were released - ammunition, medicine, fuel, and other crucial supplies. First and second brigades were directed to take defense positions toward Dhuusomareeb for potential attack from that direction, while battalions 4th and 6th took positions toward Elgal east and west, whereas brigade 5th, which is the most powerful of all, was directed toward the mountain areas of Beledweyne. The last battalion, 3rd, was stationed between Kalabayr and Elgal. General Saed Dhere, who was the army leader and who was willing to engage with clan militia to retrieve weapons and vehicles, was contacted by the president to convince him to also avoid any confrontation within Hiiraan territory and consider the objectives of the mission. Furthermore, the president told him it was not a strategic option for any confrontation as it could spread to Jowhar where there were not sufficient forces to defend the president, thus it would negatively affect the whole relocation process. For the vehicles and weapons captured by the militia, the president convinced his general that negotiations were underway and they would be returned to his hands peacefully.

However, the decision made by the President and commander Saed Dhere created tension as many soldiers and lower-level commanders insisted on engaging the clan militia and resisting against the commander's order. As a result, 2 soldiers died and 9 others were injured. However, the commander ordered that the army should be deployed back to Feer-

feer and Fadhiyare. The decision influenced a good number of the army to defect with their guns, taking advantage of transport vehicles from Puntland shipping livestock from Hiiraan to Bosaso port. As a result of this, 19 soldiers defected. As we were preparing to set out from Feer-feer to Beledweyne, having assured the support of the governor and traditional leaders, there had been propaganda portraying us as wanting to capture Beledweyne. This led to mobilization of the youth as clan and regional forces to defend against the "enemy forces" who wanted to capture the area, but it was unsuccessful. As we returned to Feer-feer and Fadhiyare, we started to repair our vehicles and the vehicles retrieved from clan militia by the governor Abdikarim Laqanyo and the Hawadle traditional leader that had been returned to us.

Two days in Feer-feer and Fadhiyare, we set out from Feer-feer and Fadhiyare to Mustaxiil. The first day we arrived at Burukur village where we remained two more days before we reached Mustahil, and the third day we finally arrived at Mustahil. Mustahil used to be a military base for the Somali National Army, Somali opposition fronts who were fighting with Somalia such as SSDF, who used to control Mustahil, and eventually Ethiopian forces after the collapse of the Central government of Somalia. Although Mustahiil lies at the border between Somalia and Ethiopia, it is worth noting that there was also some confrontation between General Aideed's forces and the Ethiopian army, and later again there was more confrontation between Alitihad Alislam fighters and Ethiopian forces. So Mustahil was notorious for being a center for conflict. Although I don't have more details about it, I can confirm people from Mustahil in the army were among the most talented and socializing people. The Shabelle River goes through Mustahil, resulting in a bridge built by Somalia, which Somalia used to defend from enemies willing to enter the country.

So by all means, Somalia was using the bridge for defense and not allowing enemies to use it as a means to cross the river during war. Due to its strength and quality of construction materials, many attempts to break it by different forces fighting there ended in failure. SSDF attempted to destroy it and failed; Ethiopian forces and even Somali forces tried to break it many times, and all were unsuccessful. Our Commanders such as General Saed Dhere and Awil Dhiig-sokeeye are familiar with Mustahil, because they used to operate during SSDF and it was once their military base to wage war against Somalia. However, our arrival at Mustahil elevated our hope to achieve our dream to be a more integrated national force, unlike the current forces which are merely from Puntland and small number from Somaliland which all our commanders emphasized in all their speeches. Although we were not selected on a clan basis and rather composed of people from across Somali clans, there was a wider perception that we were from specific districts and regions.

This is what compelled us to dream of having an integrated national force from across all regions in Somalia. A few days later, high-level officials including the President, his prime minister, members of the cabinet, and legislators visited us. Following the high-level visit, all weapons of the army were stored in a safe spot except for those of 5th battalion and the national intelligence unit, which were aimed as a foundation for the creation of national intelligence forces.

The national intelligence team included:
1. Gen. Mohamed Adan Bidar, Intelligence Commander
2. Col. Abdirizak Muse Hirsi Indhol, Deputy Intelligence Commander
3. Abwaan Mohamed Dhagafe Ilmi
4. Jamal Said Issa Ibad
5. Mohamed Koreye Ilmi (Garadoxo)

Two training camps were officially opened, and all army personnel were given crash training courses. The first few days after the training, a battalion from Abduwak and Balanbal led by Hasan Gurey Warsame, who later became Villa Somalia director, and Col. Qase (R.I.P.) joined the training. Those were the days when our hope to create an integrated national army was growing, as a large part of Somalia was embracing the goal and the difficulty we were enduring to achieve it. Although the priorities were to bring more people from across the country, those from Abduwak and Balanbal boosted the national army integration dream tremendously. The battalion led by Hassan Gurey Warsame was accommodated in a specific place and included in the army assigned for the training courses, becoming part of the 1st battalion. They were also given all logistics including uniforms and rations for each soldier. At this point, there was no salary remuneration allocated to anyone. They were using rented civilian vehicles and as such, they were given new military vehicles while the civilian vehicles were returned to the civilians.

1.5. Army battalions from Abudwak and Balanbal joined

Army battalions from Abduwak and Balanbal joined the ongoing training and harsh life. These include:

Cpt. Abdirashid Hassan Dirie Aley (Afgub)
Cpt. Ali Mohamed Artan (Ali Waranle)
Lt. Dayah Abdi Abdile

There were also some other days we were excited following the news that more forces would join us, but after delay, 4,000 soldiers joined us. Those who facilitated their mobilization include:

Gen. Omar Dheere, deputy minister for defense (AUN)
Honorable MP Gaagaale
Honorable Member of Parliament Abaadir
Late Amb. Abdikariim Farah Laqanyo, former Hiraan governor.

These four officials were responsible for making possible the existing current operating government that we all rely on. As training courses had been going on for days, it apparently became difficult for the trainees to adapt to the environment due to not only the lack of clean water but also the nonexistence of crucial supportive resources such as incentives for the trainees and extreme movement restrictions.

It was decided to set out from Mustaxiil to Qurac Joomo for fear of health issues, lack of sufficient drugs and hospital infrastructure, and more defection of the army. For the first night we camped between Mustaxil and Godey, while the second night we arrived at Gurac Joomo. However, after taking dinner, we continued our journey for hours to ElAli, where newly mobilized forces from Middle Shabelle joined the mission. They were armed with small armies and 15 military convoys. For sure, it was not easy to travel from Jowhar to ElAli through Buloburte given the huge threat and danger notorious in the area. They made a strong commitment to facilitate the relocation process on their part and achieve an integrated national army. We remained in El-Ali for one night and proceeded to Buloburte where we created a base on the west side of the city. This time the convoy was led by Col. Hassan Gacmeyo who was the commander of the Middle Shabelle brigade as he hailed from the Middle Shabelle region. We arrived smoothly at Mahaddaay district, which was close to Jowhar, and Jowhar is 90km north of Mogadishu. We then moved to Jowhar early in the morning and settled in the General Daud military training academy in Jowhar.

It was mid-June 2005 when TFG gained the support of the Puntland regions and Mudug, Galgudud, Hiiraan, and Middle Shabelle regions through democratic processes and values and decided to operate in Jowhar, the capital of Middle Shabelle region, as an interim government base. "Somalia's interim government has begun establishing itself in the town of Jowhar, where it will be based until security is restored in the capital, Mogadishu, a spokesman said on Wednesday. The government is in the process of setting itself up in Jowhar and the prime minister [Ali Muhammad Gedi] laid the foundation for the construction of a larger airport yesterday [Tuesday]," Hussein Jabiri, director of information in the prime minister's office, said"[13]

1.6. Infrastructure challenges

Although the TFG leaders were undergoing a tough process, key challenges included poor infrastructure in Jowhar city such as the poor airport which was essential for the TFG to deliver services and achieve its goals. Huge efforts were parallelly ongoing including Jowhar airport expansion. Hussein Jabiri said the expansion of the airport in Jowhar would cost US $900,000, and added that the expanded airport would facilitate the work of the government, which was expected to remain in Jowhar for "several months." Poor lighting at the airstrip in Jowhar had forced a plane transporting President Abdullahi Yusuf Ahmed from Nairobi to Somalia on June 13 to fly instead to neighboring Djibouti.

1.7. Difference within TFG

TFG leaders were also facing challenges within the government regarding whether TFG shall be operating in Jowhar or in Mogadishu. They were having different views on the whole relocation process and particularly on security and reconstitution of inclusive SNA. A section of

---

13. News 22 June 2005 IRIN News
https://www.thenewhumanitarian.org/report/55029/somalia-tfg-preparing-begin-operating-jowhar

the government disagreed with the decision to install the administration in Jowhar, and in May they moved to Mogadishu saying it wanted to restore normalcy to the city so the government could operate from there (Mogadishu). About 100 members of the 275-strong parliament, led by Speaker Sharif Hassan Sheikh Aden, earlier this month started an effort to rid Mogadishu of illegal roadblocks manned by armed militiamen, who were being asked to move to designated camps in the city.[14] However, the TFG leaders could see this move as different views regarding from military perspectives. As such, Hussein Jabiri said, "The government has no objection to that [efforts to restore security in Mogadishu]. It is a positive thing that should be supported."[15] The Inter-Governmental Authority on Development IGAD, which is made up of Djibouti, Eritrea, Ethiopia, Kenya, Sudan, Uganda and Somalia, sponsored two years of peace talks between the various Somali clans and factions, culminating in the establishment of this TFG (straddling to relocate itself from Nairobi to Mogadishu) in Nairobi in October 2004.[16]

In the second day, at General Daud academy in Jowhar, 8 brigades had been brought to a parade by the commanders in order to make more adjustments and restructuring of the army organization, knowing that President Abdullahi Yusuf was visiting the army which now comprised forces from nearly all regions in Somalia except those regions of the south and Mogadishu. Col. Fardaale, well known as Dhaq-dhaqaaq Dhaaf, a former SNA officer, was instructed to pay the presidential salute. Col. Fardaale, whom I respect a lot, was notorious in his capacity within the army for identifying individual soldiers not meeting required standards during the training from the eight brigades. He had the talent to memorize the details of every soldier in the training including full name, identification number, the unit they were part of, etc. He is remembered for his guidance and leadership during the long journey from Galkaio to Jowhar, including his own sentiments he used to say, "You fasten your belts more and more when you feel hungry, and if necessary, use a double belt."

---

14. https://www.thenewhumanitarian.org/report/55029/somalia-tfg-preparing-begin-operating-jowhar
15. Ibid
16. Ibid

President's visit to the army at General Daud academy was accompanied by his Prime Minister Ali Mohamed Geedi, Middle Shabelle Governor, the late Mohamed Omar Habeeb, and other cabinet members and military commanders. After receiving a salute from the army, the President emphasized military discipline that the army should exhibit and ordered all weapons currently in the hands of the army to be stored, with no one to be seen exposing their gun in and around the academy. While waiting for other army units mobilized from the remaining regions in the south including Lower Jubba, Gedo, Bay and Bakool, and Mogadishu and Jowhar to join the gathered national army in the academy, a new training was to be started in the academy. At the same time, there was some incentive food for the army provided by the president, and he urged them to continue to show resilience until the government would be able to meet their needs.

The first few days after the training, a battalion from Abduwak and Balanbal led by Hasan Gurey Warsame, who later became Villa Somalia director, and Col. Qase (R.I.P.) joined the training. Those were the days when our hope to create and achieve an integrated national army was growing, as a large part of Somalia was embracing the goal and the difficulty we were enduring to achieve it. Although the priorities were to bring more people from across the country, those from Abduwak and Balanbal boosted the national army integration dream tremendously. The battalion led by Hassan Gurey Warsame was accommodated in a specific place and included in the army assigned for the training courses, becoming part of the 1st battalion. They were also given all logistics including uniforms and rations for each soldier. At this point, there was no salary remuneration allocated to anyone. Hassan Gurey and his army from Abudwak and Balanbal were using rented civilian vehicles and as such, they were given new military vehicles while the civilian vehicles were returned back to the civilians.

Later on, the President along with the prime minister walked between the lines of the parade, observing the army and urging them to exhibit more resilience in this harsh time. During the observation, the president spotted a senior high-ranking soldier that he hadn't seen over past decades when he was leading SSDF. Thus, the president assumed him being close to the former President Mohamed Siyaad Barre, and by this time he was already promoted to a military general. He said, "Omg, is this General

Bussul?" Col. Bussul said, "Thank you Mr. President for promoting me to a military General, this must be a decree, thank you for publicly announcing the promotion that I was long waiting for." The president asked him, "Are you saying you didn't receive your promotion since then?" And continued to say, "Get your decree letter tomorrow." He likely became, among other soldiers, the first officer to be promoted by the TFG president. The commanders began directly to organize the army and provide responsibilities as well as define training courses and eventually to offer medical referrals for patients among soldiers to Jowhar district hospital. The hospital was functioning well and offering treatment to most of the patients in an equal manner, while referring those with severe medical conditions to Mogadishu Hospital. The hospital management never considered biased letters from the regional administration and other government officials and strictly upheld equality for all patients.

Middle Shabelle region was the headquarters for both the transitional federal government and regional administration led by H.E. Abdullahi Yusuf Ahmed and Mohamed Omar Habeeb respectively. The vast majority of the people in the region relied on farming as a source of livelihood and income and were willing to see a mature and fully functional government that could support them to enhance productivity and economic growth. They were desperate for functioning government institutions for all their needs including provision of security and achieving greater stability. Despite this, it was one of the most peaceful region among the eighteen regions of Somalia. In particular, Jowhar, which is the capital city of the regional administration, had tough security measures in place. As a result, every new comer had to register with the district police station to record their details before proceeding to the city. This led the security apparatus to know more about the details of every single person coming in and going out of the city. Those security steps taken and social progression motivated them to think to host the federal government institutions to operate there.

Under such wonderful times and environment, it was later realized that a growing division and mistrust between the federal government and regional administration was emerging, which affected government business and undermined Jowhar as a potential place where the federal government could continue to operate. The situation turned out to cause the federal government to face another difficult time just like the complicated nature of Feer-feer and Fadhiyare. Jowhar police station became a place to harass government officials including police, politicians, and senior military officers, while at other times presidential staff might be arrested arbitrarily. However, there was no military confrontation because people had already trusted the government. Despite differences with Mohamed Dhere, the governor, people from various segments of society had already endorsed and joined the government notwithstanding the position of the governor. It was during those days when it became known that warlords against the federal government had held a meeting in Daynile district in Mogadishu, with the aim of undermining the federal government operating in Jowhar. However, it was a shock when it also became known that the Middle Shabelle Governor, the late Mohamed Omar Habeeb, had been part of this plot against the government operating in his own regional offices, and he was asked by TFG leaders to clarify his political position regarding the federal government. The government forces could have taken action against Mr. Habeeb, but that was not government policies. . As such, the process was more democratic, focusing on negotiations, btoader consultation, and consensus.

In this light, the army was informed to prepare for relocation of the government from Jowhar to Baydhabo and to consider the potential confrontation from militia loyal to warlords and governor Habeeb. But, Mohamed Dhere showed another picture when he spoke with the media. At a news conference at his residence in Jowhar on Tuesday, Muhammad-dhere said he would support the government's relocation to Mogadishu, "but made it clear that he does not want the TFG to come to Jowhar," Abdikarim said. "Jowhar does not have the capacity to host the government," Muhammad-dhere was quoted as saying.

1.8. Relocating Within the Country

Unlike the relocation of the government from Nairobi to Somalia, this time is another relocation within the country, with the government relocating itself from Jowhar to Baydhabo, and probably the next one will be a relocation from Baidoa to Mogadishu. Baidoa is 200km south of Mogadishu. The mission is to relocate the government to the capital city and operate in Villa Somalia, the Somalia's Presidential Palace."The TFG has to come up with a new plan for the relocation. It really does not look good," the analyst said. The situation deteriorated increasingly, resulting in political crisis, more army defection, and emergence of new alliances.

The faction leader who controls Jowhar town in south-central Somalia said on Tuesday that interim President Abdullahi Yusuf Ahmed's Transitional Federal Government (TFG) was no longer welcome in the town. The announcement came after the faction leader, Muhammad Omar Habeb, spent the better part of Monday at the airstrip in Jowhar, waiting for Yusuf's arrival. However, Yusuf's plane did not land in Jowhar as it was diverted to the neighboring country of Djibouti.[17] Different interpretations about the conflict emerged, including that Mr. Habeeb was being influenced by warlords in Mogadishu on one hand, while on the other hand he was said to be angered by President Yusuf who diverted his flight from Mogadishu to Djibouti instead of Jowhar.

For example, Mr. Habeb, popularly known as Muhammad-dhere, was apparently angry because Yusuf went to Djibouti after leaving the Kenyan capital, Nairobi, instead of Jowhar, as planned, a local source said. Muhammad-dhere, who had mobilized "the entire town" to welcome Yusuf, and his entourage "was at the airstrip for over eight hours waiting for them,"[18] While the change of Yusuf's itinerary could have been perceived as a snub by those on the ground in Jowhar, Dahir Mire, the permanent secretary in the office of the president, said on Wednesday that Yusuf's plane was diverted to Djibouti due to insufficient lighting at the Jowhar airstrip. "We were simply late and the plane could not land on a dark airstrip," he said. "He was also angered by Prime Minister Ali Muhammad Gedi's announcement in an interview that he would go to Mogadishu instead of Jowhar," Abdikarim said.[19] The President and his Prime Minister summoned the governor Habeeb, and questioned him about his meeting with the opposition in Dayniile District in Mogadishu. He responded that he met with the opposition group and said it was an inevitable solution.

---

17. https://www.thenewhumanitarian.org/report/55029/somalia-tfg-preparing-begin-operating-jowhar
18. Abdikarim Omar, a local journalist working for Radio Jowhar, said on Wednesday. 22 June 2005. See IRIN News l
19. https://www.thenewhumanitarian.org/report/55029/somalia-tfg-preparing-begin-operating-jowhar

The president told him that the government could not function anymore there and it would be relocated to another region where regional politicians were not against their government. He added that he would lose all opportunities he had when the government institutions were operating in Jowhar, once the government was relocated to another city in Somalia, which the President meant to be Baidoa city and not Mogadishu. As the situation escalated further, including deprivation of using federal government uniform in Jowhar by the governor of Middle Shabelle region, this led to more confrontation and incidents. At least 100 members of the 275-strong parliament, led by Speaker Sharif Hassan Sheikh Aden, were in Mogadishu in a bid to stabilize the city. They had been convincing faction leaders to disarm and encamp their militias.[20]

A quick army parade was conducted at the airport in sight of the president's house, where all federal army attended including a good number of presidential security guards and prime minister's security escort and their respective vehicles. Then the president and his prime minister, accompanied by a number of senior military commanders who were involved in the relocation decision from Jowhar to Baidoa, hoping to lead the operations, stood at the podium to address the army. Commanders were not happy with what was happening in Jowhar and were championing shifting from Jowhar to Baidoa to keep building an integrated national army and achieve this goal with reduced domestic risk. The president received a salute from the army through General Osman Hassan Ali (Afdalow) and then the president came close to the parade and selected the following officers:

1. Col. Jigre Yusuf Ahmed Yey
2. Col. Abdirisaaq Mohamed Hirsi (Garcad) AUN
3. Cpt. Abdirashiid Hirsi Mohamed AUN
4. Farah Ahmed Dari (Aan) AUN
5. AbdiAsis (Jinni Iraale) AUN
6. Abdulaahi Ahmed Abdi Jubakoole AUN
7. Said Mohamed Hirsi (Siliinge) AUN
8. Lt Abdisaid Farah Guure
9. Abdifitah Mohamed Hasan (Jamhad Gagaale)

---

20. https://www.thenewhumanitarian.org/report/55029/somalia-tfg-preparing-begin-operating-jowhar

10. The author
11. Abdulkadir Ali Yuusuf (Lugey Ali Wagaafe)

This team was instructed to go to Baidoa tomorrow by air and no one was ahead to receive us. Nonetheless, I was quite happy to be part of this team going to Baidoa by air, knowing the risk involved on land. Furthermore, I was having stress due to uncertainty about who would receive our team at the airport in Baidoa; nonetheless, I knew it would always be better than Jowhar's growing tension. The president spoke with the army and informed them to set out from Jowhar to Baidoa through Buloburte road, but before reaching Buloburte, they would turn left through El Ali road, with no single stop. If a vehicle got damaged, they would leave it there and move through the night until they reached Baidoa. He identified and instructed Yassin Khamriile and Dahir Mohamed Hersi (Dahir Farur) as commander and deputy commander to lead the journey.

The president's appointment of the commanders for the different tasks was widely welcomed by the army. Then the president ordered that all logistics needed for the army in the parade to overcome challenges they might encounter as they will travel to Baidoa to be provided, including sufficient fuel, medicine, food, water, ammunition, roadside bomb detectors, compasses for guiding directions, and other crucial supplies, and to set out now to Baidoa from Jowhar. The president said, "See you in Baidoa."

Our unit selected to travel by air was accompanied by honorable Abdalla Derow Isack who was a very influential politician in Baidoa and hence, we were highly welcomed at the airport by the people in Baidoa led by Ministers Haabsade and Col. Shaati Guduud. Both Minister Haabsade and Col. Shaati Guduud had huge militias armed with heavy mortars and vehicles mounted with mortars, and they were dispersed across the airport wearing civilian clothes rather than military uniforms. So we could not distinguish militias from civilians by guns. We were also welcomed by ordinary people who were inhabitants in Baidoa and willing to see the government using their city as its base and operating. However, armed militias of Minister Haabsade and Shaati Guduud were overwhelming civilians. Honorable Abdalla Deerow Isack addressed the public and militias at the airport as arrived at Baidoa Airport and congratulated them that the federal government of Somalia would be relocated to Baidoa from Jowhar tomorrow. As such, people in Baidoa were expected to welcome the government and exhibit appropriate behavior and greater hospitality. Our team was then taken toward the city, particularly to the UNDP building which previously belonged to the Ministry of Agriculture of Somalia. The surroundings of the building were several highly populated internal displaced persons camps, a tarmac road from different directions were surrounding the building, and the opposite was the 60th army base of the Somali National Army.

No one lived in the building but sheltering birds alone, however, despite its strong structure. It required massive renovation and cleaning. There were two separate compartments, one of them seemed possible to be cleaned in a less time, but the other one would take more time as we were expecting the president to arrive the next day. We decided to clean the first compartment and make it a furnished office so that immediately the president and his prime minister arrive, they could use it as both offices and accommodation. Honorable Abdalla Deerow took the responsibility to prepare the house, and by mobilizing and using people in Baidoa, the house was renovated within 24 hours. This would be the new presidential Palace where the president and his government would operate to lead and govern the nation. The next day we prepared to go to the airport to receive the president and other officials from Jowhar. As we reached the airport, we found more than double the number of people who had welcomed Honorable Abdalla Deerow and our team yesterday. In my observation, everywhere in the airport were vehicles mounted with anti-aircraft Zu 23mm or 37mm, and you could also spot massive militias predominantly armed with PKM, AK-47, and RPG-7. About five leaders, each one escorted by close to 100 militiamen with their own uniform and ten well-armed vehicles, attended to welcome the president and other officials. Making the airport pandamonium.

The president's airplane landed safely and we took him to the new office prepared just yesterday by our team and Abdalla Deerow mobilised citizens. The TFG plan was always to engage with the local people including armed clan militias, traditional leaders, politicians, former SNA officers, and other influential eminent persons to involve them in state-building processes, providing them opportunity to contribute and criticize the process and enabling them to feel ownership and eventually engender their trust, and secure their full involvement in the relocation process and ownership. It is worth noting that the TFG leaders were desperately seeking the support of the people, this being a valuable democratic process which never enjoyed the support of the international community but was rather vilified by international media

The first meeting in Baidoa held in this new building was chaired by President Yusuf and participated in by Prime Minister Ghedi was held successfully and concluded with the following outcomes. The national army in Jowhar at General Daud academy and all other government officials were to set out from Jowhar through El Ali, Hudur, Tiyeeglow, Waajid, and then Baidoa. However, as the number of newly mobilized army in Jowhar grew faster, unexpected challenges emerged including transport vehicles, logistics, food, medical supplies, and other crucial instruments necessary for the relocation of the government from Jowhar to Baidoa.

However, despite President Yusuf having heavily counted on Puntland for key issues and challenges in telation to relocating the transitional federal government to Mogadishu, it became apparent that support from Puntland to the Somali national army in Jowhar to set oit to Baidoa was not possible due to the long distance, and the possibility of using airplanes was also ruled out during the meeting. As such, the president decided to task these activities to the following two businesswomen. These included new vehicles that would be used to transport all army and government officials and food and medicines needed to make the strategy happen:

1. Surer Abdi Firin and
2. Asha Un laaye

These two businesswomen used their network in Mogadishu, in particular Banadir region women, to facilitate purchasing required vehicles, food, medicine, and spare parts for the army journey. Immediately such vehicles and food were successfully brought to Jowhar, the army set out on their journey from Jowhar to Baidoa. However, as the army was traveling to Baidoa, a military vehicle mounted Zu 23 experienced engine failure, and hence, they remained in ElAli until the vehicle was repaired. Sureer and Asho, who had been with the army in El-Ali, now had to play their role. They communicated with women in Banadir region to buy the engine under the name of a civilian person to avoid forces against the government knowing the purpose of the engine, as they would never allow that to happen. It was depicted as if the engine had been ordered by a businessman in Baidoa, and then later the engine was transferred to El-Ali. As a result of this, the army continued their journey to Baidoa and arrived at Waajid.

It has been ordered the placements of the following four battalions of the army as follows: one for Presidential Palace in Baidoa, one battalion in Daynuunaay, one for Bardaale and two in Manaas, while all other brigades instructed to remain in Waajid. The battalions in Daynuunaay and Manaas were meant as defense positions for Baidoa in the event of attacked. We are now in Baidoa Although there was widespread illegal possession of weapons in the hands of people across the region, in our early days we were offered a warm welcome to Baidoa and greater hospitality by the people. Contrary to the prevailing harsh life and continuous harassment in Jowhar, Fadhiyare, and Feer-feer by the administration and environment respectively, in Baidoa the life was much better and inhabitants were free from warlords' influence or any administration and were proponents to the government. However, we once again encountrrd a similsr situation to those in Feer-feer, Fadhiyare, and Jowhar. Nonetheless, all of us thought that we had undergone the most difficult and horrible times in our journey to Baidoa and no more challenges lay ahead of us. As such, in Baidoa there were freelance militias and warlords who had survived the Islamic court forces disarmament program in the southern part of the country as they hadn't yet come to Baidoa.

Shockingly, in Baidoa there were militias who frequently attacked and killed the national army just to take their guns and vehicles. Thus, Baidoa again became a hostile city, contrary to the initial thought that it would be a more convenient alternative in comparison with the risks of Fadhiyare, Feer-Feer, and Jowhar. As a result, most of the army opted to stay in their camp for many days. On another note, in an effort to restore stability to the city, yielded about 170 soldiers led by the late General Ahmed Addoye (Omar Dhegad) to be sent to overseas for training, particularly to a training camp in Kenya called Mayaani. This was the first army team sent to foreign countries since the formation of the transitional federal government. The training covered VIP protection, security of military camps or bases, and police force tasks including crime investigation and establishment and investigation of crimes, taking cases in police station through criminal procedure. The training lasted for three months and the closing ceremony of the training was officially done by Somali Police Force Commissioner General Ali Madobe and his deputy General Bashir Goobe. However, the president issued a directive that the newly trained forces from Kenya join the police forces to disarm illegally armed people in Baidoa, including freelance militia, instead of serving as protection units for their respective offices including the offices of the president, prime minister, and Parliament.

The president paid a visit to the newly trained police forces aimed at disarming militias and spotted a white mark on the police hat and advised them to remove the white mark and put a red one as they were carrying out a disarmament operation. As such, the white was changed to a red mark. A few days later, they disarmed all the people who were illegally armed, while some who were willing to join the army were accepted and enrolled as new soldiers from Baidoa. The newly recruited army from Baidoa was camped at Daynuunay base under the command of Col. Med Med Deer.

1.9. Relocation from Bossaso to Mogadishu

We realized that it was a long journey to reach Mogadishu as new armed conflicts erupted between Islamic Court Unions and warlords over the control of the capital city Mogadishu and many other parts of the southern part of the country. As such, the government decided to wait and see the outcome of such huge confrontation between the sides fighting there over the control of Mogadishu and the surrounding environment, and prepare for a potential attack from whichever side won. Strangely, each side believed they would overrun and defeat the other and finally destroy the TFG government in Baidoa. This shows that the sides didn't regard the transitional federal government as potential.

To defeat any side who defeated the other side, the president ordered the federal government forces to prepare for the potential attack from one of these two fighting sides. As such the TFG forces remained in their defense positions. The Islamic court forces badly defeated the warlords and seized or captured all their armored vehicles and weapons, which resulted in gaining more public support. The shift made by the government would expand the geographical area for Islamic court forces to wage attack from Mogadishu to Bay and create challenges in terms of fuel and number of army or reinforcement. This would allow the government to leverage its resources and defeat them. The TFG leaders understood that the tasks ahead of them were not limited to relocating the government from Nairobi to Mogadishu but to engender public trust, because they were aware of the importance of getting public support and the criticality of diffusing the wrong notion that people perceived about a government formed outside their country which they were not a part of. The way people think about them and how crucial it was to engage with the people to reduce misconceptions and the significance of including more influential personnel across Somalia, in particular more SNA high-ranking officers to reconstitute a broader inclusive national army. They were also engaging other politicians and traditional leaders as well as business people. The goal was not only to relocate but to expand the government to all provinces of the country and create a conducive environment where everyone felt included, safe, and could criticize. To achieve these goals would take years depending on the appropriate strategic options applied and processes designed to meet the goal set with reduced risks. The TFG intention was to achieve its goals with highly reduced risks, and it was successful in its processes from February 2005 to December 2006.

1.10. Ethiopia's sinister intention

However, it is noteworthy to express that, although Ethiopia's sinister intention was the biggest challenge against democratic state-building processes by TFG during these two years which the TFG leaders' relocation processes had been ongoing from Garowe to Baidoa which was achieved with less risk, let alone any confrontation that might claim the lives of even 5 persons.

The achievement made during the two years of Reconciliation Conference in Kenya 2002-2004 and the subsequent two years of the TFG democratic process from 2005 to December 2006 inside Somalia was deliberately reversed and ruined by the invasion of Ethiopian National Defense Forces in less than 2 months (December 24, 2006 and January 2007). Before these two months, there was no hostility against the TFG emanating from any region in Somalia. This was due to the democratic process that the TFG applied when engaging local communities all along from Garowe to Baidoa. In light of this democratic process, and in contrary to what many agencies wrote about the invasion of ENDF into Somalia as being key ally to TFG was a destructive, horrible securitization move by Ethiopia which caused people to disown the government they had been supporting over the past two years and consequently view it as a puppet for Ethiopia and western countries. This further boldened and widely perceived as truth when the massive bombardment by Ethiopian forces on highly densely populated areas and arbitrary detention and killing of arrested civilians inside their own military bases occured What was even more striking was their desire to arrest and torture high-level SNA officers and governors and their continuous threats against politicians.

I am an avid fan of Qeylo-dhaan, the Somali patriotic music band who as of late has come to represent the true conscience of most Somalis who are deeply aching to find solutions for their country's never-ending mayhem. Thus, when I recently listened to their latest indignation song about Col. Gebregzabher Alemseged unmatched adverse intrusion into Somali politics for the last two decades,[21] I became interested to dig deep and find out who exactly Col. Gebregzabher Alemseged is and what his motives in meddling in Somali affairs are. Nevertheless, Col. Gebregzabher Alemseged record speaks for itself as a war criminal who should be summoned to justice for his wholesale genocide of massacring tens of thousands of innocent civilians in Somalia during the ill-fated Ethiopian invasion between 2007-2008. Unfortunately, Somalia's corrupted politicians decided to turn a blind eye to this war criminal walking amongst them with impunity as though he was a born-again honest peace-broker.[22]

ENDF and intelligence officers didn't spare anyone. Col. Gebregzabher Alemseged made his lasting mark during the early days of the invasion after allegedly being confronted by President Abdullahi Yusuf who became rather conflicted with the Ethiopian forces' indiscriminate use of heavy weapons in civilian neighborhoods in the capital, where tens of

---

21. https://www.hiiraan.com/op4/2015/dec/102847/who_s_afraid_of_general_gabre.aspx
22. https://www.hiiraan.com/op4/2015/dec/102847/who_s_afraid_of_general_gabre.aspx

thousands were killed and hundreds of thousands more were forced to flee.[23]

1.11. TFG Key Financial Resources in the Absence of Donor Fund

TFG relocation processes suffered from inadequate funding. The only budget TFG received was coming from Puntland State and businesspeople from Puntland. Puntland state had been donating to TFG $100,000 in cash and $150,000 in kind monthly for four years. The role of businesspeople who became bankrupt from investing in the government relocation processes and state building processes was unique and powerful.

The TFG leaders could never have met their set goals without the support of the businesspeople in the country. The international community's financial support commenced almost at the end of TFG's term, and the relocation process never benefited from it. In addition, it went through several processes that would not allow the TFG to act timely on crucial issues. As such, TFG leaders were compelled to engage with businesspeople for supplies and even direct funding to meet their daily needs, including government daily businesses and logistics including fuel, food, spare parts, and even logistic cash (air tickets and hotel accommodation for diplomats), overseas travels, and per diem. The following are the key personnel whom the TFG relied on for finance during the relocation and even after the relocation processes, as there was no revenue collected from the people to run government businesses.

Due to persistent inadequate financial support from the international community, who were the primary anticipated source of finance for the TFG to run the nascent government, these individuals had never been refunded their funds as early promised by the TFG leaders. As a result of such payment failure, they all ended up bankrupt:
1. Aden Isse Ali Hade (Aden Dhagah)
2. Dhoobis Aden Sheikh-Doon
3. Ahmed Elmi Dhagow (Tobon Tolaale)
4. Asha Uun Laye
5. Sureer Abdi Firrin

---

23. Ibid

6. Abdirahman Farah Gure

In Jowhar, the government appealed many times to Aden Isse (Aden Dhagah) for financial assistance and supply of goods that had never been refunded to date. For instance, Aden Isse spent a massive amount of money on TFG operations. Some of the funds borrowed from Aden were used to reconstruct some embassies. He passed away in 2018; a heart attack killed him in Nairobi, Kenya.

CHAPTER 2

BAYDHABO SUICIDE ATTACK (18 SEPTEMBER 2006)

CHAPTER 2

BAYDHABO SUICIDE ATTACK

> We didn't know that we were on the brink of the suicide attack aimed at the President.

[**Fig. 3:** Cars on flames after a suicide attack in Baydhabo, Somalia 18 September 2006. Image by AP.]

2.1. How the Attack Happened and What Was the Surrounding Mystery?

*A*s I was there and accompanying the president nearly all the time, while his safety and security was my primary task assigned by SNA commanders, let me begin with a brief background of the political ecosystem, who the players were, the role each player was taking, and the kind of game being played. Before the orchestrated terrorist attack to assassinate the president through suicide attack on September 18, 2006, in Baidoa, there were separate meetings between the president and the speaker, Honorable Sharif Hassan Sheikh Adam on one hand, and between Prime Minister Ghedi and President Col. Abdullahi Yusuf Ahmed on the other hand in Baidoa's Presidential Palace on September 15, 16, and 17, 2006. The parliament session was called to approve a new cabinet. Members of Parliament and cabinet ministers who had been loyal to the three leaders were also participating in the complex meeting between the leaders in which the key issue was whether or not to deploy presidential security guards (extracted from Brigade 54th which was later renamed 77th based at Presidential Palace) to the Parliament building during the Parliament session on September 18. The other issue in the discussion was concerning a new bill against the offensive attack from Islamic Court Unions and other terrorists who had captured several regions including parts of Mudug, Galgaduud, Hiiraan, Middle Shabelle, and Kismaio and were close to Baidoa.

As the discussion was ongoing, we, the special force mandated to protect the president, became concerned about the potential decision outcomes from ongoing meetings, including the one stating presidential security guards would not be allowed to access the Parliament building during the September 18 Parliament session. Together with battalion commander Late Jigre Yusuf Ahmed, who in turn shared our concern about implications of our responsibility under the new decision outcomes to the commander of Brigade 54th, General Awil Dhiig-sokeeye. On September 16, 2006, immediately after the meetings ended, the following officers met with the president in the evening in his resting room:

1. Late Gen. Awil Dhiig Sokeeye

2. General Osman Hassan Ali (Afdalow) Battalion Commander
3. Col. Abdiwahid Mohamud Hassan Lugey Chief Protocol of the President
4. Late Col. Ali Abdi Guled Duguf Specail Security of the President
5. Late Col. Jigre Yusuf Ahmed Yey company Commander presidential Guard
6. Late Col. Abdirizak Mohamed Hersi (Garcad), Commander of special security guard
7. Late Mohamed Ali Samatar (Siraaje) Specail Security of the President
8. The author: Special Security of the President
9. Late Captain Abdirashid Hersi Mohamed Specail Security of the President

However, prior to the meeting with the president, our group discussed our concerns and responsibilities for protecting the president in the face of growing insecurity and political complexity. General Awil Dhiig-sokeeye, who knew about our increasing stress concerning the outcome decision that we would not have access to the parliament building on the September 18 parliament session and the vulnerability of the associated threat to the president's safety and security, said "We will ask the president's position regarding this decision outcome." At that moment, we were all obviously under a lot of stress and confused, believing that this was our job and not the parliament's role and responsibility. As we entered the president's resting room, General Awil Dhiig-sokeeye, who was leading us, paid military salute. However, the president, who sensed what had brought us together, said while laughing at us, "I understand what is driving you to come here and visit me," and added, "Please have a seat." Then General Awil Dhiig-sokeeye, yet standing, said, "We don't like to waste your time," and told the president we were in pursuit of information about the outcome decision regarding the deprivation of our security unit's access to the parliament building on the September 18 session. He continued and said, "Mr. President, what is your view about this decision?"

The president responded: "General Awil, the September 18 parliament session is just like past challenges we met in Beledweyne and Jowhar. You need to know that Somalia is at a critical point with potential to die or survive. It is up to you to ensure Somalia survives from this point as parliament rejected our suggestions, and thus we need to show concession and approve what they are demanding. It seems that they need to keep Somalia in this terrible situation; they don't view the situation the way we view it. You should not be in the parliament building during the Parliament session on September 18 and hand over security responsibilities to the policemen." General Awil again confirmed from the president whether this was final or not, and the President said, "It is a final order. This is because we don't want parliament to blame us that we violated the decision outcomes, and we need them to pass the new cabinet. However, keep security outside and surrounding the parliament." We all realized that this was the president's final decision. We then convened another meeting for our presidential security team in which we decided that the following fifteen soldiers, including drivers and special guards who were in plain clothes, would go inside the parliament building, all of us armed with pistols.

1. Late Col. Jigre Yusuf Ahmed Yey, Commander of the Special security guard for the president
2. Late Col. Abdirizak Mohamed Hersi (Garcad)
3. Abdiweli Osman Warsame (Fadhigo)
4. Capt. Abdifatah Mohamed Hassan (Jamhad Gagaale), the second security guard unit commander
5. Late Col. Ali Abdi Guled (Cali Duguf)
6. Late Captain Abdirashid Hersi Mohamed
7. Late Mohamed Ali Samatar
8. The author
9. Late Saed Mohamed Hersi (Siliinge)
10. Adow Humey Weheliye
11. Abdirahman Farah Nuur (Fareer)
12. Major. AbdiAsiis Farah Mohamed (Istakiin), Driver Vehicle 1 for the president
13. Abdiweli Abbi Abdille, Driver Vehicle No. 2
14. Guulwade Jaaweel, Driver Vehicle No. 3
15. Jama Dhulun, Driver Vehicle No. 4

We planned to be there very early and become the first people to go inside the building. We needed to go with convoys using four private vehicles from the office of the president. We also planned for the protocol unit and some senior officers to go inside the parliament building to assess the situation.

These include:
1. General Osman Hassan Ali (Afdalow)
2. Ahmed Abdi Guled Yey (Yoole)
3. Abdiqafar Yaasiin Farah Yaquub
4. Ahmed Awle
5. Shukri Wayrah
6. Hassan Gurey Warsame
7. Ahmed Abdulaahi Yusuf Ahmed Yey

We also planned for Brigade 54th to secure the outside parameters of the parliament building and allow access to the parliament only for the designated police. On September 17, around evening time, our team held a meeting at the presidential building to design our operations, including preparing the four private vehicles, one of which was a bulletproof vehicle. We hid four AK-47s inside the bulletproof car in the event unexpected challenges arose. Guulwade Jaaweel was the driver of the bulletproof vehicle. Our team was distributed equally among the four vehicles. Fortunately, the police tasked with checking people and vehicles entering the building were comprised of three parts. The first part was those trained in Kenya training camp called Mayaani, 70 soldiers in number and tasked to secure the safety of the parliament building. Most of them were former military units of the presidential guard and familiar to us, thus, they didn't bother us as we were wearing plain clothes and armed with pistols that were not visible. They considered us as the inner circle team of presidential special security guard. They were trained for that; they knew responsibility better than politicians. They were well prepared and had received high-level training skills from Kenya. They were trained for protection of high-level officials, safety and security of premises, and inspection of people and vehicles. Consequently, the terrorists were unable to infiltrate and get inside the parliament building whatever attempts they might choose, including wearing the same uniform as the police. They secured both entrances of the building and its surroundings. Their commanders were the following:

1. Col. Mohamed Abdulkadir Hersi (Dhagaweyne Kirtan)
2. Col. Hassan Hussein Adan (Hassan dabeecad)
3. Late Col. Jama Saeed Warsame Kor-Wadaadle (Jama Afguduud)

4. Dhame Abdulkadir Jama Abbi (Khaddar Ogaadeen)
5. Abdisaed Farah Gur

The other two police units involved were a group of former Somalia Police Force who recently were given a refreshing course at Manaas and a third group composed of clan militia trained as police at Labaatan Jiroow camp. Both groups were tasked to secure the main road coming from the town to the parliament building. All presidential guard commanders and their battalions were instructed to remain in their positions while a reinforcing unit and more police officers were deployed to boost stability and, in the event that instability arose from security staff of the 275 MPs, to step in and support police at the checkpoints to tame them. On September 18, all checkpoints controlled by Brigade 54th were handed over to the police in accordance with the outcome decision regarding the parliament session. In light of this complex situation, most of the MPs didn't come to the parliament session at the scheduled time. Their delay caused the session to begin very late. Furthermore, all MPs' security staff were not allowed to get close to parliament and they remained at Shanta-jid. As a number, they were estimated to be about 200 armed militias. The same happened for the security staff of the speaker, Sharif Hassan Sheikh Adam, who were using 6 heavily armed vehicles. Police instructed him to leave all his staff and assault vehicles at Shanta-jid like other people. Similarly, the prime minister's security escort was not allowed to get access to parliament, and he left them at Shanta-jid like other government officials.

It was time for us to move to the parliament building in Baidoa for the long-awaited session on September 18, 2006, for the members of parliament to pass the new cabinet. We were a convoy of four vehicles. The first vehicle was a Mercedes Benz with five soldiers on board, the next one was a four-wheel drive Toyota Land Cruiser with four soldiers on board, the third vehicle was the president's vehicle - the president, director of the office of the president Hussein Ali Yalaan, General Mohamed Nor, and the driver Abdilatif Farah Istakiin were on board, whereas the last vehicle was carrying five soldiers including the commander of the president's security escort, late General Jigre Yusuf Ahmed. He would be killed in today's suicide attack. He was the commander who outlined the strategy we would apply in case serious problems arose. He used to advise us that things could change very quickly and we should remain vigilant and be ready to quickly adapt with the change. He was a very honest and transparent commander who cared a lot about other soldiers rather than his own interests. Over the past three days, he hadn't rested for the sake of the president's safety.

His last directives were that in the event an unexpected attack against the president happen, he said we should first protect the president, then ensure we took him away from the scene of the attack, then save anyone else who might sustain injuries during the operation. Early morning on September 18, before he was killed, he was chanting with Somali songs by celebrity singer Khadra Dahir Ige.

Adduunkan waxaa cusleeyay
caddaan baa madow amaahday
waxay nabaddii carootay kolkay
car i taabo gaartay
Guuguulihii xalay ciyaayeyna
Colaad buu sheegay yaab leh
wuxuu cirka yeerku wariyey
wuxuu cirka yeedhku wariyey
inay cawo daran inay cawo daran bogsooto
qofkii calafkii adeego wuxuu cuni laa ma waayo
wuxuu cuni laa mayo"

ENGLISH:

What has made this world burdensome
Is that the whites have taken from the black people
What enraged peace
Is when it reached "Touch me if you dare"
The Guuguule bird that cried last night
It foretold a great conflict
The Cirsan-yeedh bird says
That an unlucky person won't stay unlucky
Whoever try's hard
Will never go hungry

We drove to the road that connects the Presidential Palace to the Parliament building, which was just 3km distance. We didn't encounter any challenges and we safely entered the parliament building. As we entered the building, the president sat down in his seat and a few minutes later he was welcomed to make his opening speech. However, our plan was to take him back to the State House immediately after he finished his speech.

We, the following four officers, were tasked to ensure that immediately after the president concluded his speech, we would take him out and back to the Presidential Palace and prevent him from engaging with other officials due to security concerns.
1. The Author
2. Abdirashid Hersi Mohamed (Abdirashid Dheere) AUN
3. Abdulkadir Ali Yusuf (Lugey Ali wagaafe)
4. Said Mohamed Hirsi (Saliinge) who would be killed during the suicide attack

We were also told which vehicle of the different vehicles we would use as we were going back to the Presidential Palace. Other security team members who were in the parliament building were also informed to leave the building using available exits and ensure they got in the assigned vehicles in accordance with the plan and not any vehicle they might wish. The president, who had experience in tough situations and who was capable of interpreting people's intentions or was good at face reading, decided to follow our instructions and followed us by declining the speaker's desire to have a private talk with him in the rest room of the parliament building. Thus, we quickly left the building, boarded the presidential motor vehicle and other vehicles in order to take him to the Presidential Palace. We had no idea, as we were trying to leave, that we were on the brink of a suicide attack orchestrated by terrorists outside the parliament building to kill the president.

2.2. How the Terrorist Attack Happened

Immediately after we got out of the parliament building, all the security staff boarded the vehicles, and we secured that the president got in his car. However, before we could move, we heard the first heavy explosion; it was a suicide attack targeted at the president's car, exactly 3 meters away. This being among the first suicide car bombs that happened in Somalia, the whole environment became filled with smoke, creating a terribly confused environment, making it hard to know the direction of the attack and what would come next. Then, with that shock, extensive fire exchange followed. I rushed toward the president's vehicle, which was burning and had collided with another vehicle at the front side. I opened the window, which was already half-open, and found inside a president burning and surrounded by smoke. The president said, "This must be a suicide bomb," and I removed him from the vehicle and helped extinguish the flame on his body. I kept him on the side of the vehicle, using the rear tire as a defense wall. Members of our team quickly joined me in protecting the president. These included late Abdirashid Hersi Mohamed and Abdifatah Mohamed Hassan aka Jamhad Gaagaale, Yoole Abdi Guled, and Shukri Wayrax, who were uninterruptedly firing at the terrorists who were firing at us with all available weapons in their possession.

Lugey Ali Wagafe, another prominent soldier, rushed toward the president's vehicle without noticing that we were here at the right side of the vehicle. He checked inside the vehicle and helped evacuate General Mohamed Nor who was inside the vehicle, while the director of the office of the predident Hussein Ali Saylan, who was not seriously injured, alighted on the other side. Unfortunately, we could not help the president's driver, Major. AbdiAsiis Farah Mohamed (Istakiin) who was seriously injured. Despite massive shootings from the east side, our team continued surrounding the president to protect him while others were engaged in fighting with the terrorists who were dedicated to killing the president. We chose to move toward the east, because of less gun shooting continued from there, as it seemed not to have more terrorist fighters. We were worried about other potential suicide attacks from the north and west sides, where we spotted so many vehicles and massive fire exchange. Another suicide attack by a vehicle VBID happened 15 minutes later. Eventually, we chose to run towards east direction together with the injured president.

Although we chose to run toward the east while carrying the injured president, you may think a better option could have been going back to the parliament building. Unfortunately, the perception we held inside parliament was that some elements of terrorist forces were already inside the building. This was the reason we decided to move the president quickly from the scene, and we insisted on moving toward the east and to reach the palace for safety and treatment. The following officers joined us as we set out to move toward the east.

1. Abdifatah Mohamed Hassan (Jamhad Gagaale)
2. General Osman Hassan Ali (Afdalow)
3. Adow Humey Weheliye
4. Abdirahman Farah Noor (Fareer)

This team had already eliminated terrorist fighting from the parliament side, which was south. However, as the environment became less filled with smoke and dust, two soldiers named Adow Humey Weheliye and Abdirahman Farah Noor aka Fareer engaged in fighting with a group of terrorists shooting at us from the east side who intensified their attack. While these two soldiers were covering us from the enemy firing at us from the east direction, we put soldiers around the president to prevent further assault, though he had moderate injury. We proceeded toward the east on foot as there was no road, and the risk of using vehicles and potential more suicide attacks against our vehicles was very high. Of the four vehicles, two were totally burnt down there, while the two drivers of the last two vehicles, Awil Abbi Abdille and Guulwade Jaweel, and their vehicles were unharmed. However, we retrieved the four AK-47s from one of the two vehicles. One vehicle escaped toward Baidoa airport after seeing a chance that terrorists could not attack it. As we continued to move toward the east direction with reduced shootings and overcoming most terrorist attacks, a four-wheel drive vehicle with late Mohamed Abdirizak (Mohamed Yare) and Ali Farah (Ali Qaataa), who were using rough roads and piercing the fences of the houses, reached us.

The four-wheel drive Toyota and the two officers on board presented a significant opportunity to quickly rescue the injured president and ensure his access to medical assistance. As such, we took him using the vehicle toward the Presidential Palace. On the other hand, there was one security staff member escorting the Honorable late Hassan Abshir Farah Waraabe who was among those kept at the Shanta-jid checkpoint. This officer named Ali Muse Gabayre, really used his intelligence and, through his observations of the shootings, decided to attack the terrorists from behind. Consequently, he weakened their orchestrated attack against our team and created an opportunity for us to move faster toward the Presidential Palace. Mr. Ali Muse Gabayre made his own assessment of the confrontation and figured out where he could attack the terrorists to destroy their plans for blocking the president's movement toward the Presidential Palace. This intelligent soldier later left the army and became a businessman. There were also some officers from the 54th Brigade who later went to the scene and encountered attacks from terrorists; nevertheless, they helped all the injured team members, including the president's driver, Mr. Major. AbdiAsiis Farah Mohamed (Istakiin), and Mr. Abdulkafar Yacquub, who was the president's advisor. Both of them were severely injured. They also assessed the situation by gathering all crucial information about the suicide attacks that was merely intended to assassinate President Abdullahi Yusuf Ahmed.

As we arrived at the Presidential Palace, we badly needed a medical doctor who could attend to the president who had an injury on the neck. We requested Sheikh Door Moalim Abdirahman to find a medical doctor immediately, and he brought a military officer who was also a medical doctor. He arrived at the palace wearing a military uniform, carrying an AK-47 and a bag full of drugs. He immediately attended to the president and administered solutions and injections after cleaning the areas affected by the suicide flame. As his treatment was ongoing, the president glanced at the severely injured driver and his advisor who also were brought by the backup team. They were both bleeding severely, and the president requested the doctor to start helping them as he was no longer bleeding. However, the doctor continued to treat him, and he later examined the other two officers who also badly needed his attention. Among key people we lost in the suicide attack include the company commander, Col. Jigre Yusuf Ahmed Yey, who was also the president's brother, presidential guard officer Mr. Said Mohamed Hersi (Saliinge); and Ahmed Awle, who was the president's uncle. In his memoir, President Abdullahi Yusuf stated the September 18, 2006, suicide attack in Baidoa. He wrote in his book that he went to the parliament whose task was to pass new cabinet ministers. This was to encourage the MPs to expedite the process and pass the new government in order to deliver pressing basic services that people needed.[24]

He said, immediately after he concluded his speech, he was escorted by the speaker and the new prime minister toward his vehicle. However,

---

24. Yuusuf, Cabdullaahi Axmad. *Halgan iyo Hagardaamo: Taariikh Nololeed (Struggle and Conspiracy: A Memoir)*. (Sweden: Scansom Publishers, 2012), p.360

he said, he got a shock when the speaker asked the new prime minister whether he was also going with the president. The president, before the prime minister responded to the question, raised his objection and said, "Why is he going with me, when the parliament session will be discussing whether he and his government shall be passed or not?" He continued and said angrily, "He should be in the parliament as the MPs are here to approve him and pass his government." The speaker, who noted that the president was vigilant, said, "Yeah, exactly he should remain and wait for the result." The new prime minister also noted the president's concern and nodded his head in agreement. For the suicide attack, the president said in his book, "As we boarded the vehicles and wanted to move from the parliament building toward Villa Baidoa, my vehicle was attacked by a vehicle full of explosive material in an attempt to assassinate me, and they hit it with my vehicle which as a result got burned or ablaze. I alighted from the vehicle while flaming on the neck, and then there was fire exchange between my security and the terrorists who attacked me. I sustained an injury but was capable of moving."[25]

We went on foot toward a small road leading up to Villa Baidoa. However, walking down the small road, we luckily got a vehicle with one of our soldiers who rushed us toward Villa Baidoa.[26] Later, the prime minister and the speaker visited the president and realized that the president was not seriously injured and was capable of recovering from minor injuries through the support of local medical facilities, and they then returned to their respective offices. Equally important, more civilians and senior military officers came to visit the president to know about his medical situation. As a result, we later decided the president should speak to the media, particularly the BBC Somali service, to share with the citizens and army brigades in Wajed, Tiyeeglow, Hudur, Manaas, and Maayo Fuulka, who were eagerly interested to know about the president's medical situation. The BBC reporter Yusuf Garad Omar interviewed the president and aired his interview through BBC. However, other media also wrote about the attack in Baidoa, including The Guardian, and said:

---

25. Yuusuf, Cabdullaahi Axmad. *Halgan iyo Hagardaamo: Taariikh Nololeed (Struggle and Conspiracy: A Memoir).* (Sweden: Scansom Publishers, 2012), p.364
26. Yuusuf, Cabdullaahi Axmad. *Halgan iyo Hagardaamo: Taariikh Nololeed (Struggle and Conspiracy: A Memoir).* (Sweden: Scansom Publishers, 2012), p.364

"Somalia's president survived an alleged assassination attempt after two bombs were detonated outside a parliament building, killing at least five people. A car thought to have been driven by a suicide bomber exploded as the president, Abdullahi Yusuf, was driving away from parliament, a converted grain warehouse in the temporary capital of the country, Baidoa."[27]

He was not injured but his brother, Abdulsalam Yusuf Ahmed, was thought to be among those killed. Witnesses said eight cars in the president's convoy were destroyed, including three "technicals", pick-up trucks with mounted machine guns.[28] Fifteen minutes later there was a second explosion. Somalia's foreign minister, Ismail Mohamed Hurre, said the bombing had al-Qaida's fingerprints all over it.[29]

"This is the first suicide bomber in Somalia," he said. "This was an attack aimed at assassinating the president to destabilize the government. The attackers knew the president was addressing parliament." The dead included members of Mr. Yusuf's security team. Mr. Hurre said six "attackers" were also killed by militiamen loyal to the president in a gun battle after the explosions.[30] Despite 11,500 well-trained and disciplined army troops across from central regions and Puntland being ready in Baidoa, Wajid, and its surroundings, there had been international media vilifying the TFG capabilities, which was tamed by democratic values. For instance, the following were the ways international media were depicting the TFG as faltering instead of seeking accurate information about the TFG. Mr. Yusuf's Transitional Federal Government is struggling to assert any authority over the country. Although supported by the international community and the UN, it has no army or police force and controls no territory outside Baidoa, a small town west of the capital Mogadishu. It has also been racked by infighting, and yesterday a parliamentary session was called to approve a new cabinet.[31]

Unlike the above, the TFG had trained 11,500 military and police forces, some of them trained in Kenya. They were based in Wajid, Manaas,

---

27. Xan Rice and agencies in Nairobi, "*Somali president escapes car bomb suicide attack,*" The Guardian, September 19, 2006, https://www.theguardian.com/world/2006/sep/19/mainsection.international11.
28. Ibid
29. Ibid
30. Ibid
31. Ibid

Baidoa, and other bases such as Maanyofuulka, when the media was portraying the TFG as if it had no military or police forces. Attempts to establish authority beyond Baidoa had been threatened by the recent rise of the Supreme Islamic Council of Somalia, which now controlled much of the southern and central parts of the country, including the capital. The government and Islamist leaders had held two sets of talks to find a way forward, but little progress had been made. Nobody had claimed responsibility for the attack.[32] Ethiopia's ally, the TFG, was corrupt and feeble, and it welcomed the Ethiopian military support. In 2006 it had a physical presence in only two towns, provided no useful services to Somalis, and with the ICU's ascendancy was becoming increasingly irrelevant.[33]

Despite all media propaganda against the TFG such as it was receiving international support, there was no support from regional body IGAD, AU, and other international bodies. Although AU and IGAD made pledges to deploy peacekeeping forces early 2005, the first IGAD soldier set foot in Somalia in December 2006, and it was Ethiopia's invasion defending its sovereignty and irredentism and not to support Somalia.

Unlike the way Western countries and Somalia assumed, Ethiopia invaded Somalia to defend its sovereignty and irredentism and viewed a powerful, strong Somali Government as a threat to its sovereignty.

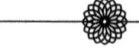

---

32. Ibid
33. Human Rights Watch, "So Much to Fear: War Crimes and the Devastation of Somalia," December 8, 2008, https://www.hrw.org/report/2008/12/08/so-much-fear/war-crimes-and-devastation-somalia.

CHAPTER 3

THE DEFEAT OF ISLAMIC COURT UNIONS BY TFG AND MILITARY STRATEGY

CHAPTER 3

THE DEFEAT OF ISLAMIC COURT UNIONS BY TFG AND MILITARY STRATEGY

> *former government military experts developed a military strategy to defeat Alshabaab.*

[**Fig. 4:** The Islamic Courts Union, in Somali: *Midowga Maxkamadaha Islaamiga.*]

3.1. TFG Strategy Deployed to Defeat ICU

In this chapter we will cover the military strategy developed and used to defeat the Islamic Courts Union who captured, in a very short period of time, and controlled a large part of South Central Somalia. In other words, from Bandiiradley in the Mudug region of central Somalia to Raaskambooni in southern Somalia's Lower Jubba region, exactly where Somalia borders with Kenya. Only small parts of the Bay and Bakool regions weren't under their control. Before we state the unique strategy deployed by the TFG to defeat the Islamic Courts Union (ICU), we will begin with how the Islamic Courts Union came into play and became relevant in Somalia's security and political ecosystems. The Islamic Courts Union emerged from the combination of continuous oppression of the people by warlords, who disconnected the flow of business and people across the country, and the new US contracts for the warlords to arrest suspected non-Somali terrorists in Somalia. The Mogadishu warlords named themselves ARPCT (Alliance for Restoration of Peace and Counter Terrorism) after receiving the US contract to arrest suspected terrorists and hand them over to the US.

As the ICU consolidated control in Mogadishu, Washington came to view it as a terrorist threat. In mid-2006 the United States sought the handover of several non-Somali terrorist suspects who it believed were being sheltered by the ICU, but ICU leaders reportedly ignored those requests. Washington responded by backing a coalition of Somali warlords, each in command of personal militia forces, in a bid to oust the ICU from Mogadishu. The warlords, who played upon US terrorism concerns by branding themselves the "Alliance for the Restoration of Peace and Counterterrorism," were defeated by the ICU in mid-2006.[34] The newly named alliance triggered the Islamic Courts Union to unify their resources and forces against the ARPCT and provided an opportunity to sway the hearts and minds of the people behind their vision, labeling the ARPCT as being against "practicing the Islamic religion". The Islamic

---

34. Human Rights Watch, "So Much to Fear": War Crimes and the Devastation of Somalia, 1-56432-415-X, 8 December 2008, https://www.refworld.org/reference/countryrep/hrw/2008/en/64117 [accessed 26 February 2025]

Courts Union successfully managed to win the support of the people, thus mobilizing massive forces, predominantly untrained. The first half of 2006 was characterized by intense fighting between the ICU and the ARPCT, a group of allied warlords who enjoyed a degree of support from the US.[35]

While sporadic inter-clan violence was not uncommon in Somalia between the collapse of the Barre regime in 1991 and 2006, the ICU-ARPCT struggle was particularly consequential, as the ARPCT represented the last barrier to the ICU's rise to power.[36] Warlords under the name ARPCT failed to develop shared meaning, purpose, and strategy for seizing the suspected terrorists sought by the USA and defending against the ICU attacks. The ARPCT never unified their militias and resources, thus they were facing the massive unified ICU forces separately or individually. This poor strategy by ARPCT led the ICU to defeat them and capture all their weapons. By July, the ICU had routed ARPCT forces and effectively established control over Mogadishu and parts of central and southern Somalia.[37] The Union of Islamic Courts, a group of Sharia courts supported by majority of clans inhabiting in southern defeated various warlords constituting the Alliance for the Restoration of Peace and Counter-Terrorism (ARPCT) in 2006, and thus seized control of much of southern and central Somalia, including the capital city of Mogadishu.[38]

The ICU advanced their agenda to win more public support across the country by taking action against other elements generating insecurity in Mogadishu. Upon securing the capital city, the ICU removed freelance militia checkpoints and improved freedom of movement throughout the city. The ICU's ascendancy ushered in a brief period of relative calm that allowed the "opportunity to enhance already existing and on-going humanitarian activities, in particular in favor of around a quarter of a

---

35. Civins, Braden. *Ethiopia's Intervention in Somalia, 2006-2009*. (Seoul, South Korea: Yonsei University, 2010), p.125
36. Civins, Braden. *Ethiopia's Intervention in Somalia, 2006-2009*. (Seoul, South Korea: Yonsei University, 2010), p.125
37. Civins, Braden. *Ethiopia's Intervention in Somalia, 2006-2009*. (Seoul, South Korea: Yonsei University, 2010), p.126
38. Civins, Braden. *Ethiopia's Intervention in Somalia, 2006-2009*. (Seoul, South Korea: Yonsei University, 2010), p.123

million [internally displaced persons] IDPs residing in the capital who ha[d] been receiving very limited assistance over the years." Furthermore, in mid-July the ICU actively encouraged UN agencies to reinforce their support to IDPs that were residing in overcrowded settlements in Mogadishu.[39] Although the TFG was not part of the fight between ICU and ARPCT, its senior military officers and the president had been regularly monitoring the situation and potential new developments from both sides, and in particular they had been assessing their military capabilities and public support lost or gained by one of the two sides fighting for control of Mogadishu.

With the ostensible purpose of facilitating dialogue between the TFG and the ICU, the United Nations Security Council passed Resolution 1725 (UNSCR 1725) in December 2006.[40] The Resolution called for the deployment of a multinational peacekeeping force made up of Intergovernmental Authority on Development and African Union personnel to facilitate peace talks between the TFG and ICU, maintain security in TFG-controlled Baidoa, protect TFG government officials, and train TFG security personnel.[41] Immediately after its passage, the ICU, adamantly opposed to the measure, began attacking TFG-held territories in and around Baidoa.[42] These attacks catalyzed the offensive deployment of the ENDF-TFG forces toward Mogadishu and marked the beginning of the end for the ICU.[43] The result was that "[b]y the end of December the ICU had folded under an Ethiopian-led TFG advance, with some ICU leaders and troops retreating south from Mogadishu, and others **melting back into the city's population**."[44] Fortunately, the TFG had former Siad Barre military officers who possessed higher military skills and experience and, as a result, believed that the ICU was not a great technical threat to the TFG.

---

39. Civins, Braden. *Ethiopia's Intervention in Somalia, 2006-2009*. (Seoul, South Korea: Yonsei University, 2010), p.126
40. Civins, Braden. *Ethiopia's Intervention in Somalia, 2006-2009*. (Seoul, South Korea: Yonsei University, 2010), p.124
41. Ibid
42. Ibid
43. Ibid
44. Ibid

The TFG military officers identified that the ICU lacked sufficient military experts on the terrain. Furthermore, what they identified as a weakness was the absence of superiority in terms of weapons, military hardware, and assault vehicles from the TFG side. They just wanted support in terms of superior weapons to easily defeat them. This was the major reason the TFG leadership requested Ethiopian troops' entry into Somalia, primarily because of the arms embargo on Somalia. Ethiopia, at the request of the TFG, deployed an unspecified number of ENDF soldiers to Baidoa in July 2006 following the capture of a nearby city by militias loyal to the ICU.[45] The United States, which denounced ICU leaders for harboring wanted terrorists, supported Ethiopia's actions with political backing and military assistance.[46] The Ethiopian military easily routed the ICU's militias. For a few days it appeared that they had won an easy victory and that the TFG **had ridden Ethiopia's coattails** into power in Mogadishu. But the first insurgent attacks against Ethiopian and TFG forces began almost immediately and rapidly built toward a protracted conflict that has since grown worse with every passing month.[47] This is where Ethiopia's crippling agenda commenced.

3.2. ICU's Perspective on TFG Before Their Fight Against ARPCT

The ICU leaders, based on the democratic process that the newly formed TFG had been applying, knew they could not confront them, and it was hard for them to get public support for that reason. But the TFG efforts in building an inclusive, powerful democratic government never received international media support and international community moral support over the past two years. In addition to this, people in Somalia, including ICU leaders and supporters, underscored the TFG process as powerful, transparent and inclusive. The TFG relocation process from

---

45. Ibid
46. Human Rights Watch, "So Much to Fear": War Crimes and the Devastation of Somalia, 1-56432-415-X, 8 December 2008, https://www.refworld.org/reference/countryrep/hrw/2008/en/64117 [accessed 26 February 2025]
47. Human Rights Watch, "So Much to Fear": War Crimes and the Devastation of Somalia, 1-56432-415-X, 8 December 2008, https://www.refworld.org/reference/countryrep/hrw/2008/en/64117 [accessed 26 February 2025]

Nairobi to Garowe and to Baidoa was breathing in with more democratic values, including engagement with the various political groups and local communities across Somalia, and more consultation seeking their input on the process by creating a conducive environment enabling people to contribute, criticize safely, and feel ownership. Ethiopia never wanted to see a powerful democratic government in Somalia, as Ethiopia itself was not practicing democratic values and good governance; as such, they viewed the TFG as a threat.

3.3. TFG Democratic Efforts Vilified by International Media and International Organizations

Although, all international media, human rights organizations, and UN agencies relentlessly vilified the democratic values the TFG adopted and labeled it as a weak government that didn't even control beyond Baidoa city, yet the TFG had broad support from Garowe all the way to Baidoa and Gedo and Lower Jubba regions. Furthermore, it's worthy to note that the TFG had 11,500 soldiers, of which only 5,000 were from Puntland regions, and the remaining 6,500 joined from other regions through TFG engagement with the people during the two years (from February 2005 to November 2006).

Despite relentless vilification of the TFG quality and the democratic process that nurtured it, the truth about the TFG forces and their capacity and capabilities had been recognized after Ethiopia's withdrawal and securitization move in early 2009.

Despite continuous disparaging of the TFG's true democratic process it had adopted, the true value of its military army had been exposed during the unity government when the former ICU leader, the then president, recognized the qualities and discipline of the TFG army in the villa and instructed them to liberate Mogadishu instead of the ICU fighters he came with.

3.4. TFG Without the Ethiopian Intervention

The TFG, post Ethiopia's invasion and securitization move, liberated all Al-Shabaab bases in Mogadishu without the support of Ethiopia, but with other AU forces. This was proof that without Ethiopian intervention, the TFG alone could have fought with ICU forces and defeat them without the displacement of millions and the death of tens of thousands of people

3.5. TFG Commanders from USA and USSR Military Academies in Baidoa and Strategy They Developed

Contrary to many published reports which portrayed negatively about the facts of the TFG, for example, that Ethiopia's ally the TFG was corrupt and feeble and it welcomed the Ethiopian military support - in 2006 it had a physical presence in only two towns, provided no useful services to Somalis, and with the ICU's ascendancy was becoming increasingly irrelevant[48]; And Unlike the perception that the TFG came to power through ridding coattails of the ENDF, the TFG had a good number of former military commanders trained both in USA and USSR military academies and 11,500 well-disciplined and skillful army personnel in Baidoa. This was the first time that TFG leaders at all levels, including political leaders and military commanders, changed their approach to the peaceful relocation process. This was compelled by the aggressive attack of the Islamic Courts Union. The Islamic Courts Union was a powerful force that emerged as a result of the warlords who lost their territories to the ICU militia as well as their influence in society, while the ICU started gaining public trust in a very speedy manner. This led Islamic Courts Union forces to wage war against all warlords controlling large parts of south central Somalia. They disarmed and humiliated all warlords and were willing to also disarm the Transitional Federal Government forces and destroy the government. Thus, everyone knew they would never spare Baidoa, which was defined as their next target.

It is noteworthy that the Defense Minister of the Transitional Federal Government, who was among the warlords and controlling the port city of Kismaio, was the last warlord they defeated. Despite being a former military officer of SNA and skilled in guerrilla warfare, he managed to fight with the powerful Islamic Courts Union forces for weeks but eventually

---

48. Human Rights Watch, "So Much to Fear": War Crimes and the Devastation of Somalia, 1-56432-415-X, 8 December 2008, https://www.refworld.org/reference/countryrep/hrw/2008/en/64117 [accessed 26 February 2025]

lost to them. He came to Baidoa from Kismaio seeking support to continue to fight with them and regain control of the Kismaio port. However, the President said to the Defense Minister, Col. Barre Adam Shire, that he was focusing on defending Baidoa as ICU forces were planning to attack Baidoa and destroy the government, adding, "You are the Minister, so I propose you join us in defending Baidoa." However, Col. Barre Hiiraale declined the president's proposal and insisted on proceeding with his plan of regaining Kismaayo and requested the president to consider his request. As a result, the president provided him all the military logistical support he requested.

As Col. Barre Hiiraale and his forces were close to Kismaayo, the ICU orchestrated a coordinated attacks against his forces and Burhakaba district of Bay region to deter potential military backup from the Federal government in Baidoa. It became apparent that Col. Barre Hiiraale will once again be defeated. In Burhakaba, after confrontation between ICU forces and Transitional Federal Government forces, it was decided that TFG forces would withdraw at midnight from this front and were brought back to Daynuunaay base. For Col. Barre Hiiraale, backup forces were sent to help him survive from orchestrated various flanks, and he returned safely to Baidoa. In light of growing concern about the ICU's potential attack to capture Baidoa, in southern Somalia which the Transitional Federal Government operated from, the situation became stressful. This quickly led to the development of a military strategy comprising both offensive and defensive elements. The ICU forces were not only successful in all battlefields but won the hearts and minds of the people, including defeated warlords' militias who recalled their confrontation with ICU forces in many battlefields. They said they fought like Mujaahidiin who don't fear death, which is why they always win in every battlefield. Despite this, the Transitional Federal Government forces and ICU forces had not yet come face to face in any battlefield and had no idea about each other. Among the key military experts who joined in military strategy development was General Ade Muse Hersi. A successful military strategy was consensually agreed upon by all Transitional Federal Government commanders. The following was how the strategy was outlined.

Having in mind the potential attack by ICU forces to capture Baidoa, the strategy formulated two strong defenses that would deter ICU massive forces from proceeding further to capture Baidoa. These were:

Mood Moode and Idaale defenses. The planned duration that the confrontation could go on was two weeks; hence, brigades placed in these two defense positions were provided all resources they needed and instructed to remain there for two weeks as defense and not attempt any offensive even if they felt the enemy weakened. For the offensive, having in mind the stretched power of the ICU from Bandiiradley to Raaskambooni, the **strategy outlined the following offensive steps**. Knowing that they would wage massive attacks on Moode Moode and Idaale to capture Baidoa, and there would be a need to get more backup forces, it was decided to attack ICU forces stretched from Mudug, Hiiraan, Galgaduud, Middle and Lower Shabelle regions to weaken them and deter them from sending reinforcing forces to their forces fighting in Idaale and Mood Moode. The strategy offered them reinforcement from Gedo and the two Jubbas, which is another forested land and strategic for them to vacate and join Idaale where powerful TFG forces were deployed to finally defeat them. This design was deliberately made for the strategic defeat of the ICU forces across Somalia by the TFG commanders and experts. There was one more direction that the ICU might come from but far from Baidoa: the north side toward Waajid, Tiyeeglow, Hudur, and QuraJome. Brigades from the TFG that had been based there were involved to defend this direction.

3.6. On the Offensive Strategy

Step one of the offensive strategy: As ICU stretched from Mudug, which is east from Baidoa geographically, a brigade led by General Ade Muse, General. Abdi Qeybdiid, Col. Hiif Ali Taar and Minister Warsame Abdi Shirwa (Seefta Banaanka) attacked ICU forces in Bandiiradley, Adaado, Dhuuso Mareeb, and Guri-ceel through Beledweyne, where there was another TFG brigade, and unified their forces to reach Mogadishu. **The second offensive strategy**, which started from Beledweyne, was led by General Mukhtar Hussein Afrah, Governor Mohamed Omar Habeeb, and General Tawane, who were tasked to regain the Beledweyne area, Buloburte, Mahaddaay, Jowhar, Balcad, and East Mogadishu.

3.7. On the Defensive Strategy

Step 3 of the defensive strategy was primarily Iidaale, but also included Safar Nooleys, Habaallo Barbaar, Dharqo, and Diinsoor defense. ICU flooded tens of thousands of their forces to defeat the TFG forces and proceed to Baidoa where the government operated. The TFG forces led by the Defense Minister Col. Barre Hiiraale and General Saeed Mohamed Hersi were ordered to remain in their defensive position for two weeks. The objective was to defeat them and deter them from proceeding to Baidoa, while offensive operations were going on in the peripheral areas to destroy their bases that might extend any reinforcement. However, this defensive brigade led by Minister of Defense Col. Hiiraale was tasked to pursue them in the event they defeated them after days, all the way to Raaskambooni, as they had not left any soldiers behind at Raaskambooni.

Step 4 of the defensive strategy: This brigade was led by the Prime Minister Ali Mohamed Ghedi and the Deputy Defense Minister Salad Ali Jeele. This was the Mood Moode defense position, and after two weeks in defense, the plan for them was to proceed toward Mogadishu. All strategy plans, offensive and defensive, became highly successful. Despite huge casualties on both sides and major losses of vehicles and other resources, we finally captured all territories under the control of ICU forces. However, during the battlefield engagements, the ICU forces viewed both Mood Moode and Iidaale defenses as strong enough, but they later obtained intelligence information that Iidaale was more fortified and prospects to defeat Iidaale were narrow. Hence, they focused on attacking the Mood Moode defense, but the TFG forces defeated them viciously. As a bitter war continued for four consecutive days, one of the toughest wars in Africa in battlefields for the warring sides only, where each side was committed to be the winner, the only competitive advantage was military skills, experience, and logistics, which would determine success and defeat. As a result, the former Somali Generals defeated ICU forces through tacit knowledge on the battlefields. In light of this TFG success, the global media has still been depicting the TFG as weak and claiming that without Ethiopian forces they could have been destroyed by ICU forces.

This government was known as an ally of Ethiopia (one of its main weaknesses in the eyes of the Somali population), and dependent on foreign support, not only from the US or EU, but Ethiopia as well, as their openly admitted good relationship showed.[49] This implies that the securitization move of the Ethiopian government regarding the events in Somalia in 2006 and after helped not only to secure the Ethiopian state but also to reshape the image of the Ethiopian regime and its political project.[50]

Ethiopia Launches Attack on Somalia. Contrary to what international media assumed, Ethiopia didn't come to provide the support requested by TFG leaders in Baidoa. The Ethiopian Prime Minister admits his troops are waging a war against Islamic Courts fighters, but the truth was Ethiopia waged war against Somalia and its newly formed government with the support of the international community. The international community's intention was pretty much appreciative as it spent millions of dollars to reestablish a government that could restore law and order and deter risks of being taken ovet by terrorists. "Ethiopian defense forces were forced to enter into war to protect the sovereignty of the nation and to blunt repeated attacks by Islamic Courts terrorists and anti-Ethiopian elements they are supporting," Meles said in a televised address. Ethiopia had in mind something else as the then Prime Minister said: "Protecting sovereignty and irredentism. Our defense forces will leave as soon as they end their mission." Berhan Hailu, Ethiopia's Information Minister, said earlier his country's forces had targeted several fronts including Dinsoor, Bandiradley, Belet Weyne, and the town of Buur Hakaba – close to the interim government's encircled base of Baidoa. "The Somali government will defend the people it is responsible for and Somali sovereignty," Ali Mohamed Gedi, Somali PM. The continuation of Ethiopian forces' presence in Somalia enabled the terrorists to regroup and keep fighting. This is because Ethiopia never wanted to destroy the terrorists but rather it wanted them to flourish.

This hidden agenda undermined both Somalia's and western countries' efforts in Somalia and their common strategic interest. Despite the defeat of the ICU, violence persisted largely unabated for the next

---

49. Aimé, Elsa González. "The Security Issues Behind the Ethiopian Intervention in Somalia (2006-2009)". *State and Societal Challenges in the Horn of Africa*, edited by Alexandra Magnólia Dias, Centro de Estudos Internacionais, 2013, p.33
50. Ibid

two years as former ICU loyalists, Islamist militias such as al Shabaab, and elements of the newly formed Alliance for the Re-Liberation of Somalia (ARS) waged an insurgent campaign against the ENDF-TFG.[51] The power vacuum left by the ICU's collapse turned Somalia into a proxy battlefield of sorts, as a host of combatants sought to achieve a diverse set of aims in the resulting chaos: (1) the US targeted suspected al Qaeda members; (2) Eritreans armed and trained Somali militias to inflict losses upon their chief rival, Ethiopia; (3) Islamist militias and foreign jihadists waged war to dislodge the US-supported ENDF and establish a foothold in the Horn of Africa; and (4) Somali warlords sought to aggrandize their power.[52] ICU remained strong enough since December 2006, and the TFG was weakened by ENDF who withdrew from all their military bases unilaterally, while Alshabab took over all those bases. The TFG leader requested Ethiopian troops to leave the country, which led to a new initiative, particularly the formation of a unity government.

In October 2008, an agreement signed between TFG and ARS officials in Djibouti called for the formation of a joint police force of 10,000 to maintain security in Mogadishu following an envisaged relocation of ENDF troops from much of the city.[53] The formation of a unity Government that enjoyed a measure of support in both Ethiopia and Somalia was perhaps a turning point in addressing the humanitarian crisis. The success of the new government hinged on its ability to assert control over central and southern Somalia, a formidable challenge considering the continued violence in those regions caused by inter-clan fighting and militant Islamists.[54] If the unity government proved capable of stabilizing Somalia and reintroducing the rule of law, Ethiopia's intervention, it can be argued, will have played at least some role in paving the way for long-term improvement in humanitarian conditions in

---

51. Civins, Braden. *Ethiopia's Intervention in Somalia, 2006-2009*. (Seoul, South Korea: Yonsei University, 2010), p.124
52. Civins, Braden. *Ethiopia's Intervention in Somalia, 2006-2009*. (Seoul, South Korea: Yonsei University, 2010), p.124
53. Human Rights Watch, "So Much to Fear": War Crimes and the Devastation of Somalia, 1-56432-415-X, 8 December 2008, https://www.refworld.org/reference/countryrep/hrw/2008/en/64117 [accessed 26 February 2025]
54. Civins, Braden. *Ethiopia's Intervention in Somalia, 2006-2009*. (Seoul, South Korea: Yonsei University, 2010), p.138

Somalia.⁵⁵ Ethiopia's true agenda was to weaken the TFG and empower the terrorists because Ethiopia viewed the presence of terrorists in Somali territory as an opportunity to milk the western countries on one hand, while on the other hand it viewed a strong Somali government with strong institutions and military forces to defeat as a threat to its existence.

However, it claimed it invaded Somalia to destroy terrorists. Ethiopia decided to intervene militarily against the ICU and empower the TFG later that year, and the United States provided staunch political and material support.⁵⁶ Ethiopia received sufficient support from the USA through the fig leaf and committed huge human rights violations, including mass civilian casualties, displacement, and bombardment. Ethiopia ended its two-year occupation of Somalia, claiming to have nullified the threat of Islamist rule, even though much of the country remained in the hands of violent insurgents.⁵⁷ Over the past two years, hundreds of thousands of people fled their homes because of the fighting. At least 16,000 civilians were killed.⁵⁸

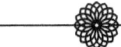

---

55. Ibid
56. Human Rights Watch, "So Much to Fear": War Crimes and the Devastation of Somalia, 1-56432-415-X, 8 December 2008, https://www.refworld.org/reference/countryrep/hrw/2008/en/64117 [accessed 26 February 2025]
57. Xan Rice and agencies in Nairobi, "*Somali president escapes car bomb suicide attack,*" The Guardian, September 19, 2006, https://www.theguardian.com/world/2006/sep/19/mainsection.international11.
58. Xan Rice and agencies in Nairobi, "*Somali president escapes car bomb suicide attack*," The Guardian, September 19, 2006, https://www.theguardian.com/world/2006/sep/19/mainsection.international11.

CHAPTER

THE 5ᵀᴴ BRIGADE

THE 5TH BRIGADE

Major Abdirahman O. Warsame "Jeeniqaar"

CHAPTER 4

THE 5ᵀᴴ BRIGADE

> *One of the most fearless armies that Somalia counted on for relocation processes.*

4.1. Introduction

In countries with militarily strong establishments, there is always a powerful brigade notorious for their competency to dominate enemies in the battlefield. As a result, this brigade is often deployed to dangerous battlefields to destroy enemy forces and capabilities. For instance, Stalingrad, formerly known as Volgograd, is well documented in the history books of the Second World War. Stalingrad was a notorious city in the history of World War II and featured prominently in many books written by historians. This Russian city witnessed a ferocious war between the powerful German 6th Army and the Russian Red Army. In 1942, German leader Adolf Hitler sent the 6th Army Wehrmacht to capture Stalingrad, while his counterpart Joseph Stalin gave a standing order known as "Not One Step Back" to the Russian Red Army. The German 6th Army was commanded by General Friedrich Paulus, whereas the Russian army sent to dig in was commanded by General Timoshenko. The bitter war in Stalingrad lasted a year. Eventually, the German forces commanded by General Friedrich Paulus were defeated, resulting in his capture as a prisoner of war. As stated above, the 5th Brigade was an army that President Abdullahi Yusuf Ahmed regarded as comparable to the German 6th Army Wehrmacht. We need to examine the potential challenges that the Somali 5th Brigade, commanded by General Abdirizak Afgudud, encountered in the battlefield during fighting with terrorist forces. These terrorists were dedicated to overthrowing the internationally backed government struggling to relocate itself back to Somalia's capital city, Mogadishu.

In terms of army brigade competency, the 5th Brigade was one of the most significant brigades known to have unique experience, skills, and an undefeated record in battlefields. It was a powerful brigade that existed prior to the formation of Puntland State of Somalia and was remembered for the fierce fighting against Al-Ittihad Al-Islami, who had arrested the traditional and political leaders in Puntland who were involved in the formation of Puntland State. The Puntland state comprised the following regions: Sool, Sanaag, Mudug, Karkaar, Bari, Nugaal, and Buuhoodle district of Puntland. The 5th Brigade defeated Al-Ittihad Al-Islami fighters in Garowe, Ligle, 54th base, 22nd base, and Bihin Valley. It waged a fierce war against the main base of Al-Ittihad Al-Islami located in the mountains of Sanaag region and Saliid, while it carried out ferocious military operations in the Galgala Mountains of Bari region. President Ade Muse of Puntland and President Abdullahi Yusuf of Somalia quarrelled over the deployment and involvement of 5th brigade for the relocation processes. For Ade Muse, he never wanted to release the 5th brigade and instead wanted it to remain in Puntland, while Abdullahi Yusuf demanded the 5th brigade to lead the SNA reconstitution processes and facilitate the relocation process Finally, President Abdullahi Yusuf succeeded on use the 5th brigade in his mission.

4.2. The 5th Brigade Defense of the Federal Government against ICU Forces

Iidale in Bay region was the main battlefield where the two forces confronted each other. At this time, the 5th Brigade had to face the Islamic Courts Union forces who were moving swiftly and had rapidly captured most parts of south-central Somalia. President Abdullahi Yusuf, who had heard extensive propaganda about their prowess in battle, considered the 5th Brigade as the only potential force which could defend Baidoa from the Islamic Courts Union forces' attempt to capture it.

4.3. How Did the Ferocious War Between the Two Forces Happen?

The president ordered the 5th Brigade, which was based in Wajed, to be deployed to the front line to defend against the massive ICU forces advancing toward Baidoa with the intention of capturing it. It is noteworthy that there were other brigades in and around Baidoa, including the 1st Brigade and two Ethiopian brigades; however, the president had confidence in the 5th Brigade as the only potential force which could destroy the ICU forces. The 5th Brigade was immediately deployed to the front line to face ICU forces in an environment where word of mouth spread tales of the Islamic Courts Union forces' power and their likelihood of capturing Baidoa.

In this light, a garrison team from the 5th Brigade armed with a military vehicle known as "Jemis" and other motor vehicles were sent to maneuver and assess the situation of the ICU forces who were not far from them in the battlefield. This led to an immediate confrontation with another garrison unit from the enemy. In the confrontation, the 5th Brigade showed bravery and determination but lost the military vehicle and two other motor vehicles to ICU forces. This led the 5th Brigade to open their eyes and dig in against the enemy.

This was followed by fierce fighting that uninterruptedly continued for four consecutive days in which the rapidly moving ICU forces were prevented from advancing even one step ahead and suffered huge casualties that they had never experienced since the inception of their war against warlords controlling large parts of south-central Somalia. As a result, the ICU commander deployed all of their forces and reinforcements from Mogadishu and Kismaio to dislodge the 5th Brigade and achieve their goal to capture Baidoa.

On the fifth day, as the ferocity of the war intensified, the 5th Brigade forces who were dug in spotted one of their military vehicles captured in the first confrontation between the two garrisons in which two prominent soldiers named Mohamed Farah (Gaandaa), and Abdirizak

Ismail Warsame were killed. Having seen their military vehicle very close to them, now being used by the Islamic Courts forces, the 5th Brigade soldiers and commanders decided to break the standing order to remain in defense and moved to attack the Islamic forces to regain their vehicles and defeat them. This happened without even informing artillery units bombing ICU forces target areas. As a result, the artillery units were ordered to stop bombing as the 5th Brigade was no longer in a defensive but rather in an offensive position.

Consequently, the 5th Brigade sustained huge casualties, despite Islamic Courts Union forces being totally defeated. Equally important, as the artillery support was suspended, ICU took advantage and moved towards the 1st Brigade and other two Ethiopian brigades and destroyed them badly. This also led to massive casualties on all sides. Despite all sides sustaining huge casualties, ICU's case was more severe and this led them to withdraw. As a result, it was decided to chase them and not provide an opportunity to regroup. Despite ICU forces taking advantage of the suspension of artillery support from TFG forces, they on the other side intensified using more artillery which caused increased death and destruction of the 5th Brigade. The 5th Brigade captured 15 vehicles from ICU forces including their own vehicles that changed the game. Ma'ayste Hassan Aw-Osman, a prominent soldier in the 5th Brigade, captured the 5th brigade vehicle better known as Jemis. However, the 5th Brigade realized the massive casualties of their army and decided to return to their positions, but not yet, as the Islamic Courts forces who destroyed the 1st Brigade and two other Ethiopian brigades attacked the 5th and sought support from the artillery support garrison. The 5th Brigade lost command and control, and it became hard to support them as the other supporting 1st Brigade and two other Ethiopian brigades were totally destroyed.

As a result, two more battalions were quickly deployed, one from the Presidential Palace and a battalion from Bakool, to support the 5th Brigade in evacuating the injured and dead for medical assistance. As we reached the 5th Brigade base, we found plenty of injured soldiers who had not received any treatment since the morning. However, a number of medical teams from Puntland and Mogadishu accompanied us and immediately started providing necessary treatment. Unfortunately, due to the large number of casualties, which was higher than initially estimated, the available stock of drugs was not enough to meet the treatment needed to assist the huge number of injured soldiers. As a result, a good number of the casualties had to be taken to Baidoa. On the other hand, the ICU artillery attack came close to where patients were receiving treatment, thus we evacuated them, while reinforcement from the TFG side arrived late at night to support the weakened 5th Brigade. As such, a new plan was set out to attack ICU forces early in the morning.

We decided to fight alongside the 5th Brigade and take the offensive; thus, the subsequent days, the ICU forces were totally defeated. Both the 5th Brigade and the 1st Brigade were unified and merged as one new 5th Brigade. General Abdirizak Afgudud was named as commander and tasked to chase the defeated ICU forces up to Kismaio where they had retreated. General Saed Mohamed Hersi was also named to lead the whole Kismaio operations. Once we recognized ICU forces were defeated in battlefields across Somalia, the next morning we flew to a place called Arbiska, which is between Afgoye district (30km from Mogadishu) and Mogadishu, the capital city of Somalia. This was a decision made by the president to go by air to Arbiska to deter Islamic Courts forces from running towards Mogadishu. It was a step taken by the president to prevent them from entering Mogadishu as other military officers pursued the defeated scattered ICU forces.

The defeated ICU forces ran away using the road that connects Baidoa to Mogadishu. However, while they were on the run between Walaweyn and Bali Doogle area, two war planes accompanied by the president bombed them, while the presidential brigade led by Prime Minister Ali Mohamed Ghedi was in pursuit, following them to further attack them. As the team who flew to Arbiska, we went to the Baidoa airport early. The driver of the vehicle that took us to the airport was called Saleban Abdille Khalaf. Our team who traveled by air were the following:

1. President Abdullahi Yusuf Ahmed
2. Late Gen. Mohamed Warsame Darwiish, Intelligence Chief (AUN)
3. Late Gen. Awil Dhiig-Sokeeye, 54th Brigade Commander
4. Hussein Ali Saylaan, Chief of Staff of Villa Somalia
5. Col. Gebregzabher Alemseged, Ethiopia's Intelligence Officer
6. Late Col. Abdirizak Mohamed Hersi (Garcad)
7. Col. Abdiwahid Mohamud Hassan (Abdiwahid Lugey)
8. The author

9. Late Captain. Abdirashid Hersi Mohamed (Abdirashid Dhere)
10. Captain. Abdifatah Mohamed Hassan (Jamhad Gaagaale)
11. Abdiweli Osman Warsame (Abdiweli Fadhigo)
12. Adow Humey Weheliye
13. Late Mohamed Ali Samatar (Siraaje)
14. Late Abdulahi Mohamed Abdi Jubba Koolle
15. Dr. Door Moallim Abdirahman, Military Medical Doctor

We landed at Arbiska airstrip, close to Afgoye district, it is a flat area with green grass and fenced with forest trees. This was indeed a base for Islamic Courts Union forces where they used to orchestrate attacks against the Transitional Federal Government based in Baidoa, and even there was also a large workshop for repairing military vehicles and defected artilleries. It was a risk area, where there was no a prior dispatched military units to assess the situation except the two military planes which flew at low altitude towards Mogadishu. As we alighted from the plane, we were 15 passengers comprising 8 presidential escorts and a medical doctor, the president and 6 other officials. Our presidential guard team embarked on to make a security setup and positioned the different directions of the airstrip. We left the president, his doctor and other officials wandering around the airstrip, while we focused on our obligations to protect the president and officials. We were only eight well-trained military officers and deployed all our skills, including removing our red hats and inserting them on the trees nearby to portray that we were more forces than our number to confuse potential enemies. In the event we were being attacked by any group, we were instructed to remain in defense of the president as he was getting in the plane to use it as a means of escape. As such, we would keep fighting until a backup reached us.

On the west side of the airstrip, there was the main highway that connects Mogadishu and Afgoye. This is the main road that public transport known as "Caasi" uses, and it was a busy road. There is a bus stop between Arbiska and Afgooye which is not very far from the airstrip. Having seen our presence on the road side, drivers of the busy road stopped their movement for fair of our presence. Two officers, Mohamed Ali Samatar and Abdullahi Mohamed Abdi, were communicated with by General Awil Dhiig-sokeeye and instructed to inform the public using the transport and drivers to feel free and continue their business as usual. For the two officers tasked to diffuse the traffic jam on the main road as a result of the army presence, Abdullahi Mohamed Abdi, who was not familiar with Ethiopia except during the course of the relocation from Puntland to Mogadishu, was sent to talk to the drivers and inform them to continue their business as usual. The other officer was tasked to cover him as he is engaging in with the peole.

Officer Koole, as he reached the main road, signaled drivers to keep moving; however, only one driver moved, the rest were not courageous enough to keep moving. As a result, officer Abdullahi Koolo impersonated an Ethiopian soldier and communicated with drivers using his own new vocabulary, "Gina Gina," and signaled drivers to move and they continued their travel. This is because Somalis have concerns about ethiopian forces. A passing Somali girl who assumed Koole was an Ethiopian soldier told drivers, "The Ethiopian soldier is signaling you to keep moving." Eventually, Koole communicated back to us and confirmed the smooth transport movement. Most of the transport was from Afgoye with limited transport from Mogadishu to Afgoye. As we stayed in defense longer than expected, we felt more thirst. Knowing that it was hard for us to fetch water from the area due to our small number, we heard a communication from the main road towards the Afgoye side, indicating a convoy of assault vehicles was appearing. Our mood changed to a hostile mood, and we didn't feel any thirst anymore.

The officer in charge of that direction, Officer Abdirizak Garacad, informed us about two assault vehicles coming. We all became alert for a potential attack. However, it was later confirmed that it was our own army escorting Prime Minister Ali Ghedi from the battlefield. We then stood down from the tension and felt more relieved as we now had more reinforcement from our own presidential guard brigade. A few hours later, we received a full convoy led by Prime Minister Ali Mohamed Ghedi. Then there was a discussion about possibility of proceeding towards Mogadishu. As such elders from Mogadishu were invited to the discussion, covering primarily the possibility of disarmament and security and the way in which the government could be relocated to Mogadishu and operate there. This was the official policy that TFG had been applying over the past two years to form an inclusive democratic government.

One of the key points proposed was that we should move to Mogadishu on the same day. This resulted in the president questioning everyone's opinion about that point to gather more information and consider divergent views and insights from all. The discussion took longer than expected; however, the president was happy with that because he never wanted to go back to Baidoa as he was now close to Mogadishu. Among the notable suggestions was one offered by Mohamed Omar Samriye, also known as Shaaweeye. He said, "Mr. President, Mogadishu enjoyed six months of remarkable peace, in which people changed their lifestyle from that of 1990 whereby people were wearing their best clothes, and there were no thieves and armed militias to rob you. We need you to maintain such hardly gained peace, and if you go to Mogadishu with these brigades, I want to let you know that you will just fail as the previous two presidents, namely Abdikasim Hassan and Ali Mahdi Mohamed, became failures."

He continued his suggestion discourse and pointed out that Mogadishu is a large city badly destroyed by the civil war, with massive bloodshed, while all government infrastructures were either out of order or occupied by civilians. On the other hand, "Mr. President, once your army brigades enter Mogadishu, they will likely encounter remnants of the defeated Islamic Courts Union forces. As such, you better stay and operate in Baidoa for two years." In my view, it was the best suggestion, and I heard the same insight from the president himself. As the discussion was still ongoing and the sun was setting, the president said, "We don't have more time now, and I see this Mogadishu discussion requires more time. I will leave with the prime minister who will go with you to Mogadishu to pave the way for government relocation, and I will be coming to Mogadishu in a few days." We then walked toward the airplane to return to Baidoa. We landed in Baidoa at exactly 6 PM and moved to the Presidential Palace. Prime Minister Ghedi proceeded with his journey together with Mogadishu elders toward the capital city. On his first night, he stopped at Hawo Abdi area close to Mogadishu, and the next morning he entered Mogadishu.

In light of growing efforts by the TFG to overcome challenging assumptions through democratic processes key international bodies described it: Ethiopia's ally, the TFG, was corrupt and feeble. However, here's where the true agenda of Ethiopia emerged.

4.4. Misalignment Between TFG Leaders and ENDF Commanders Over How to Proceed to Mogadishu

Great misalignment between TFG and ENDF emerged over how to proceed towards Mogadishu. The Somali Government wanted to keep its inclusive and participative policy dialogue and not resort to military means or use of forces, while ENDF had its own hidden agenda including ignoring the TFG and its leadership and unilaterally proceeding to enter Mogadishu with its own military tanks and multiple rocket launcher, 12 tube 107mm. The President engaged with Ethiopian commanders and shared with them the TFG tested and proven democratic approach to enter Mogadishu, but ENDF commanders ignored it. From this point forward, Ethiopia's ENDF commanders and Intelligence officers would act as if they were the sole authority in Mogadishu through unprecedented harassment against Somali government politicians and senior SNA commanders and indiscriminate bombardment of highly civilian populated areas in Mogadishu, using multiple rocket launchers - we will discuss more about this in the following chapters. Both Western efforts and the desire of the Somali people to be a stable, peaceful and prosperous democratic nation would be crippled by these killers and arrogant Ethiopian commanders who applied total securitization policies against all of Somalia.[59]

---

59. Human Rights Watch, "So Much to Fear": War Crimes and the Devastation of Somalia, 1-56432-415-X, 8 December 2008, https://www.refworld.org/reference/countryrep/hrw/2008/en/64117 [accessed 26 February 2025]

CHAPTER 5

VILLA SOMALIA

CHAPTER 5

VILLA SOMALIA

> *The peaceful democratic value process that the TFG chose to convince civilians sheltering in Villa Somalia to vacate by themselves.*

[Fig. 5: From right to left: President Abdullahi Yuusuf and Ethiopia's Foreign Minister Seyoum Mosfen. At the back from the right to left: the author, and General Mohamed Nuur.]

5.1. Introduction

The rise of the Islamic Courts Union (ICU) in Mogadishu was the primary reason for Ethiopia's military intervention in Somalia in late 2006. Many analysts characterized the decision to intervene as disastrous and ill-conceived although Ethiopia had genuine concerns. Ethiopia and Somalia have a long history of mutual enmity, and the two countries fought a costly war in 1977 when Somalia's military invaded Ethiopia in a doomed attempt to annex what is now Ethiopia's Somali Region.[60]

In 2006, some ICU leaders took actions and made statements that stoked Ethiopia's fears of what a resurgent and hostile Somalia could mean for its own stability.[61] Hardliners within the ICU declared war against Ethiopia. Some also publicly voiced irredentist claims on Ethiopia's Somali Region—the same claims used to justify Somalia's 1977 invasion. The ICU also courted the support of Ethiopia's arch-foe Eritrea, which has made a policy out of waging proxy wars against Ethiopia through client rebel movements. All of this took place while Ethiopia was waging a brutal counterinsurgency campaign at home against the ethnic Somali Ogaden National Liberation Front—an armed group Ethiopia did not want enjoying the patronage of any potential ICU-led government.[62] But irrespective of Ethiopia's motives for intervention in Somalia, there is no justification for the numerous violations of the laws of war and human rights abuses committed by Ethiopian forces in the country.[63]

---

60. Human Rights Watch, "So Much to Fear": War Crimes and the Devastation of Somalia, 1-56432-415-X, 8 December 2008, https://www.refworld.org/reference/countryrep/hrw/2008/en/64117 [accessed 26 February 2025]
61. Ibid
62. Ibid
63. Ibid

5.2. Untrue Diplomatic Picture Between TFG and ENDF Painted by Analysts

Diplomatically, Ethiopia has also by and large failed to play a constructive role. The Ethiopian government has more diplomatic leverage over Somalia's Transitional Federal Government (TFG) than any other foreign power—most analysts believe that the TFG would crumble without the backing of Ethiopian National Defense Force (ENDF) troops on the ground. In August 2008, Ethiopia made important diplomatic efforts to mediate a dangerously widening political rift between TFG Prime Minister Nur Hassan Hussein and TFG President Abdullahi Yusuf.[64] But Ethiopia has applied no discernible pressure on TFG officials to rein in the abusive conduct of their security forces and militia fighters. Instead, ENDF forces have themselves committed serious human rights abuses in operations they have conducted alongside those TFG forces.[65]

5.3. Ethiopia Denied Violations

Ethiopian government officials have refused to investigate or respond in any meaningful way to allegations of international human rights and humanitarian law violations by ENDF forces. Instead, Ethiopian officials have dismissed and angrily denied all such allegations of abuse, no matter how well documented. A November 2008 communiqué from the Ethiopian Embassy in Washington, DC to Human Rights Watch stated that the government was "unaware of any specific instance" where Ethiopian troops fired indiscriminately into civilian crowds or indiscriminately fired mortars or "Katyusha" rockets (the latter being inherently indiscriminate weapons unsuitable for use in urban environments). This mirrors the Ethiopian government's response to criticisms over its domestic human rights record, including war crimes and crimes against humanity committed by ENDF forces in Ethiopia's own Somali and Gambella regions.[66]

---

64. Ibid
65. Ibid
66. Ibid

Villa Somalia is a building inside Somalia's Presidential Palace, where Somalia's president sits to lead the country and run government business. Villa Somalia was built before independence, and it is not as big as someone might assume when hearing it described as the house where decisions regarding the country's destination are reached. It consists of 4 rooms and three sitting rooms. The building was named Villa Somalia because it is the oldest construction in the Presidential Palace. However, other buildings in the palace include the following:

1. Villa Somalia
2. Villa Hargeisa for the Speaker of the Parliament
3. President's Underground House
4. Office of the Prime Minister and other ministries
5. Office of the President
6. Military Police Base
7. Presidential Exhibition building, also known as "Uganda House"
8. The red building for one more battalion

People often use the name Villa Somalia when they want to talk about the Presidential Palace; however, Villa Somalia is just the smallest building among those in the Presidential Palace. During peacetime, it's an excellent vacation spot due to the well-developed landscape and the city view that allows you to see Mogadishu from above. In contrast, during wartime, it is easily targeted by snipers, artillery barrages, RPG-7s and other rifles, making it feel like a very insecure place. During wartime, the Underground House is very often chosen as a safe place to be, as it was built with concrete that cannot be easily destroyed by artillery bombardment and other mortar shells.

Immediately after our return from Arbiska, our brigade, the 54th, was informed on short notice to come to the parade at Baidoa Presidential Palace. A report was given to the president that the brigade was ready for his attention and instruction.

After the report, the president divided us into three groups. Thirty soldiers, including myself, were instructed to step aside from the rest of the 54th brigade and assigned as presidential escorts who would travel with the president in his trip to Mogadishu the following day. A battalion led by Col. Abudwak was told to step aside and tasked to remain in Baidoa Palace and perform their duties. The third battalion, led by General Awil Dhiig-sokeeye, was ordered to prepare for Mogadishu, particularly Villa

Somalia, by land. Early in the morning, our presidential guard team went to Baidoa airport to depart for Mogadishu. Three airplanes, including one for the president, were ready at the airport. We planned for the first two flights boarded by our teams to take off first, with the president's plane to follow us a little bit later. Importantly, we agreed to land at Mogadishu airport before landing the president's plane to ensure it was safe for him to land or to take him back to Baidoa if Mogadishu airport was deemed unsafe. Fortunately, we found Mogadishu airport to be a safe place where the prime minister, other government officials, and members of the public were waiting to receive the president.

As we alighted from the airplane, the president was received by government officials led by the prime minister. Before we moved toward vehicles to take the president to Villa Somalia as planned earlier, Prime Minister Ali Mohamed Ghedi proposed to the president to go to Hotel Lafweyn, saying they had prepared it for him because Villa Somalia was not currently suitable for him to reside and operate from. However, in response to the prime minister's proposal, the president looked at me with frowning eyes and said, "Where is our tent? Didn't you bring it with you?" I responded, "Yes, Mr. President, the tent is ready." The president then told the prime minister that there was a tent with air-conditioning fixed, asking, "Is there not a space at Villa Somalia where we can install the tent?" We knew there was no tent we came with, but this was a communication code between us and the president when there was disapproval of something or in times of difficult situations. The president preferred using codes and reading faces or body signals instead of explicit statements, particularly in difficult situations including when he sensed a security threat, or when someone was suspected of being a threat. There were levels of codes used at different stages depending on the severity of the situation.

5.4. From Mogadishu Airport to Villa Somalia

We came to Villa Somalia through KM-4 and Maka-Mukarama Avenue. However, I found surprising the difference between the Mogadishu I grew up in and how it looked now. The former was a booming city, with a lot of traffic jams where police officers used to help people cross the main road. At night, commercial flights flying at low altitude were numerous. I remember the white sand everywhere where we used to play football together with other children.

Although I found a different Mogadishu in respect of its beautifulness, yet as we proceeded to Villa Somalia from Mogadishu Airport, I couldn't understand the landscape of 1989 and the one of today—entirely different. I thought this might not be the area I was familiar with in my youngest age. Buildings destroyed, roads depleted, and massive destruction of all known places. I put a lot of effort to reconstruct how the city used to be from the rubble, depleted roads, and closed streets with illegally, roughly built business premises. However, there was a woman much more familiar with Mogadishu than I was. She was with us after requesting to travel with us, seeking to reach Mogadishu. I found her also thoroughly busy identifying locations known to her, just as I was busy trying to find the playing grounds I used to play in during my childhood. But she was more experienced in figuring out what had changed and what was left as it was before the civil war.

In addition to this confused state, we were bearing in mind the potential of roadside bombs; hence, drivers were moving faster. Our driver, named Jama, and other drivers were well-connected drivers with the same pattern of driving vehicles in tough situations. They were driving with speed despite the rough roads. As the old woman was in a state of shock, she burst out questioning about the well-known monuments including Sayid Mohamed, Ahmed Gurey, and Dhagax Tur, asking, "Where are all those historic monuments?" A young soldier who had no idea about the names of these well-remembered heroes assumed that she was talking about individuals known to her and replied, "I think those guys left Mogadishu. When was the last time you heard about their whereabouts?" She didn't respond to him and kept mourning the devastating destruction of the city. We finally arrived peacefully at Villa Somalia.

Villa Somalia, as we entered, we could immediately spot the massive destruction that it shared with Mogadishu city. However, it was also used as a military camp by warlords leading warring factions in Mogadishu. On the other hand, there were restaurants for food and some shops and a small fruit and vegetable market. Furthermore, the main roads leading to Villa Somalia and those around it which were forbidden for public transport were now being used by public transport and donkey carts fetching water for families sheltered in government buildings including the Presidential Palace. However, as we entered Villa Somalia, we went into the underground house, where Hussein Farah Aideed was residing. The president used the sitting room as a rest place and had discussions with officials who received us at the airport. He also fixed an appointment to meet with various elders from Mogadishu.

The 54th brigade, who also came to Mogadishu by land, arrived today and established a base inside the Presidential Palace. Indeed, civilian inhabitants in and around Villa Somalia extended a warm welcome to the 54th brigade. The army felt a bit of relief about the horrific travel from Baidoa to Mogadishu and Villa Somalia and two years of horrible situation. A few hours later, the meeting between the president and elders from Mogadishu gradually started. It was a very fascinating meeting. Nevertheless, as the meeting was going on, Hussein Aideed's wife entered the meeting room and told us that after the elders' meeting, there was a lunch at Hotel Lafweyn for the president where politicians had already prepared for him. However, we told her we would let her in to share the message with him directly immediately after the elders' meeting was over.

Now, in the room, the president, Captain. Abdirashid Hersi Mohamed, and I remained after the elders left. We informed the president about the lunch event at Hotel Lafweyn, where other politicians and members from civil societies were waiting to meet him and exchange views. However, the president refused the invitation for the lunch and said he was not leaving Villa Somalia, adding that this was what failed the previous two presidents, namely Abdikasim Hassan and Ali Mahdi Mohamed. He instructed us to find a place to sleep, and we embarked on the process of finding a suitable place for the president. Captain. Abdirashid on his part communicated with Asho Unlaye, one of the Somali businesswomen offering funding to the relocation process, and briefed her about the new situation and the president's position of not leaving Villa Somalia. He told her we needed to prepare a suitable place for the president to sleep. Asho immediately ordered the necessary matters and other supplies to facilitate the process. She told him we would receive a vehicle delivering all we requested in a very short time. We communicated with the 54th brigade commander to let in the vehicle delivering those supplies. We then received the requested items delivered by a very old off-road type vehicle. On my part, to assess the environment and figure out an appropriate place for the president to sleep, I called Asiya Mohamed Hassan who was sitting not far away from me and requested her to help me in setting up a place for the president to rest and sleep. She was a very humble lady who had been with the president since we left Garowe. She was a well-educated lady who didn't secure a job from the Puntland administration due to the 4.5 clan system. This system deprived many educated people of their rights to employment.

She immediately spotted a tree next to where she was sitting and said, "Hey, why don't we set up under this tree as it has good enough shade?" I agreed with her and we started preparing the shade of the tree, putting two mattresses on top of one another, and adding a mosquito net. We then went to inform the president, who was having a serious discussion with Captain. Abdirashid, and told him we had set up a place to sleep. They both came with me and we brought the president to his new bed in Villa Somalia and left him to relax or sleep. But shortly, Madam Ayan Dahir Anshur, who is the lady inhabiting the underground house and Hussein Aideed's wife, came to us and asked, "Where is the president?" I told her he was taking a nap. With disapproving behavior, she went directly to the president and said, "My uncle, why are you vilifying me? This is not an appropriate place to sleep. There is a better arrangement made by government officials at Hotel Lafweyn."

"Here in the villa there is no running water or electricity or any other basic services. Please, only tonight go to the hotel as I am now embarking on preparing the house." The president smiled, sat down, and said to her, "Uncle, sit down here," but she didn't sit down and turned towards us while she was on the phone. As she finished her phone call, she requested we help her prepare the underground house as she had changed her mind. She realized the president was happy with the villa and not Hotel Lafweyn. Madam Ayan Dahir Anshur was not only the wife of Hussein Aideed but also a close matrimonial relative to both President Abdullahi Yusuf Ahmed and the late General Aideed. As a result, she decided to vacate the underground house and let the president reside in it instead of under the tree outside the house. She then called the deputy prime minister and her own husband and plainly told him that the president was not coming to Hotel Lafweyn.

For President Abdullahi Yusuf, this tree and the two mattresses had a great significance that other government officials didn't understand.

This was because he had undergone 12 years of military prison before assuming the responsibility he now held. He didn't want to go and sleep in a simple hotel only to have many excuses created for him to return to the Villa. He has also experienced several attempts to assassinate him in the course of coming to Villa Somalia over the past two years from Garowe. Furthermore, it was the realization of his ambition since 1969 to sit in Villa Somalia and rule the country.

The president's decision to remain in the villa and use the tree as a place to sleep stemmed from his in-depth understanding of the political game played by Mogadishu politicians to undermine any new president. Any new president who opted to operate in other buildings or hotels outside Villa Somalia experienced legitimacy challenges; it portrayed them as someone weak, contrary to a sitting president from Villa Somalia. He was refusing to fall into a trap that would lead to him being perceived as a powerless president lacking legitimacy. These were the same challenges that Presidents Abdikasim Hassan and Ali Mahdi Mohamed faced, which prevented them from operating in Villa Somalia. Ethiopia's ally, the TFG, was corrupt and feeble, and it welcomed Ethiopian military support. In 2006, it had a physical presence in only two towns, provided no useful services to Somalis, and with the ICU's ascendancy was becoming increasingly irrelevant.[67]

The United States, which denounced ICU leaders for harboring wanted terrorists, supported Ethiopia's actions with political backing and military assistance.[68] The Ethiopian military easily routed the ICU's militias. For a few days, it appeared that they had won an easy victory and that the TFG had ridden Ethiopia's coattails into power in Mogadishu. But the first insurgent attacks against Ethiopian and TFG forces began almost immediately and rapidly built toward a protracted conflict that has since grown worse with every passing month.[69]

We, the security team, were not happy with the circumstances we were in, including lack of electricity, running water, great insecurity, and disorder among public transport using the villa roads in and around Villa

---

67. Human Rights Watch, "So Much to Fear": War Crimes and the Devastation of Somalia, 1-56432-415-X, 8 December 2008, https://www.refworld.org/reference/countryrep/hrw/2008/en/64117 [accessed 26 February 2025]
68. Ibid
69. Ibid

Somalia. Despite being quite shortsighted of the situation, President Yusuf not only could interpret the situation to his advantage, but he was also considering the challenges he had encountered in achieving his vision, including 12 years in prison and denial of promotion to higher military rank by the Somali National Army for 21 years as of October 1969. The deputy prime minister, Mr. Hussein Aideed, and his wife, Madam Ayaan Dahir Anshur, vacated the underground house, taking all their belongings out and allowing the president to move in. In addition to that, Hussein Aideed also instructed his security staff and assault vehicles to be removed from Villa Somalia. We then mobilized other people to act immediately for the repair of electricity and water supply systems in Villa Somalia. A good number of workers from both the water and electricity sectors stepped in and started installation and repair of the systems. Within hours, electricity was restored and people could enjoy light. For the water supply, employees started to repair the water well, water points, and supply system. Change was felt within Villa Somalia.

5.5. Warlords' Disarmament and Challenges Encountered

The international community facilitated a Somali National Reconciliation Conference in Kenya between October 2002 and October 2004. The Reconciliation Conference, guided by IGAD frontline states—namely Kenya, Ethiopia, and Djibouti—invited all warlords, existing administrations, the Transitional National Government (TNG), and civil society organizations to participate in the National Reconciliation Conference in Kenya. The purpose was to form a government consisting of all armed warlords, administrations, the TNG, and civil society in order to facilitate the disarmament and demobilization of militias loyal to them as well as freelance clan militias, and to form an inclusive government that could restore law and order and deliver urgently needed public services. However, as the government is now operating at Villa Somalia, this is the right time to put crucial efforts toward realizing the above-stated goal. The vast majority of the warlords are cabinet members and members of parliament and are required to disarm themselves and shift toward participation in building a peaceful environment where only government forces can possess arms. This means they must disarm their militias or integrate them with the reconstituted Somali National Army.

They are now the government and they should take responsibility for disarmament of their own militias. Their president is Col. Abdullahi Yusuf, who had been fighting over the past decades to hold the highest position of the government and is now The President. It is now his primary task to implement the above-stated disarmament processes and convince them to lead the process across Somalia. Each and every warlord holding a position of authority in the government, whether they are in the legislature or cabinet ministers, is required to start disarmament on themselves and set the tone for the process. Then warlords based in Mogadishu, together with the government now operating in Mogadishu, had agreed to convene meetings to discuss the way in which an integrated disarmament process led by the warlords could be implemented in Mogadishu and other regions of Somalia. In particular, a meeting between all warlords and the president had been agreed to be convened. However, all warlords attending the meeting were informed that during the meeting inside Villa Somalia, they should come without weapons and militias armed with heavy weapons. They should leave their security staff outside the premises of the meeting.

Whenever the security convoys reached the villa main gate, they were not let in but directed towards the east direction where the staff used to wait for the warlords, now ministers or MPs. There was a hotel named Balihigis. Although the vast majority of the warlords' convoys obeyed and upheld the introduced security measures and parked their vehicles at Balihigis, however, several Toyota 4WD vehicles disobeyed and entered inside Villa Somalia. Nevertheless, the military brigade didn't take action against those vehicles that entered inside office premises and violated agreed security measures. The four vehicles which disobeyed the standing order belonged to late Mohamed Qanyare, one of the most prominent warlords in Mogadishu. They had been stopped at the next checkpoint before the underground house and were diverted towards the 54th brigade base was located. There were 19 more vehicles mounted with automatic rifles caliber 12.7mm, well known in Somalia as "Dhashike," and about 100 militia each with AK-47s, which instantly mobilized themselves to react should tension arise.

They created their own defense zone around the Prime Minister's House and Ethiopian embassy, which were close to the main gate of the villa. Tension erupted between soldiers from Qanyare's men and the presidential guard commander. It is worth noting that Qanyare was attending a meeting whose agenda was the disarmament and demobilization process led by the same warlords. The 54th officers at the gate engaged with the militia to diffuse the tension and convinced them they were enforcing the standing order while allowing some of them to go inside after leaving their guns behind.

Due to Qanyare's militia's perceived superiority, as no one could block them from proceeding where they wanted in Mogadishu, instead of upholding the standing order, they opted to use force and get inside the villa where their boss was meeting with other officials. However, the tension was diffused, and Qanyare's militia went back to where other militia were staying. Both Qanyare and Muse sudi Yalahow became champions of disarmament processes. On the other hand, the president's Protocol Officer, Col. Abdiwahid Mohamud Hassan, was tasked with making arrangements for the meeting, and all the attendees' names were placed at the gate, thus allowing all warlords to smoothly pass through the gate with their private vehicles. Media outlets and other stakeholders, including Colonel Gebregziabher Alemseged Abraha of Ethiopia, head of Ethiopia intelligence were allowed to enter Villa Somalia after leaving their security staff outside at the Balihigis area.

As the president's VIP Protection, I was in the meeting room where the president and the ministers and MPs (former warlords) were discussing their agenda, which was, as mentioned above, the disarmament process that would be led by the warlords themselves, as they are now holding highest positions in the government. These efforts by TFG leaders were being ruined by Ethiopia's securitization move, which resulted in massive bombardment across Mogadishu. This government was known as an ally of Ethiopia (one of its main weaknesses in the eyes of the Somali population), and dependent on foreign support, not only from the US or EU, but Ethiopia as well, as their openly admitted good relationship showed. Ethiopia's securitization move entirely destroyed the international community's goal, which was to form a government consisting of all armed warlords to disarm themselves and avoid deploying international peacemaking forces. The TFG leaders, including warlords, were committed to implementing the disarmament process, but Ethiopia's securitization move jeopardized everything and reversed all past achievements.

In fact, Ethiopia's invasion of Somalia had an agenda different and in many ways opposite to the one pushed by Western countries. Ethiopia never wanted to support the TFG in its efforts to defeat Islamic Courts Union forces but rather it wanted to weaken the TFG and strengthen the terrorists in order to consolidate its global strategic position in the war against terrorism and maintenance of global order, thus continuously exploiting Western military, financial, and diplomatic support.

Along with these processes was the withdrawal of ENDF (the massive number). Ethiopia agreed to the withdrawal processes, but changed its mind and camped at Stadium Mogadishu. They removed their army. Fire exchange at Mogadishu stadium. The arrest of traditional leaders who requested Ethiopia's withdrawal from Somalia. Then ENDF attacked former President Abdiqasim Hassan. They eventually wanted to arrest the president. Indiscriminate attack against everyone by ENDF happened rather than a withdrawal. The disarmament processes were cancelled as Ethiopian forces started. Ethiopia intelligence developed propaganda saying ENDF wanted to withdraw but it was the TFG which was seeking that ENDF remain further. For example, when the former president's house was raided by ENDF, it was said the attack was carried out by the Somali intelligence office.

CHAPTER

ASSASSINATION ATTEMPT AGAINST THE PRESIDENT BY ETHIOPIA IN VILLA SOMALIA

CHAPTER 6

ASSASSINATION ATTEMPT AGAINST THE PRESIDENT BY ETHIOPIA IN VILLA SOMALIA

> Ethiopia National Defense Forces orchestrated an assassination to kill the president in his office in collaboration with terrorist group.

6.1. Introduction

With a little stability and good weather, clouds bearing huge amounts of water hover over us. One could have spring season imaginings, and I particularly recall my nomadic years herding camels in Doollo, Mudug, Togdheer Nugaal And Sool. I then joined Bali Busle training camp as a new cadet and later the 54th training camp in Garowe. However, the season is neither Gu nor Dayr; there have been massive rains in Mogadishu, well known as Hagaa, and it has rained uninterruptedly throughout the whole day. A proverb often used by people in Mogadishu states that Mogadishu without Hagaayo rains is Mogadishu without its niche. The situation changes at night. Unlike the good old days of uninterrupted electricity and water supply, busy city and good citizens, we now experienced pervasive darkness across the city, except for Villa Somalia, which is the only hope for reinstituting government institutions. From 1991 until 2006, Villa Somalia experienced a lack of electricity and running water, while people occupied or sheltered in all public infrastructure, using small lighting tools fueled by kerosene. During this period, the Villa became a forest, which furthermore complicated sight seeing, with disorganized business premises that people opened without permission. However, in 2007, a change was being spotted as a result of the restored electricity system and water supply in the villa Somalia. On this night, there was a meeting between the president and his prime minister which took longer than expected. There were also other high-level government officials, including members of Parliament, who were also expecting to meet with the president. The place was the underground house of the Villa where the president lived as his residence.

Once the meeting between the president and his prime minister was over, the prime minister was taken to his residential house in Abdiaziz district by his security convoys. The prime minister's convoys used the 15 May gate. President's protocol officers set out arrangements for other officials wishing to meet with the president, serving on a first-come, first-served basis. Unfortunately, a few minutes later, insurgents waged a fierce attack from the 15 May side, targeting the president's house and surrounding buildings, using all types of weapons including P10, P9, PKM, RPG-7, mortars, 12.7mm, and Jeep-106mm. They were coming from behind, near the interior minister's house which was not far from us.

The 15 May Gate security was under the control of ENDF, but they deliberately vacated without informing the SNA to take over. It is widely believed they were in collaboration with insurgents who waged the attack on the president's building. The shooting became point-blank, and presidential escort forces were engaging and also using all means available to them to defend the president. Our VIP Protection team quickly set up a plan to protect the president by positioning ourselves in potential areas terrorists might enter the presidential residence. Some of us prepared vehicles, including bulletproof vehicles, to take the president out of the villa in the event our presidential guards were defeated. I quickly started monitoring the back door, which was the east side towards 15 May road.

I saw massive fire exchange, some bullets hitting the road and exploding again with massive destructive power. I also saw Col. Abdirizak Mohamed Hersi with an AK-47 in hand firing at terrorists as much as possible.

Given the severity of the situation and how highly intensified it was, it was not possible to keep the president there, and we needed to take him out of the place to a more safe and secure location. Captain. Abdirashid Hersi and Officer Ali Abdi Guled were inside the house with the president whenever there was an ongoing meeting. After assessing the situation outside and my observations on the intensity of the attack, I rushed towards the underground house and reported about the situation to the two officers and the president. We all agreed to take the president to another location as the potential of the terrorists to break our defense was highly possible The president, however, resisted taking our decision.

The president urged us to keep fighting. He said we would be better killed in defense rather than on the run. He insisted we keep fighting. However, as I entered the room and listened to the president's position, Emotionally, i broke down a small table next to the president and grabbed his right hand without further explanation to take him out of the house. He stood up to go with me. The president was very respectful and capable of sensing when someone he trusted made a decision as final. Nevertheless, with the first step or as we made small movement, an RPG-7 fired by the terrorists hit the wall of the house exactly where the president had been sitting. The RPG shooting came through the outer wall and the wall behind the room we were in at that time. Fortunately, the RPG-7 lost power and became defective, causing no harm.

Despite the RPG-7 shooting being harmless due to the several walls it went through, it convinced us to move the President towards a safe place. Thus, we moved faster to avoid a second RPG-7 shooting which could kill all of us. We left the house through the south gate as we knew all other directions were already battlefields with heavy fire exchanges. As we came out of the underground house and sought a safe concrete building to protect the president from heavy shelling, we were guided by the commander of the flank we moved who told us to go towards Sargudud, changing our plan which was to go to another building well known as Mine Store (guriga miinad) However, the Sargudud, which literally translates to "the red building," was occupied by Ethiopian forces who were firing in all directions to defend themselves. It became challenging to seek safety from the red house because Ethiopians had difficulty discerning Somali army from terrorists, thus they would likely fire at us too. We turned towards Sargudud and found a small space at the corner, where General Bashir Mohamed Jama, aka Goobe Deputy Somalia Police Commander, and General Nur Shirbow Somalia intelligence officer were sheltering from the shelling.

The president repeatedly urged us to keep fighting against terrorists to the extent that we all went to engage with them and abondoned him with only two soldiers, Jamal Said Isse Ib'ad and Mohamed Ali Samatar (Siraaje). At the same time, General Dhiig-sokeeye and I went to reassess the situation and figure out a safe place forbthe president and moved to where there had been heavy fire exchange. We went to the site where heavy close fighting was going on and then moved to the opposite side where we saw two vehicles with one open doors. General Awil spotted someone in the vehicles and that he had to move towards vehicles. He came close to the open door and shouted to the soldier he spotted"Said are you out of your mind?" and said "Move! Move!" Unfortunately, the guy in the vehicle had already been hit with an RPG-7, and while his body was in the cabin of the car, his stomach had already fallen to the ground. He responded, "don't step on my stomach." The soldier was among the fearless fighters and named Aweis. But now he was no longer a fighter, bleeding and his body torn apart, in that he was in the cabin of the car while his stomach was on the ground. We moved to the next vehicle mounted with a machine gun; however, both the soldier and the driver of the second vehicle were injured (named Burhan Nabadoon and Shine Waraaq, respectively). General Awil Dhiig-sokeeye immediately came up with a plan to attack the terrorists from the national theatre flank. In the meantime, he ordered us to go back to the president and stay with him.

Nevertheless, as we came back to the president's location, it was darker and we found all people flocked and extending assistance to someone injured. I suddenly assumed it was him (the President) because of poor visibility. I became emotional; however, as I came close to the injured person, I saw it wasn't the president, but General Mohamed Ali Samatar. We were in a confined situation, where we had to evacuated the president from his residence following extensive attack and potentiality terrorist to get in. We felt we were defeated and this might be the end of Villa Somalia as our presidential office. Our goal now was to ensure the president survived from this attack. The situation deteriorated increasingly in the next hour. We didn't know about whereabouts of General Awil Dhiig Sokeeye to make a good devision. However, a few minutes later, the shooting drastically reduced, a sign that showed the attackers had changed their mind and retreated. We moved the president back to his residential house alongside General Bashir Goobe and the late General Nur Shirbow. The morale of the presidential guard forces had become higher despite huge casualties.

6.2. Other Events in Villa Somalia, March 2, 2007.

We set out from Baidoa to Mogadishu by land as a presidential security guard team along with several other officials led by Col. Ali Abdi Guled. Other officials along with us included the late Mohamud Yaasiin Tumey, who was then director general of Villa Somalia and later became the Galkayo mayor, and Haaji Sayn. We were using four vehicles, and although the road was depleted, there was no tension on the road that connects Baidoa to Mogadishu. Although we arrived smoothly throughout our journey and, being tired, wished to relax from the travel, we were greeted with massive heavy mortar shelling in Villa Somalia by insurgents. It deprived us of getting even a little rest. The first shell hit next to us, causing all of us to lie down and stop movement. We then started assessing the situation to determine whether someone was hurt and the direction of the attack.

However, as I tried to stand up to see the situation, I was told to keep lying down by Abdulahi Ahmed Abdi Jubba Koole, and we all remained prone to another shelling. Normally in the battlefield during fierce fighting, some soldiers lose control and are unable to bear with massive shelling, attempting to seek shelter. As a result, they are given new names by other soldiers regarding their inability to resist the attack. To avoid such embarrassment, you better bear the situation you are in together with your colleagues. Whenever shelling intensified, we kept communicating while lying down, and in many cases we remained silent, alternating between silent moments and communicating from our prone positions. However, one soldier named Haji Sayn was unable to maintain his composure in the situation and opted to run under the roof that we used as parking for the President's vehicle. I saw him running towards the parking roof and told him that it was more risky there and he would be better off remaining in his position.

CHAPTER 7

HOW ETHIOPIA'S AGENDA CRIPPLED BOTH SOMALI AND WESTERN EFFORTS IN STABILIZATION AND STRATEGIC INTERESTS

CHAPTER 7

HOW ETHIOPIA'S AGENDA CRIPPLED BOTH SOMALI AND WESTERN EFFORTS IN STABILIZATION AND STRATEGIC INTERESTS

> Ethiopia's Prime Minister Meles Zenawi said 'terrorists melted in the Somali people.' He meant it is impossible to distinguish terrorists from the large civilian population, thus ENDF killed 70,000 across Somalia and displaced 1.3 million.

[**Fig. 6:** Ethiopian Forces on march.]

7.1. Introduction

Ethiopia's claim of sending its troops to Somalia for fear of its existential security and to support the TFG in fighting Islamic Courts Union forces was a fig leaf for its hidden securitization agenda against the emerging TFG and Somali people. This hidden agenda increasingly ruined the collective Western and Somali efforts to restore law and order, achieve stability, and deter terrorists from making the country a safe haven. Ethiopia prioritized its interests in a way that undermined both the interests of the Somali people (existing stability and desirable future state) and the interests of Western countries committed to supporting Somalia's efforts to restore law and order. Western nations backed the Ethiopian intervention of 2006-2009 intended to help the TFG stabilize the country.

Despite contradictions in Ethiopia's speech acts—which claimed to defend its existential security and integrity from ICU forces while also defending the TFG and law and order in Somalia—its application of securitization measures against the TFG government and people of Somalia rather than Islamic Courts Union forces revealed the truth of its hidden agenda. It is important to note that the Ethiopian forces and TFG have never been on the same page on this war, though TFG was hoping at the beginning of the intervention for honest support from Ethiopian forces to thoroughly defeat the Islamic Courts Union forces. Although both international media and human rights organizations had very often lumped in their reports the terms TFG and ENDF as partners or allies with shared meaning and purpose against the Islamic Courts Union, the truth has been the opposite. Ethiopia and TFG have never been on the same page since Ethiopia's invasion of Somalia in December 2006. TFG leaders very often sought to engage with ENDF commanders and political leaders in an attempt to develop shared meaning, strategy, and options for dealing with the Islamic Courts Union. Unfortunately, TFG had no knowledge about Ethiopia's securitization move and hidden negative agenda.

For TFG, they were hoping Ethiopia would view the ICU and other terrorists in the country as common threats and anticipated significant military support to fight them and deter their ideology from taking root in Somalia and beyond. Contrary to what TFG believed, Ethiopia had its own hidden agenda in which it viewed Somalia within an adversarial framework, pertinent to historical enmity. However, it is noteworthy that before TFG's request for military support from Ethiopia in its efforts to defeat the ICU, Ethiopia had its own intervention plan using speech acts in relation to ICU's "Greater Somalia" discourse. Ethiopia claimed there was a tremendous threat to its existential security from Mogadishu by pointing the finger at ICU.

Although both TFG and Ethiopia pointed their fingers at the potential threat from ICU, they never had shared perspective, objectives, purpose, or core strategy to follow. There was no joint military operation discussed by the two countries. For Ethiopia, its campaign to invade Somalia began in the middle of 2006; thus, whether the TFG leaders requested military support in December or not, Ethiopia would have invaded Somalia regardless. When in 2006 the UIC gained force and presence in the country, especially after June when they succeeded in controlling Mogadishu, the Ethiopian government expressed concern about the unfolding events.[70] The takeover of the country by the UIC was perceived as a threat to the integrity of the Ethiopian State for several reasons: the UIC's "Greater Somalia" discourse and their claims on the Ethiopian Somali region, a region already troubled by the Ogaden National Liberation Front's (ONLF) demands for independence (Hagmann, 2007); the hosting of the Oromo Liberation Front (OLF) by fundamentalist movements in Somalia to add another destabilizing factor for Ethiopia; fear of attacks in other parts of Ethiopia, reminiscent of the 1996 and 1997 bombings in public buildings such as the Ghion Hotel in Addis Ababa, claimed by Al-Itihad, then led by Sheikh Hassan Dahir Aweys who was one of the leaders of the UIC in 2006; and the Eritrean connection with the UIC and other armed movements, documented in the November 2006 Report by the UN Monitoring Group on Somalia (UN Monitoring Group on Somalia, 2006).[71]

Based on these issues, Ethiopia was dedicated to invading Somalia on its own terms and not on the terms requested by the TFG leaders.

---

70. Aimé, Elsa González. "The Security Issues Behind the Ethiopian Intervention in Somalia (2006-2009)". *State and Societal Challenges in the Horn of Africa*, edited by Alexandra Magnólia Dias, Centro de Estudos Internacionais, 2013, p.34

71. Ibid

Although the TFG made assistance requests to Ethiopia for military support, its troops used to cross the border more frequently to fight with movements against the regime. At least since 1997, Ethiopia had been making—although denying it—incursions into Somalia. The consolidation of the UIC in Somalia and the jihad they declared against Ethiopia in July 2006 catalyzed the attention of the government, which started a securitization move concerning the conflict in Somalia, and particularly the role of the UIC in it. In this regard, it is possible to identify a shift in The Ethiopian Herald's coverage of the issue. Until that month, international information in this newspaper focused primarily on bilateral relations with the countries of the Horn (Eritrea and the role of the UNMEE regarding the border dispute, diplomatic relations with the TFG and Djibouti), other countries such as China, the US and UK, and international organizations (EU, IGAD).[72]

Although there was no shared military strategy and options to respond to the unfolding ICU control over eight regions of the eighteen regions of Somalia, Ethiopia invaded Somalia with overwhelming forces compared with the TFG who was seeking support from them. Somalia was seeking military support from Ethiopia, but Ethiopia sent four times the number of TFG forces. The Ethiopian forces have been equipped with huge military tanks, artillery, 63 multiple rocket launchers, 12-tube, 107mm rocket launchers known Katyusha, BM21 122mm multiple rocket launchers, MIG 17, and helicopters which were not in the possession of TFG. This doesn't mean support for TFG but it really means invading and conquering Somalia. The Ethiopian government never publicly acknowledged the size of the forces deployed in Somalia during the intervention, but it is estimated that 30,000-40,000 Ethiopian soldiers took part in operations in 2007 and 2008.[73] By comparison, TFG soldiers involved in offensive operations and the defense of Mogadishu numbered approximately 5,000.[74] In late 2006, TFG forces, with ENDF ground and air support, engaged and effectively dispersed the ICU, which

---

72. Ibid
73. Aimé, Elsa González. "The Security Issues Behind the Ethiopian Intervention in Somalia (2006-2009)". *State and Societal Challenges in the Horn of Africa*, edited by Alexandra Magnólia Dias, Centro de Estudos Internacionais, 2013, p.127
74. Ibid

had previously "gained control of 8 of the country's 18 administrative regions" by early January 2007.[75]

7.2. Displacement

At the peak of this brief period of fighting, an "estimated 65,000-70,000 people were displaced, some of them having already been displaced by the flooding," but most cited conflict as the primary motivation for their flight.[76]

7.3. The Purpose of Ethiopia's Invasion in Somalia

The purpose of Ethiopia's invasion was to conquer Somalia, while depicting Somalia as a threat to Ethiopia's existential security and global order forever. Thus, it must be understood in the context of historic enmity between the two countries as a result of territorial dispute. Ethiopia's securitization move was not meant to fight terrorists and stabilize but rather to cripple TFG efforts and empower terrorists, in order to always portray Somalia as a threat country. As such, Ethiopian forces never fought with terrorists during the two years of invasion but instead killed tens of thousands of civilians, with many others tortured and 1.3 million displaced. According to estimates provided by Somali medical institutions, 6,501 Mogadishu civilians were killed and 8,516 wounded in 2007.[77]

These numbers do not take into account civilian casualties that occurred throughout central and southern Somalia, a figure that is unlikely to be definitively determined.[78] Between February and June 2007, 406,000 Somali civilians were displaced.[79] United Nations Office for the Coordination of Humanitarian Affairs (OCHA) estimates place the total number of displacements from Mogadishu in 2007 as a result of the

---

75. Ibid
76. Ibid
77. Aimé, Elsa González. "The Security Issues Behind the Ethiopian Intervention in Somalia (2006-2009)". *State and Societal Challenges in the Horn of Africa*, edited by Alexandra Magnólia Dias, Centro de Estudos Internacionais, 2013, p.128
78. Ibid
79. Ibid

conflict at over 700,000.[80] While an estimated 1,000,000 IDPs were living in Somalia by late 2007, the US Agency for International Development also estimates that 335,000 Somali refugees who sought asylum abroad were displaced in 2007.[81] While it must be acknowledged that a portion of the 2007 displacement is likely attributable to drought brought upon by weak spring rains in 2007, there is ample evidence to suggest that the majority of displacement was driven by conflict.[82] This conclusion is shared by the UN, which categorically claimed that "the main cause of displacement was the conflict between the TFG/Ethiopian forces and the ICU."[83]

The UN's claim is supported by the fact that during the height of the conflict between the ENDF-TFG alliance and the ICU, between 65,000-70,000 people were displaced within two months. A subsequent report indicates that 40,000 were displaced in February as a direct result of the unrest.[84] Furthermore, OCHA noted that violence in "November 2007 alone was of such intensity that it triggered the movement of more than 240,000 people out of the city [Mogadishu]."[85] These individual instances of displacement suggest that a substantial proportion of displacements in 2007 were a direct result of the conflict between the ENDF-TFG and the insurgency.[86] President Abdullahi Yusuf wrote in his book, although he retired from Somali politics, that there are two lingering problems in Somalia's stability: the first lingering problem is Ethiopia's fear and concern for a strong and united Somali people and rebuilding of a powerful government with its fully functional institutions to take responsibility of the nation. The second lingering problem is the growing terrorist influence in Somalia.[87]

---

80. Ibid
81. Ibid
82. Ibid
83. Aimé, Elsa González. "The Security Issues Behind the Ethiopian Intervention in Somalia (2006-2009)". *State and Societal Challenges in the Horn of Africa*, edited by Alexandra Magnólia Dias, Centro de Estudos Internacionais, 2013, p.129
84. Ibid
85. Ibid
86. Aimé, Elsa González. "The Security Issues Behind the Ethiopian Intervention in Somalia (2006-2009)". *State and Societal Challenges in the Horn of Africa*, edited by Alexandra Magnólia Dias, Centro de Estudos Internacionais, 2013, p.127
87. Yuusuf, Cabdullaahi Axmad. *Halgan iyo Hagardaamo: Taariikh Nololeed (Struggle and Conspiracy: A Memoir)*. (Sweden: Scansom Publishers, 2012), p.360

Ethiopia never came to Somalia, as most of the Western countries assumed, to fight with the terrorists but rather it came to further advance its own strategic interest in conquering Somalia. Thus, during these two years, Ethiopia carried out not only massive gross killings and displacement of millions of people but even destroyed the SNA reconstitution process and brigades formed, the democratic process that TFG was applying, and created its own profound political influence across the country. Although the ENDF-TFG alliance had soundly defeated the ICU, establishing order proved a more complicated task, especially in Mogadishu. The obvious reason was that: "[A]fter the fall of the ICU [sic], the semblance of order and security that the ICU had created in Mogadishu began to deteriorate."[88] Banditry, violence, and assassination of TFG-loyalists by insurgents became commonplace in the early months of 2007. The deterioration of the situation is reflected in statistical data compiled throughout the year.[89]

7.4. ICU Forces Melted

However, what is contradicting was the speech act made by the Ethiopian government and how easily the ICU forces were defeated by TFG and ENDF in 6 days. This defeat was not a true defeat and as Ethiopia's then Prime Minister Meles Zenawi said: **ICU forces melted.** What does "melted" mean to Ethiopia? This means Ethiopian military would remain in Somalia until separation of the melted solution happens. Although Ethiopia's Prime Minister announced Ethiopia would withdraw from Somalia, it has remained in Somalia to date. And today, the Federal Government of Somalia is publicly declaring Ethiopian forces cannot be part of a new peacekeeping transitional mission to Somalia because of its past security implications on the country. The truth about ICU being connected with international terrorists—other researchers have pointed out that the connections with international terrorist networks were not

---

88. Aimé, Elsa González. "The Security Issues Behind the Ethiopian Intervention in Somalia (2006-2009)". *State and Societal Challenges in the Horn of Africa*, edited by Alexandra Magnólia Dias, Centro de Estudos Internacionais, 2013, p.127
89. Aimé, Elsa González. "The Security Issues Behind the Ethiopian Intervention in Somalia (2006-2009)". *State and Societal Challenges in the Horn of Africa*, edited by Alexandra Magnólia Dias, Centro de Estudos Internacionais, 2013, p.128

self-evident, and that as a consequence the importance of the threat might have been overstated; cf. Marchal (2007: 1105).⁹⁰

And even in one week as stated by Meles Zenawi: THE (2006), "Union of Islamic Courts has simply melted away –Prime Minister Meles Zenawi", December 30th, pp. 3-10; THE (2006), "The Six-Day war. Ethiopia's successful military operation against Somali extremists", December 31st, p. 3. One month after the beginning of the operation, it was said that the Ethiopian troops had begun their withdrawal: THE (2007), "Ethiopian troops begin Somali withdrawal, says ministry", January 24th, p. 1. "[...] the Ethiopian army then found itself (like Western militaries in Iraq and Afghanistan) in the classic tar-baby dilemma, where every attempt to attack the problem led to its being still more firmly stuck to it." (Clapham, 2009: 190).⁹¹

7.5. TFG Democratic Process Distorted and depicted as Weak Government

The true image of TFG and its democratic process over the past two years since it came back to Somalia from Kenya where it was formed, has been distorted by nany and depicted as follows"Ethiopia's ally the TFG was corrupt and feeble and it welcomed the Ethiopian military support" "in 2006 it had a physical presence in only two towns, provided no useful services to Somalis, and with the ICU's ascendancy was becoming increasingly irrelevant."⁹²

Howere, contrary to above distortion TFG was having 11,000 well-trained forces in Baidoa and gained more trust and support from the people of central and Puntland regions who contributed the 11,000 TFG forces. The distortion continued and said "The Ethiopian military easily routed the ICU's militias. For a few days it appeared that they had won an easy victory and that the TFG had ridden Ethiopia's coattails into power

---

90. Aimé, Elsa González. "The Security Issues Behind the Ethiopian Intervention in Somalia (2006-2009)". *State and Societal Challenges in the Horn of Africa*, edited by Alexandra Magnólia Dias, Centro de Estudos Internacionais, 2013, p.33
91. Ibid
92. Human Rights Watch, "So Much to Fear": War Crimes and the Devastation of Somalia, 1-56432-415-X, 8 December 2008, https://www.refworld.org/reference/countryrep/hrw/2008/en/64117 [accessed 26 February 2025]

in Mogadishu. But the first insurgent attacks against Ethiopian and TFG forces began almost immediately and rapidly built towards a protracted conflict that has since grown worse with every passing month."[93]

7.6. The Truth About TFG

The truth about TFG emerged after the Ethiopian invasion ended in December 2008, at a time "when the situation reached an impasse following dramatic gains by insurgent forces." By the end of 2008, the ENDF-TFG alliance had relinquished control of much of central and southern Somalia to the insurgency.[94] "TFG and Ethiopian forces...lost the ability to exercise even limited influence across most of the country and appear[ed] to have given up trying to recapture territory they have lost." This happened following when TFG lost trust with ENDF, as ENDF made unilateral wuthdrawal from all terrotories lost to Alshabab. ENDF commanders deliberately stopped the close collaboration with TFG commanders and withdrew all their positions in the battlefield. It is also widely believed that they were in collaboration with Alshabab and provide sufficient ammuniations and other logistics, because Alshabab attack intensifies whenever ENDF makes unilateral withdrawal from the battlefield. The TFG-ENDF's area of operations was limited to Baidoa and a handful of districts in Mogadishu, a military situation similar to that of early 2007.[95] Shockingly, TFG alone was later tasked to restore stability in Mogadishu and while Ethiopian forces were removed from Mogadishu and parts of south central Somalia. It had then been recognized that TFG was the right SNA to take responsibility for liberating Mogadishu from Al-Shabaab. Insurgent elements who came with President Sheikh Sharif were sent to Sudan for training. TFG successfully liberated all Al-Shabaab bases in Mogadishu through a military strategy developed and led by General Gordon. Although tangible progress was made in providing a

---

93. Human Rights Watch, "So Much to Fear": War Crimes and the Devastation of Somalia, 1-56432-415-X, 8 December 2008, https://www.refworld.org/reference/countryrep/hrw/2008/en/64117 [accessed 26 February 2025]
94. Aimé, Elsa González. "The Security Issues Behind the Ethiopian Intervention in Somalia (2006-2009)". *State and Societal Challenges in the Horn of Africa*, edited by Alexandra Magnólia Dias, Centro de Estudos Internacionais, 2013, p.129
95. Ibid

measure of security largely absent in the previous two years, the situation continues to remain volatile.[96]

Conflict and resultant civilian casualties, displacement, and emigration have been commonplace in Somalia throughout the last twenty years. However, since the last major Somali Civil War following Barre's fall, humanitarian crises in Somalia had not reached the level of severity that occurred during Ethiopia's intervention.[97] These displacements and deaths of civilians were among Ethiopia's goals to weaken TFG and the Somali people to its advantage and didn't exist before December 2006. The TFG was controlling the country from February 2005 to December 2006, and it was gaining more legitimacy from the people. According to the Internal Displacement Monitoring Centre, approximately 300,000 Somalis were displaced in 2008 as a result of the fighting, including 870,000 or 60 percent of Mogadishu residents. The IDP count in Somalia totaled 1.3 million by the year's end. A joint statement released by 52 NGOs in October 2008 describes how conflict, drought, and escalated food prices led to a situation in which "[n]early half of Somalia's population, or 3.25 million people, are now in need of emergency aid," a 77 percent increase since the beginning of the year.[98]

TFG had been operating from Bosaso of Puntland through Galkkaio, Galgudud, Hiiraan, Lower Shabelle, Bakool, and Bay region. It had successfully managed to engage with the people in those regions with minimal conflict and decisively gained their military and political contribution to the newly formed government. It was hard to comprehend why those reports vilifying TFG efforts could not see the peaceful process that TFG had chosen. It seems in their view, if TFG could oppress people, they could call TFG a strong government that controlled half of the country. They emphasized military approach as a powerful way to control rather than democratic process which takes root and achieves sustainable peace. Ethiopia viewed Somalia purely within the

---

96. Aimé, Elsa González. "The Security Issues Behind the Ethiopian Intervention in Somalia (2006-2009)". *State and Societal Challenges in the Horn of Africa*, edited by Alexandra Magnólia Dias, Centro de Estudos Internacionais, 2013, p.130
97. Ibid
98. Aimé, Elsa González. "The Security Issues Behind the Ethiopian Intervention in Somalia (2006-2009)". *State and Societal Challenges in the Horn of Africa*, edited by Alexandra Magnólia Dias, Centro de Estudos Internacionais, 2013, p.130

framework of long-term adversarial relations between the two countries and never conformed to or aligned with Western countries' perspective, particularly regarding democracy, global order, and strategic interests in the region and beyond. Despite there being two wars between Ethiopia and Somalia over Somali territory and the Ogaden region in 1964 and 1977 respectively, Ethiopia's ambitions of conquering Somali territory never changed, and remain the same to this date as it focuses on the Red Sea and remains committed to annexing part of Somalia.

It is noteworthy that in the 1977 war, the Soviet Union and Warsaw Pact countries, including Cuba, drove the Somali army out of the Ogaden region which they had captured in the 1977 war. Nevertheless, Ethiopia's desire to increasingly weaken Somalia and capture part of Somalia by applying its securitization agenda and labeling Somalia forever as a threat to its existential security and a safe haven for terrorists to attack Ethiopia has remained the same to this date.

7.7. A Lost Opportunity

Opportunities lost include political reconciliation between TFG and ICU before Ethiopia's invasion in December 2006. It seems there was intentional vilification of such importance, but it appears it was deliberate to destroy the TFG democratic process. This can also be seen in the result of the two-year intervention which ended with all territories captured being lost to ICU and other insurgents.

The trick of Ethiopia's securitization was serving on its own interest, including establishing and empowering the new Al-Shabaab to prolong Somali problems and continue its strategic positioning in the global war on terrorism and maintain its legitimacy in Ethiopia in the light of the 2005 devastating election in Addis Ababa.

7.8. Different Tactics Deployed by Players

Somali insurgents opposed to the ENDF-TFG used the civilian populace to their tactical advantage. A common method of attack against ENDF-TFG forces involved firing mortars from positions deep within residential areas, effectively "using populated neighborhoods as unwilling shields."[99] The insurgents, having launched their initial barrage from concealed positions in populated areas, immediately fled the scene, leaving the local populace to face the inevitable reprisal from ENDF-TFG artillery. But those reprisal was only from ENDF alone as TFG didn't have artillery or other hard ware machineries in the position of Ethiopian forces. TFG never possesed any of these: The 120mm M95 Long Range Mortar is a 120 mm (4.7 in) mortar that was developed by Serbian Military Technical Institute, The 82 mm Mortar M82 is used to support its own military units using indirect fire and The M2 60mm mortar was a widely used infantry support weapon in World War II, the Korean War, and Vietnam. This lightweight and portable mortar provided close-range indirect fire support to U.S. Furthermore, there has been arms embargo on Somalia (UN arms embargo on Somalia. In January 1992 the UN Security Council imposed an arms embargo on Somalia. In February 2007 the embargo was amended to allow arms supplies to Somali Government Forces under certain conditions), thus TFG could not purchase such weapons. An arms embargo on non-state Forces continues to be in place.

The insurgents also added to civilian casualties by failing to "regularly use spotters to guide their mortar fire, so frequently attacks f[e]ll on civilians caught in the general vicinity of their targets."[100] However, residential neighborhoods were not the only means of providing cover to launch attacks. Insurgents also used IDP camps as staging points for offensive operations, drawing ENDF-TFG attention to densely populated areas largely comprised of legitimate IDPs.[101]

Since the Ethiopian Invasion to Somalia on December 2006, TFG and ENDF have never sat down to develop a unified strategy and option, in the fight against terrorist groups thus, the two forces were always separate, even in the battlefields. Lumping the terms TFG and ENDF together as if they are one was totally false. It was merely ENDF who were making indiscriminate bombardment on populated areas. It was impossible for SNA soldiers to carry out indiscriminate firing or bombardament. This is because your own relatives or family members could be around in the populated areas. This is

---

99. Aimé, Elsa González. "The Security Issues Behind the Ethiopian Intervention in Somalia (2006-2009)". *State and Societal Challenges in the Horn of Africa*, edited by Alexandra Magnólia Dias, Centro de Estudos Internacionais, 2013, p.131
100. Ibid
101. Ibid

far from logic. According to extensive research by Human Rights Watch, another troubling practice commonly employed by Al-Shabaab was the forced recruitment of child soldiers. Al-Shabaab reportedly used schools as recruiting grounds,[102] promising financial reward in return for service or otherwise coercing the children to enlist through threats.[103]

Many families fled Mogadishu as a result of this practice. Insurgent elements frequently threatened and assassinated TFG officials, opposition party members willing to reconcile with the TFG, and civilians who "disagreed with or simply failed to express sufficient enthusiasm for insurgent goals and tactics."[104]

7.9. The Truth About the Tactics Employed by the TFG and the One Employed by ENDF

Although the TFG was comprised of an eclectic mix of the Somali National Army, militias, police, Ethiopian-trained forces, and various other elements, this analysis considers the military tactics employed by each component of the TFG in the aggregate.[105] As documented by Human Rights Watch, search and seizure operations conducted by TFG forces with the intent of apprehending insurgents hiding among the local populace often resulted in theft and violence.[106] The US Department of State described TFG police as "generally ineffective, underpaid, and corrupt," and acknowledged the existence of "continued allegations that TFG security officials were responsible for extrajudicial killings, indiscriminate firing on civilians, arbitrary arrest and detention, rape, extortion, looting and harassment."[107] Unlike the above US statement about TFG, it is noteworthy that TFG didn't commit a single human right violation over the past two years (from Feb 2005 to December

---

102. Ibid
103. Ibid
104. Ibid
105. Aimé, Elsa González. "The Security Issues Behind the Ethiopian Intervention in Somalia (2006-2009)". *State and Societal Challenges in the Horn of Africa*, edited by Alexandra Magnólia Dias, Centro de Estudos Internacionais, 2013, p.132
106. Ibid
107. Ibid

2006). During this period of time TFG managed to mobilize 11,500 soldiers from nearly all regions of Somalia.

7.10. Why didn't TFG act this way over the past two years that it had been working in Baidoa and Jowhar?

Our argument is that Ethiopia's securitization was totally to undermine the democratic process that TFG had been operating, deter a strong militarily Somali government and make Somalia a safe haven for more terrorists instead. Despite the historical enmity between Somalia and Ethiopia, the ENDF in Somalia, which numbered between 30,000-40,000 throughout the duration of the conflict, was initially praised by many Somali civilians for being "disciplined in their day-to-day interactions with Somali civilians."[108] However, when confronted with attacks from a growing and diffuse insurgency, ENDF frequently responded with bombardment of highly populated urban areas. ENDF relied on the use of **Katyusha rockets** launched from Grad multiple-rocket-launchers in response to insurgent attacks.[109]

7.11. Humanitarian Access

A survey of the humanitarian assistance community's access to Somali civilians throughout 2006-2009 also indicates the greater picture of humanitarian conditions in Somalia throughout the period. At the outset of fighting in 2007, the TFG immediately closed the borders and prevented flights carrying humanitarian personnel and goods from entering Somalia. The closure prompted the UN and several NGOs in Somalia to relocate to Nairobi. Humanitarian assistance to the Somali populace, such as "flood response and other life-saving activities virtually ground to a halt." Flights carrying humanitarian personnel and materials were eventually permitted to land in Somalia under limited circumstances.[110] In January 2008, relief efforts were subjected

---

108. Ibid
109. Ibid
110. Aimé, Elsa González. "The Security Issues Behind the Ethiopian Intervention in Somalia (2006-2009)". *State and Societal Challenges in the Horn of Africa*, edited by Alexandra Magnólia Dias, Centro de Estudos Internacionais, 2013, p.133

to unprecedented restrictions; roadblocks, checkpoints, banditry, and taxation significantly impeded the transportation of essential goods. Humanitarian personnel increasingly became "targets of roadblocks, kidnapping threats, harassment and roadside bombs, culminating on 28 January in the killing of three aid workers in an explosion near Kismaio."[111] By October 2008, 111 incidents of violence against aid workers had been reported. Over the course of that year, 34 aid workers were killed; this grim statistic led OCHA to conclude that Somalia was "the most dangerous place for humanitarian workers to operate in the world."[112]

This analysis examines statistical data regarding the rates of internal displacement, emigration, and civilian deaths from December 2006-January 2009.[113] Although frequent droughts, seasonal flooding, famine, extreme poverty, and overcrowding are common causes of death and displacement in Somalia, such factors must be taken into account when trying to determine what additional displacement, emigration, and deaths were caused by the intervention.[114] In many instances, the number of civilian casualties and displacements will also reflect the nature of the combat tactics employed by all sides of the conflict. These tactics will be examined through civilian accounts, NGO reports, and UN documentation to determine the extent to which the combative parties either intentionally or recklessly inflicted suffering upon the Somali populace.[115] The United Nations Office for Coordination of Humanitarian Affairs Somalia estimated that 400,000 protracted IDPs had been living in Somalia for at least a decade prior to 2006.[116] The humanitarian crisis in Somalia is ongoing. While the Ethiopian Military intervention both directly contributed to and exacerbated the humanitarian situation in terms of civilian casualties, displacement,

---

111. Ibid
112. Ibid
113. Civins, Braden. *Ethiopia's Intervention in Somalia, 2006-2009*. (Seoul, South Korea: Yonsei University, 2010), p.125
114. Ibid
115. Ibid
116. Civins, Braden. *Ethiopia's Intervention in Somalia, 2006-2009*. (Seoul, South Korea: Yonsei University, 2010), p.126

emigration, and access to humanitarian aid, there is still a possibility that Ethiopia's actions will yield long-term benefits for the Somali population.[117]

Since then the United States has failed to publicly criticize the Ethiopian government over the serious and widespread abuses carried out by ENDF forces in Somalia or even acknowledge that those atrocities have taken place—the same approach Washington has taken with regard to ENDF abuses, including war crimes and crimes against humanity, inside of Ethiopia. High-level US officials have equally failed to demand accountability for TFG officials who are responsible for those abuses or to support the conditioning of donor support for TFG security forces on improvements in their appalling human rights record.[118]

7.12. TFG Before Ethiopian Invasion (Feb, 2005-Dec, 2006)

The TFG before the invasion adopted democratic process. It started its operations from Bosaso Puntland through Jowhar and Baidoa. More about this TFG and democratic processes it applied refer to chapter 1. As such the TFG before the Ethiopia invasion engaged with a variety of communities in all the regions and never made armed confrontation with any group of clan. Unlike the tremendous misinterpretation about TFG made by many during December 2006-2009 Ethiopia intervention, TFG was a more inclusive army capable of defeating the untrained offensive ICU forces who lacked military tactics and experience in comparison to TFG commanders trained in USA, former USSR, Egypt, and Italy among others. However, it is worth noting that both TFG political and military leaders never wanted to use the power at their discretion, because they had in mind it was time to bring people together, time to build strong inclusive democratic institutions, time to engender trust and build legitimacy. Thus, the key orientation provided to its 11,000 army personnel was that they were in the process of forming a more inclusive National Army responsible for protecting citizens rather than oppressing them, and until that goal was achieved, any military action taken by

---

117. Civins, Braden. *Ethiopia's Intervention in Somalia, 2006-2009*. (Seoul, South Korea: Yonsei University, 2010), p.138
118. Human Rights Watch, "So Much to Fear": War Crimes and the Devastation of Somalia, 1-56432-415-X, 8 December 2008, https://www.refworld.org/reference/countryrep/hrw/2008/en/64117 [accessed 26 February 2025]

them could be seen as an operation carried out by an SNA brigade from a particular region with sinister intentions against the target. As such, more training was continuously given to them. Another point in the orientation was that they were being reconstituted to protect the people from the enemy and not to oppress them. But they were well-trained and well-disciplined army numbering 11,500 (5,000 from Puntland, 500 from Galguduud, 4,000 from Hiraan, 300 from Jowhar, 250 from Hargeisa, and 500 from Gedo and Lower Jubba and 1,000 from Baidoa). This was the most successful stage in Somali's state building processes. The leaders were seeking both legitimacy and inclusivity to engender public trust.

7.13. TFG During Ethiopian Invasion (Dec, 2006-Aug, 2008)

TFG had been subjected to a huge securitization move by the Ethiopian Government. TFG made a military support request to Ethiopia, but Ethiopia brought an unspecified number of army which some independent bodies estimated in between 30,000 to 40,000 equipped with more military tanks, MIG 17, helicopters, artilleries, multiple rocket launchers etc. In addition, Ethiopian military officers mistreated the SNA commanders who sought to collaborate with ENDF commanders in offensives against ICU militia. As a result the TFG was increasingly wrecked and destroyed in many fronts by Alshabab. During this period of time, the media outlets labelled TFG as a weak and corrupt government when there were no revenue collections made by TFG and limited financial support from western countries were available. Although, the two were lumping TFG/ENDF together as if they have common goals, instead they were having different goals, different objectives and different purposes and different strategies.. During this time Ethiopia empowered Alshabab and weakened TFG to meet its real objectives.

7.14. TFG After Ethiopia's Withdrawal (2009 and Beyond)

Following massive failure in the fight against terrorist, which led Alshabab to capture all liberated area and siriation turned to be as it was before the Ethiopian invasion on 24th December 2006, accompanied by displacement of 1.3 million people, and killing of thousands of civilian through indiscriminate bombardment and indiscriminate firing, it has been recognized TFG as the sole army capable to defeat Alshabab and defend the newly coalition government. The recognized TFG forces are actually the remnants of the 11,500. As such, TFG has regrouped and new senior military officers scattered across the country were requested to join in the new offensive against Al Shabaab. Among key senior military commanders was General Gordon. General Gordon led the new offensive to liberate Al Shabaab from Mogadishu. He developed a robust strategy and he successfully liberated Mogadishu and surrounding districts. This time it was a TFG offensive and Not TFG/ENDF offensive which ended in failure. The newly revamped TFG didn't only liberate a large part of the country but created a conducive environment which made possible the first election to be held in the country and a shift from Transitional Government to Permanent Government in Somalia. TFG later received direct support from USA and other EU countries which enabled it to further develop its capabilities.

During this period of time, the United state of America made a determination to supporting Somalia. On August 6, 2009, Hillary Rodham Clinton, Secretary of State met in Nairobi, Kenya. Secretay Cluntin said "President Sheikh Sharif and I have just concluded a very thorough and productive discussion – thank you – about the challenges facing his country and the efforts of the international community to support the Transitional Federal Government as it stands up for the people of Somalia and against the threat of violent extremism. The United States pledges our continued support for President Sheikh Sharif's government. And we have joined IGAD-the Intergovernmental Authority on Development, the Arab League, the Organization of the Islamic Conference, and the African Union, in endorsing the Somali-led Djibouti peace process.

I want to reiterate our support for that process today. I conveyed to President Sheikh Sharif very strong support that President Obama and I have both for the peace process and for his government. We believe that his government is the best hope we've had in quite some time for a return to stability and the possibility of progress in Somalia. A strengthened Transitional Federal Government would have positive consequences not just for Somalia, but for the region and the wider global community. It would contribute to greater regional stability and start to alleviate the growing refugee crisis afflicting Somalia's neighbors, especially Kenya, which is hosting nearly 300,000 Somali refugees today.[119]

7.15. USA Position in Ethiopia's Invasion of 2006-2009 regarding ENDF indiscriminate killings and bombardments.

The same policy framework has driven United States policy in Somalia. As in Ethiopia, Washington has turned a blind eye to ENDF laws of war violations in Somalia. US law forbids the US government from providing assistance to foreign military units involved in serious human rights abuses. But US officials have made no credible effort to investigate and determine whether ENDF units implicated in abuses in Somalia are past or potential beneficiaries of US military training and assistance to Ethiopia.[120]

As the ICU consolidated control in Mogadishu, Washington came to view it as a terrorist threat. In mid-2006 the United States sought the handover of several non-Somali terrorist suspects who it believed were being sheltered by the ICU, but ICU leaders reportedly ignored those requests. Washington responded by backing a coalition of Somali warlords, each in command of personal militia forces, in a bid to oust the ICU from Mogadishu.[121] The warlords, who played upon US terrorism concerns by branding themselves the "Alliance for the Restoration of Peace and Counterterrorism," were defeated by the ICU in mid-2006.[122] When Ethiopia decided to intervene militarily against the ICU and empower the TFG later that year, the United States provided staunch political and material support.[123] Since then the United States has failed to publicly criticize the Ethiopian government over the serious and widespread abuses carried out by ENDF forces in Somalia or even acknowledge that

---

119. U.S. Department of State. 2009. "*Remarks from Secretary Clinton.*" U.S. Department of State Archive (2009-2013). Accessed March 31, 2025. https://2009-2017.state.gov/secretary/20092013clinton/rm/2009a/08/126956.htm
120. Human Rights Watch, "So Much to Fear": War Crimes and the Devastation of Somalia, 1-56432-415-X, 8 December 2008, https://www.refworld.org/reference/countryrep/hrw/2008/en/64117 [accessed 26 February 2025]
121. Ibid
122. Ibid
123. Ibid

those atrocities have taken place—the same approach Washington has taken with regard to ENDF abuses, including war crimes and crimes against humanity, inside of Ethiopia. High-level US officials have equally failed to demand accountability for TFG officials who are responsible for those abuses or to support the conditioning of donor support for TFG security forces on improvements in their appalling human rights record.[124]

The US government designated Al-Shabaab itself a terrorist organization on March 19, 2008. There is strong evidence that US policies in Somalia have aggravated the very concerns about terrorism they seek to address. Because of Washington's unreserved backing of Ethiopia's military intervention in Somalia, many Somalis see the United States as complicit in the military occupation of their country and in the atrocities they have suffered at the hands of ENDF forces.[125]

7.16. Securitization Against TFG: Unexpected Tension between TFG and ENDF Emerged

Although TFG leaders were not familiar with the Ethiopian hidden securitization move and placed blind trust on Ethiopia as an ally, in fact, the decision process around the securitization move was characterized by its secrecy, with Parliament being consulted in November/December 2006 just to approve the measure. Although some opposition deputies tried to question the intervention, they had no capacity to impede the resolution, as any questioning of it **implied an accusation of betrayal**.[126] As such, Ethiopia always sought an opportunity to weaken the Somali people and exerted considerable efforts and resources to capitalize on the invasion to its advantage. Ethiopia's set of goals included dividing and destroying Somalia while justifying intervention to "protect rule of law and stability in Somalia" as well as "defending its sovereignty and integrity" but this was merely a fig leaf to weaken Somalia and empower Alshabaab to strengthen its global war on terrorist position. They portrayed themselves as if they were there to support the TFG and to stabilize the country.

---

124. Ibid
125. Ibid
126. Aimé, Elsa González. "The Security Issues Behind the Ethiopian Intervention in Somalia (2006-2009)". *State and Societal Challenges in the Horn of Africa*, edited by Alexandra Magnólia Dias, Centro de Estudos Internacionais, 2013, p.37

They presented themselves as if operating in the country as genuine peacekeeping forces when in actuality they had been destroying the SNA, killing and detaining hundreds of thousands of civilians and members of SNA, and eventually displacing more than a million civilians from Mogadishu and the south central part of the country.

As we said, Ethiopia never came to Somalia to help stabilize the country by supporting TFG to defeat ICU forces, but instead it empowered the terrorists and weakened the Somali people and the government of Somalia. Look, according to Gonzalez's report on securitization move, page 36, 2013, Ethiopian media, particularly The Ethiopian Herald loyal to the then government, published reports to mislead the world by emphasizing the huge threat from the ICU forces and importance of securitization move. For instance, "Then, after mid-June and particularly July, the information in the newspaper experienced a clear shift. Coverage of the conflict in Somalia started to be much more prominent because of the consolidation of the UIC, challenging the TFG, Ethiopia and the Horn.[127] Immediately after the TFG government achieved its goal through democratic process and relocated the newly formed government to Villa Somalia to operate officially in the Somali Presidency, Mogadishu, unexpected tension erupted between Somali National Army and Ethiopian National Defense Forces in Beledweyne district, 330km north of Mogadishu, to the extent that the tension was on the brink of turning into full-blown war.

The tension was triggered by the unilaterally arrest and detention of the local people by Ethiopian forces who consequently planned to take them to Ethiopia for interrogation. This was a move that SNA commander in Beledweyne, General Mukhtar, saw as unlawful and outside of their jurisdiction. He thus refused to allow the detainees to be taken to Ethiopia. Among the detainees were prominent Somalis including Farah Moallim Mohamud (in the picture), a well-known person in Hiiraan, along with key business people and youth members from Beledweyne. These violations and subsequent ones occurred despite Ethiopia having already convinced the West that it would promote democracy and rule

---

127. Aimé, Elsa González. "The Security Issues Behind the Ethiopian Intervention in Somalia (2006-2009)". *State and Societal Challenges in the Horn of Africa*, edited by Alexandra Magnólia Dias, Centro de Estudos Internacionais, 2013, p.36

of law through The Ethiopian Herald newspaper published in Addis Ababa. For instance, two news items—on July 29th, "Lasting peace, stability in Somalia crucial for overall security of the Horn," and August 12th, "Ethiopia committed to ensuring dependable peace, security in Somalia: MoFA"—illustrate the securitization move happening around the conflict in Somalia. Securing the TFG was underlined not only as fundamental to protecting peace, stability, and the rule of law in Somalia, Ethiopia, and East Africa, but as the only option.[128]

The president and General Mukhtar discussed the issue on the phone, and the president backed his decision to oppose Ethiopia's desire to take Somali detainees to Ethiopia for potential torture and killings. The president informed Ethiopia they would take responsibility for any consequences of their decisions should they insist on their position and military confrontation occur. Beyond the defense of peace, stability, and the rule of law in Somalia, the newspaper's articles affirmed the Ethiopian government's commitment to other principles such as democracy, tolerance, and cooperation, and portrayed this political project as threatened by both parties. The SNA commander in Hiiraan, politicians, and members from civil society were unable to understand why prominent people were detained by ENDF commanders and why they weren't investigated in the territorial jurisdiction instead of being taken to another country. This concern fueled the situation, thus SNA was compelled to protect its citizens.

This led the SNA commander to demand that Ethiopian forces hand over all detainees to the Somali government. If he didn't act in this manner, civilians in Hiiraan would likely view the TFG SNA as complicit in Ethiopia's torture and killings of prominent people. General Mukhtar then secured the handover of the detainees from Ethiopian forces, and after interrogation and recording statements from all detainees, he set them free to appease the local populace who were angry about the way Ethiopian NDF had been behaving since their invasion in December 2006. This move in turn annoyed the Ethiopian commanders and prompted their decision to arrest General Mukhtar. While behaving

---

128. Aimé, Elsa González. "The Security Issues Behind the Ethiopian Intervention in Somalia (2006-2009)". *State and Societal Challenges in the Horn of Africa*, edited by Alexandra Magnólia Dias, Centro de Estudos Internacionais, 2013, p.36

in a manner contrary to foreign military policies in another country, deceptively Ethiopia aligned itself with the African Union, the IGAD, the "international community" and Ethiopia behind a common objective: defeating terrorism, combating Al-Itihad and Al-Qaeda and their Eritrean connections in Somalia.[129]

Ethiopia was then participating with other international actors in the global war on terror and portrayed as defending core international values such as order and stability.[130] The arrest of the Somali General sparked tension and led Somali SNA forces to retreat from defensive positions and orchestrate an attack against the Ethiopian forces. The Ethiopian commanders decided to take the arrested General to Mogadishu to diffuse the tension. However, in Mogadishu, the president took two steps: he summoned Ethiopian commanders in Mogadishu and informed them they must hand over the arrested General to the Somali government, and on the other hand, he instructed the commanders of the 54th brigade (which protects the president) to prepare for potential confrontation with Ethiopian forces in Mogadishu should they take General Mukhtar to an unknown location. The plan for the president and Somali commanders was to take military action against Ethiopian forces in Villa Somalia should they refuse to hand over the Somali military General (Mukhtar) to the Somali Government. Ethiopia's move was viewed as a securitization move against the TFG forces and in many ways opposite to what The Ethiopian Herald depicted.

But this securitization move through speech acts in this newspaper is especially noticeable since December, when the utterances about security multiplied, depicting the UIC as an existential threat to Ethiopian sovereignty, expecting the people to gather around the government to stand against this aggression for the survival of the state. Nevertheless, these articles are interesting not only because of how they securitize this issue but also for what they imply about the way the securitization move happens. Fortunately, the detained General was handed over to the Somali Government as the president demanded, and the President

---

129. Aimé, Elsa González. "The Security Issues Behind the Ethiopian Intervention in Somalia (2006-2009)". *State and Societal Challenges in the Horn of Africa*, edited by Alexandra Magnólia Dias, Centro de Estudos Internacionais, 2013, p.36
130. Ibid

instructed General Awil Dhiig-sokeeye to provide him security guards to protect him from potential threats from Ethiopian intelligence units.

7.17. Unilateral Decision by Ethiopian Forces

As anticipated, the government of Ethiopia took several steps in response to the Somali stance over the arrested General Mukhtar, including unilateral retreat from joint battlefield defense with SNA forces operating from Galkaio to Mogadishu in the north direction and from Hudur to Mogadishu in south west, and from Raaskambooni to Mogadishu in the south direction. Ethiopian forces retreated unilaterally from those joint operations with SNA in all those various directions, leaving SNA alone to face potential threats from well-armed terrorist fighters, especially given that Somalia could not afford to buy weapons and ammunition due to the Security Council arms embargo. SNA forces obviously were counting on ENDF forces for military hardware support, and the situation turned out to make SNA forces vulnerable to terrorist attacks. As a result, SNA forces in all those directions and scope had to rethink their strategy immediately as they were unable to keep fighting with terrorist forces due to lack of a well thought out plan and shortage of ammunition. This occurred because there was a joint military operations plan which changed instantly. Al-Shabaab took advantage of scattered SNA and the unilateral withdrawal by the ENDF and waged massive attacks on all scattered SNA outside Mogadishu. Al-Shabaab weakened TFG, while Ethiopian Defense Forces were those who created the opportunity for the terrorists to weaken TFG with shortage of ammunition.

Even as media outlets reported Ethiopian troops fighting militant Islamist group al-Shabab have withdrawn from a key military base in central Somalia's Galgudud region, according to residents.[131] Heavily armed al-Shabab fighters took control of El Bur following the pullout of Ethiopian troops and a small number of Somali National Army soldiers

---

131. Voice of America. (2017, March 26). "Al-Shabab Seizes Key Somali Town After Ethiopians Pull Out." VOA News. Retrieved from
https://www.voanews.com/a/al-shabab-seizes-key-somali-town-after-ethiopians-pull-out/3794065.html

early Monday.[132] The fall of El Bur was confirmed by **Nur Hassan Gutale**, the town's district commissioner, who **said Ethiopians did not tell them the reason for their withdrawal.**[133] The Ethiopians and our troops withdrew from the town and now it is under the control of the militants. The Ethiopians did not inform us about their withdrawal plan and once we saw them abandoning, our troops also abandoned," Gutale said.[134] Residents of El Bur say al-Shabab militants traveling in pickup trucks moved into the town early Monday without a fight. "The militants traveling in more than six pickup trucks mounted with anti-aircraft machine guns moved into town this morning. They took up the strategic positions, raised their black flags on the top of some buildings," one of the residents told VOA on the condition of anonymity.[135]

Gutale has accused both the al-Shabab militants and the Ethiopian troops of mistreating civilians. Al-Shabab forced most of the residents to leave the town when the Ethiopians came three years ago. And the Ethiopians mistreated those who remained in the town," Gutale said. "The civilians had only two choices: to stay in the town and face the Ethiopian mistreatment or live as hostages under al-Shabab.[136] Ethiopia's ENDF unilateral withdrawl from all battlefields led Alshabab to take advantange of this move and orchestrate a fierce fight to destroy SNA forces. Only one brigade led by General Gacmoduule based in North Mogadishu survived. He managed to keep his soldiers in their position and respond to the situation they found themselves in.

Although the intention of the international community backing the newly formed government was to provide Somalia peacekeeping forces, Ethiopia's agenda was just crippling such good intentions and billions spent on peacekeeping forces. All these are happening through Ethiopia's fig leaf as The Ethiopian Herald published in mid-2006. Beyond the defense of peace, stability and the rule of law in Somalia, the newspaper's articles affirmed the Ethiopian government's commitment to other principles such as democracy, tolerance and cooperation and portrayed

---

132. Ibid
133. Ibid
134. Ibid
135. Ibid
136. Ibid

this political project as threatened by both parties.¹³⁷ The scattered or dispersed SNA encountered massive attacks from terrorists. As a result, many of them were killed, while others became disillusioned with the government of Somalia and joined clan militia fighting against the federal government and even terrorist groups.

7.18. Other undermining

As Ethiopian forces had already fully destroyed SNA across various parts of the country, through unilateral withdrawal and empowering Alshabaab, their focus now turned towards the destruction of the only SNA brigade defending Villa Somalia, that is to say, the 54th brigade which was based inside Villa Somalia.

7.19. Civilian Securitization

However, knowing how SNA in the region were being weakened by Alshabaab through massive ammunition support from ENDF, the Ethiopian forces in Mogadishu, which one could expect to behave as genuine peacekeepers, acted aggressively in the adversary framework and as if they were enemies of the Government and people of Somalia by carrying out widespread barrage attacks across Mogadishu indiscriminately, inflicting massive destruction, death, and civilian displacement. Critics of ENDF tactics claimed the Katyusha was an inherently indiscriminate weapon incapable of offering the targeting precision necessary to minimize civilian casualties—assuming that targets were even located to begin with.¹³⁸ Firsthand accounts detail several instances of civilian casualties that occurred as a result of Katyushas.¹³⁹ In one incident, ENDF responded to an insurgent attack launched from

---

137. Aimé, Elsa González. "The Security Issues Behind the Ethiopian Intervention in Somalia (2006-2009)". *State and Societal Challenges in the Horn of Africa*, edited by Alexandra Magnólia Dias, Centro de Estudos Internacionais, 2013, p.36
138. Aimé, Elsa González. "The Security Issues Behind the Ethiopian Intervention in Somalia (2006-2009)". *State and Societal Challenges in the Horn of Africa*, edited by Alexandra Magnólia Dias, Centro de Estudos Internacionais, 2013, p.132
139. Ibid

the town of Beledweyne by shelling the city for three days in July 2008.[140] Reports estimate "that at the end of July, 74,000 people—more than 75 percent of the town's population—had been displaced as a direct result of the bombardment and related fighting." Such episodes were reportedly commonplace throughout 2008.[141]

ENDF soldiers were also accused of using indiscriminate small arms fire that resulted in further civilian casualties. In an August 2008 incident, ENDF soldiers responded to the detonation of a roadside bomb with wild gunfire that left approximately **40 Somali civilians dead**.[142] In addition to recorded instances of reckless use of force, human rights groups also claimed that **search and seizure operations conducted by the ENDF**, like those carried out by the TFG, occasionally resulted in assault, rape, looting, and killing of Somali civilians.[143]

7.20. Ethiopian Influence on Somalia's Federal Institutions and Broader Political Ecosystem

Unlike other peacekeeping forces, Ethiopia, instead of promoting democracy and rule of law, invested in having influence across all Somali institutions in order to have greater influence and control on the direction and destination of the Somali people to its advantage, thus crippling all joint efforts and intentions of the Somali people and the interest of western countries backing to restore law and order and fully functional democratic nation.

It was the year 2006, the first time that Col. Gebregzabher Alemseged was catapulted into the vortex of Somalia's messy politics as the top Ethiopian commander in Somalia. This was the darkest era in Somalia's war trajectory, when Ethiopian forces illegally invaded southern Somalia with the invitation of then warlord President, Abdullahi Yusuf and his rapacious prime minister, Mohamed Ali Ghedi in order to defeat the Islamic Courts Union (ICU) that was then in control in the capital and much of

---

140. Ibid
141. Ibid
142. Ibid
143. Ibid

the south of Somalia.¹⁴⁴ According to friends who met with him more than once and closely watched him up close and personal, they were awestruck at how wicked the General is in his wheeling-dealings with various Somali politicians by pretending to be their best friend and looking out for the country's best interest while actually behind the scenes he's working hard to put them on a collision course. In fact, he is no less than a fox pretending to be safeguarding the chicken house and those poor Somali politicians who seem to entrust the country's fate on such a figure are no less than traitors, which should be condemned in the strongest terms.¹⁴⁵

Ethiopia has become involved in the selection process of members of Parliament, who is going to be a cabinet member, and while anyone with ambition to be a president or prime minister has first to engage with the Ethiopian intelligence officials and military commanders to appease them and get approval. As a result, this influence adversely affected the genuine desirable future state of Somalia and the Western countries' strategic interests. The outcome became politicians in positions of authority and even military officers having the same mindset as Ethiopia's desirable state of Somalia, which is a weak, poor Somalia under the control of Ethiopia. Ethiopia, having terribly failed to militarily conquer Somalia in its darkest moment, entrusted General Gabre to work his magic of playing the "divide and conquer" odious game, which rather seems to have worked.¹⁴⁶

Indeed, it's tragic whenever you see well-educated Somali leaders who seem to be more comfortable conferring with the likes of Col. Gebregzabher Alemseged and Ambassador Afey, instead of other Somali leaders.¹⁴⁷ Not to mention other regional Somali leaders who seem to have pledged allegiance to these enemies of the State in order to keep their paper tiger power.¹⁴⁸ This phenomenon has become familiar throughout Somalia, driving many youth to join insurgents and resistance groups committed to fighting with SNA and other peacekeeping forces in Somalia.

---

144. Dahir, A. (2015, December). Who's afraid of General Gabre? Hiiraan Online. Retrieved from https://www.hiiraan.com/op4/2015/dec/102847/who_s_afraid_of_general_gabre.aspx
145. Ibid
146. Ibid
147. Ibid
148. Ibid

Every Somali citizen developed the perception that whatever kind of government formed in Somalia that the international community backed merely represented the interests of Ethiopia and Western countries rather than Somalia. People felt a lack of ownership of the key peace and state-building processes. An example worth noting was how Ethiopia's influence affected General Awil Dhiig-sokeeye's dismissal. He was the commander of the 54th brigade which was based at Villa Somalia to provide protection to the president. The president was compelled to fire him following pressure from MPs, Ministers, and even the prime minister loyal to Ethiopia intelligence team. It was widely seen that they were all engaging with the president merely serving the interests of Ethiopia. General Awil Dhiig-Sokeeye was removed from the commander position to appease politicians and other eminent persons who in turn just wanted to placate Ethiopian intelligence. However, the president never wanted to remove him from the commander position. In contrast, it was in the interest of Ethiopia, who viewed him as a well-trusted military General who was loyal to his country and to the president.

If the international community backing Somalia were deeply aware of how Ethiopia's securitization policies had been severely crippling the collective effort in restoring stability, law and order, and democracy in Somalia, which cost billions of dollars of their taxpayers' money, they could have already changed their policies in relation **to their blind trust of Ethiopia and their strategic interests in Somalia**. This is because the intention of Ethiopia about the kind of Somalia it wanted, the international community backing up Somalia's view and strategic interests and the desirable future state that Somalis were in pursuit of were pretty much inconsistent with one another.

7.21. Salary of the National Army Payment

Shockingly, in the light of this securitization move, Ethiopia's involvement and influence of the Western countries, reached to the extent that they were trusted with not only TFG war against ICU but also to manage the SNA payroll and payment of their salary. So when Somali officers wanted to get their salary, they should first go to the Ethiopian army office and get approval from an Ethiopian officer and then queue for their salary. Upon my arrival to Mogadishu from an overseas military course, I queued in a line with other high-ranking military officers to sign a payment payroll for an office run by Ethiopian officers. I couldn't discern whether I was an Ethiopian soldier or a Somali soldier, whether I was under the Ethiopian government or Somali government. We all knew the situation we found ourselves in, including the securitization move by Ethiopia against TFG and Somali people, but we continued working with it until change happened.

7.22. General Dahir Aden Elmi Indho-Qarsho

Immediately after General Indho-Qarsho was appointed as SNA commander in 2013, he, pertinent to his experience in military management, changed Ethiopia's orchestrated policies towards SNA and introduced new policies to ensure an effective institution for SNA to be nurtured. Those policies, which included new military salary payments to come through the Ministry of Finance and directly to the officers' accounts, had deterred Ethiopia's growing influence on the Ministry of Defense. General Indho-Qarsho not only improved management but he also created new SNA units such as Danab special force and Gorgor force. These two newly introduced SNA units demonstrated the quality of SNA forces and created a new capability to respond to the growing threat from the terrorists and engendered possible public trust to the government. Individuals with necessary military skills didn't only bring about management change, performance improvement, and public trust but also encouraged junior officers to become inspired.

Unfortunately, previous successive governments failed to recruit people with military experience to fight with terrorists and create a peaceful conducive environment for people to exercise their democratic rights. This is the reason why the set goals were not achieved in a timely manner. Ethiopian influence on all institutions made possible the removal of 54th commander General Awil Dhiig-sokeeye, and Col. Gaalkayo Warsame Olol was named as the new 54th brigade commander. There had been well-known Ethiopian intelligence and military officers in Somalia, whose influence reached to the extent they were entitled to sit in the Somali cabinet meetings and parliament sessions. These include Colonel Gebregziabher Alemseged Abraha, Col. Tesfay, and Yohanes (we will talk more about them in the following pages). Throughout Somalia, it's now a well-known fact that Col. Gebregzabher Alemseged employs numerous spies who work for him to collect classified information from various Somali government institutions, including the parliament, ministerial cabinets, military and the police, as well as Somalia's National Intelligence and Security Agency.[149] In the background of all Somali reconciliation conferences, there's no doubt that he's a destabilizing factor because there is no telling what the incorrigible General might contrive, and he could be inflaming all reconciliation talks and undermining any peace deals that might propel the country forward. It's needless to say neither Col. Gebregzabher Alemseged nor the Ethiopian government have Somalia's interest in their deep involvement in Somalia's reconciliation and development process and only present a dangerous potential that jeopardizes any future democratically elected government in the country.[150]

54th brigade was facing dual attacks, one from joint insurgents and al-Shabaab forces and the other from Ethiopian forces who were relentlessly shelling intensified artillery barrages. As a result of this, 54th brigade sustained huge casualties and was weakened within 24 months. Ethiopian forces were shelling barrages of artillery bombardment equally on both Mogadishu and Villa Somalia. The following three SNA officers were killed by the bombardment:

1. Presidential Guard Commander Col Abdirizak Mohamed Hirsi (Garcad)
2. Platoon Commander for Presidential Guard. Abdikafi Ali Hussein (Wagas)
3. General Duty Of State House Abdulahi Daahir haruun (Afweyne)

7.23. Office of the President hit by Katyusha by ENDF

The worst attack in those days by Ethiopian forces against the 54th brigade happened in the morning at around 9 am in late 2008, when

---

149. Dahir, A. (2015, December). Who's afraid of General Gabre? Hiiraan Online. Retrieved from https://www.hiiraan.com/op4/2015/dec/102847/who_s_afraid_of_general_gabre.aspx
150. Dahir, A. (2015, December). Who's afraid of General Gabre? Hiiraan Online. Retrieved from https://www.hiiraan.com/op4/2015/dec/102847/who_s_afraid_of_general_gabre.aspx

they fired twice with BM type 63, 107mm rockets and hit the office of the president in the villa, at a time when a meeting between the Somali President and SNA commander was ongoing. In that attack, both security staff of SNA commander and those for the president, as well as Ugandan forces staying there as AMISOM, were killed and injured.

7.24. Concealing Evidence of Villa Somalia Bombardment

Concealing evidence of Villa Somalia bombardment by Ethiopian forces. When the Ethiopian forces target Villa Somalia for bombardment, immediately after they hit their target, while SNA TFG is busy dealing with the death and injury, ENDF commanders send three to four soldiers to collect evidence of weapons used. This was many times spotted by SNA officers who were helping victims. Here isn't the front line where al-Shabaab militia stationed but it was the office of the Somali president, and the world assumes that Ethiopian forces are providing support to the nascent government in Mogadishu. But Ethiopian forces are bombing with barrages of BM 63 with 107mm ammunition. The situation escalated as both Ugandan forces and Ethiopian forces deployed military panzers against each other as a result of casualties caused by Ethiopia's bombardment. Both of them are based within Villa Somalia. Consequently, Ethiopian forces closed the main gate of Villa Somalia with their tanks and their commander Col. Tesfay put a chair and sat in the middle of the tanks. This was extremely unethical and unprofessional behavior not expected from peacekeeping forces. Having seen the situation, the Somali government and Ugandan forces opted to use another gate called 15 May gate, which was a gate at the backside of the villa to avoid confrontation and massive casualties. Col. Tesfay was the commander of the Ethiopian brigade based in Villa Somalia as peacekeeping forces.

7.25. The arrest of Mogadishu Mayor by Ethiopian Intelligence

Gabre and Tesfay, two Ethiopian military colonels, decided to arrest Mohamed Omar Habeeb, the then Mogadishu governor and Mayor for his support of the president and the 54th brigade. Another reason that the two colonels wanted for his arrest was that, as he was a powerful man in Mogadishu, he might orchestrate attacks against Ethiopian forces, predominantly Tigrayan, as there had been a vacuum following the president's resignation. Their concern was that he might take advantage of the gap since the successor would come to the office after an election. They arrested Mohamed Omar Habeeb in his house in Shangani district. Col. Gebregzabher Alemseged is notorious for being well-versed with the Somalis' Achilles' heel—"tribalism"—and he never misses an opportunity to use it in his machinations to manipulate every Somali politician to bid against those of other clans.[151] Indeed, he is ubiquitous in most Somali "reconciliation"[152] conferences, clad with his pistol on his back belt, intimidating anyone who doesn't follow to his decisive agenda to keep the country in line with Ethiopian interests.

Consequently, the arrest of the governor and the president's resignation plagued the 54th brigade with a disillusioned situation, thus they retreated from all defense positions as they were unable to bear the pressure from Ethiopian forces in the villa who aimed to torture them.

[**Fig. 7:** Mogadishu Mayor (right) and his security escort - a military officer handcuffed by the Ethiopian forces in Mogadishu, with TFG leadership present]

---

151. Dahir, A. (2015, December). Who's afraid of General Gabre? Hiiraan Online. Retrieved from https://www.hiiraan.com/op4/2015/dec/102847/who_s_afraid_of_general_gabre.aspx
152. Ibid

7.26. SNA and Ethiopian Forces Confrontation Over Indiscriminate Bombardments in Mogadishu

Although the second day Mogadishu was relatively stable and there was no confrontation between insurgents and Al-Shabaab forces against SNA or AMISOM forces, the Ethiopian forces in the villa, using BM Multiple Katyusha rocket 63mm, fired on the city, and when asked about the situation and who are they targeting? they claimed they were covering their forces who had been under attack of insurgents and Al-Shabaab somewhere far in the city.

[**Fig. 8:** Katyusha rocket belonged to Ethiopian defense forces which they frequently used for the bombardment of highly populated areas in Mogadishu and Beledweyne]

SNA officers who communicated across Mogadishu bases to verify ENDF claim regarding bombardament, realized there were no Ethiopian forces in Mogadishu bases who had been under attack of insurgents and Al-Shabaab. As a result, TFG officers got annoyed and became concerned about such massive indiscriminate bombardment of civilian inhabitants across the city, and it provoked the morale and angered an SNA officer named Saed Talohun who came close to the Ethiopian soldier firing the city with the Katyusha PM 63mm rocket and beat him with his AK-47. This resulted in both SNA and Ethiopians in the scene withdrawing their guns and pointing at each other.

Col. Tesfay, who was the Ethiopian commander ordering his soldiers to fire indiscriminately on Mogadishu, was the Ethiopian officer in charge of the operation. However, the tension was immediately diffused following the 54th brigade Somali commander who instructed the arrest of Saeed Talohun and ordered his stressed forces to step down and get back to their positions. While Col. Tesfay also impersonated as a genuine officer and instructed his forces to step down, their bombardment of the rocket to the city was stopped. However, despite efforts to reduce the tension between SNA forces and Ethiopian forces, the arrest of the Somali military officer in the Ethiopian base in Villa Somalia changed the whole atmosphere and heightened mistrust emerged, which led more SNA to show disinterest in remaining in their defense positions because of the arrest decision of their colleague by their own commander and made a quick retreat including those stationed outside Villa Somalia in response to the situation.

Ethiopian commanders, having assessed the situation, deployed a special force unit to contain SNA and orchestrated the murder of the arrested officer Said Talohun, not in their base but rather outside to avoid blame for his death. By midnight they set him free to go to his camp, and on his way they shot him and left him bleeding and blocked all the roads leading to incident scene

They wanted him to die there from bleeding. However, SNA forces on patrol and at their main base communicated about the shooting, and the patrolling unit was instructed to verify the incident. Unfortunately, they were denied by ENDF access to the scene of the shooting. After several attempts, they reported back to their commanders and said no one could access the incident scene because Ethiopians had set up new blockades everywhere. Another tension arose, which led a Somali SNA driver to make his own decision to disobey Ethiopian forces' blockade. He crossed by force and reached the scene, where he reported finding a fallen SNA soldier, Said Talohun, who was bleeding severely. Furthermore, Ethiopian forces started roaring their panzer engines to divert SNA attention away from their officer Said Talohun, who was bleeding to death and appealing for help. This was happening inside Villa Somalia where both TFG forces and ENDF were based. Two soldiers and I reached the driver officer named Waharey who wanted to transport the injured officer. Ethiopian forces were also seeking to arrest him. In our effort to take him to hospital,

ENDF blocked our exit with A military tank, as such, an SNA officer clumped the Tank and forced the Tank to be removed from the road. The tank was forcible removed and we proceeded towards hospital. We all rescued the bleeding officer and took him to Medina Hospital, where he received emergency treatment.

However, the same time Villa Baido building a temparary office as a MoD Somalia, next to Madina Hospital was being targeted by ENDF shelling, which killed head of finance Col Timo jilic.

7.27. The Confrontation Between SNA and Ethiopian Forces Over a Somali Girl in SYL Hotel

This incident showed that Ethiopia's hostility was not limited to the destruction of SNA forces, indiscriminate bombardment of civilians and control of all institutions to their advantage. A confrontation occurred between SNA and ENDF over the deliberate assault of a Somali girl running her business at the SYL building by Ethiopian forces. SYL building is just opposite Villa Somalia. In this case, an Ethiopian unit comprising 11 soldiers entered a small hotel belonging to a Somali girl and requested to serve them tea. As she began serving them, one soldier rubbed his leg against hers from behind in an attempt to seduce her. She reacted angrily by pouring a cup of hot tea on him. Unfortunately, another soldier then hit the girl in the upper stomach, causing her to fall down. A nearby Somali soldier spotted the Ethiopian soldier who had assaulted the Somali girl and confronted him. Subsequently, the entire Ethiopian unit attacked and severely beat the Somali soldier who had stepped in to protect the girl. The situation escalated between the Ethiopian unit and civilians in the area, who intervened and rescued the soldier. The Somali officer was taken to a hospital for medical treatment. The Ethiopian unit later escaped the scene toward their embassy in Villa Somalia. This incident exemplified the scale of ENDF hostility against Somalis. The Ethiopians were supposed to function as peacekeeping forces and exhibit behavior in accordance with peacekeeping rules and regulations. But they were careless about peacekeeping policy and regulation and were merely doing securitization moves against everyone.

7.28. Ethiopia Withdrawal

Although ENDF said it will withdraw from Mogsdishu, the truth is they never fully withdrew from Mogadishu. They partially withdrew, and those who left went to other Somali regions such as Bay, Gedo, and Hiiraan, where they continued their unabated destruction and securitization move. Those who remained in Mogadishu, particularly inside their embassy, were given AU insignia and continued their malicious attacks in Mogadishu. However, their devastating destruction, killing, and displacement inflicted upon citizens, and their increasing influence within both security and political ecosystems remained unchanged. The world is aware of what Ethiopia inflicted upon people in Somalia during these two years, particularly people in Mogadishu and central Somalia, but the world remains unaware of how Ethiopia undermined both the TFG and Western nations' efforts to stabilize Somalia. The parallel attacks from Ethiopian NDF against the TFG and other African Union forces, and the rocket, P10, and BM bombardment toward Villa Somalia reflected Ethiopia's long-term enmity with Somalia.

Ethiopia's military presence in Somalia effectively came to an end in January 2009 as the TFG and the Djibouti-based wing of the ARS formed a government of national unity.[153] Upon Ethiopia's withdrawal, ARS and TFG troops, along with limited support from AMISOM, were tasked with bringing security back to the country. Incidents of violence, while fewer in number and intensity than in the past two years, continued nonetheless. In the first few months of 2009, for example, opposition groups including more radical elements of the ARS, clans hostile to the new government, and al Shabaab launched a series of attacks on AMISOM forces, government officials, and humanitarian workers.[154]

---

153. Aimé, Elsa González. "The Security Issues Behind the Ethiopian Intervention in Somalia (2006-2009)". *State and Societal Challenges in the Horn of Africa*, edited by Alexandra Magnólia Dias, Centro de Estudos Internacionais, 2013, p.129
154. Ibid

7.29. Proof of How Ethiopia Crippled Both Western and Somali Interests: Performance Evaluation System

What is worth noting is that when ENDF was leaving Somalia, Ethiopia refused to hand over the MOD to the FGS, particularly SNA leadership. Instead, they handed over the MOD facilities to AS. It was not only the MOD but also all their other bases in Mogadishu. The million-dollar question that TFG commanders were asking themselves was what made it possible for AS to take over all ENDF military bases, including MOD infrastructure, and not the TFG?. The answer was very clear to my commanders: the ENDF had a hidden collaboration with al Shabaab not only in Mogadishu but across Somalia.

ENDF command was later moved to Halane as CCC center. By the end of 2008, the ENDF-TFG alliance had relinquished control of much of central and southern Somalia to the insurgency.[155] In December 2008, "the situation reached an impasse following dramatic gains by insurgent forces. TFG and Ethiopian forces had lost the ability to exercise even limited influence across most of the country and appeared to have given up trying to recapture territory they had lost." The TFG-ENDF's area of operations was limited to Baidoa and a handful of districts in Mogadishu, a military situation similar to that of early 2007.[156] Nevertheless, for SNA, it was preferable that MOD was now in the hands of AS instead. This was because they knew they could dislodge them and occupy the facilities rather than confronting Ethiopian forces for control.

7.30. Gen Gordon's Strategy

General Gordon developed a military strategy to seize all military bases and MOD from AS. It was a very successful strategy. He himself died during one of those operations. As a result of his experience and courage, a current military base in Mogadishu was named after him: General Gordon Military Base. Gordon's plan deterred Ethiopia's sinister motive

---

155. Aimé, Elsa González. "The Security Issues Behind the Ethiopian Intervention in Somalia (2006-2009)". *State and Societal Challenges in the Horn of Africa*, edited by Alexandra Magnólia Dias, Centro de Estudos Internacionais, 2013, p.129
156. Ibid

against SNA, allowing the Somali military to become more effective in managing its own forces and implementing strategic initiatives to achieve the vision of a strong SNA capable of controlling the country's security and providing protection to Somali citizens. VIP Protection included Captain Abdirashid Hassan Diriye Afgub, President Farmajo, Abdikafi, and Abdullahi Dool. These teams were responsible for VIP Protection. A new trainee serving as VIP Protection and commander of the presidential guard was hit by a shell fired by the Ethiopian forces at the gate of Villa Somalia. Another shell hit two other officers who had been trained by the Ethiopians themselves. We rushed with Mr. Afgub to the hospital for medical treatment.

7.31. About General Gabre Yohannes Abate: The Ethiopian Troop Commander in Somalia

If Somalia was a stable country, or even relatively stable under a dictatorship like in the past, there would be nothing at all worrisome about the threats and machinations from such neocolonial elements as General Gabre.[157] Gabre Yohannes Abate, the Ethiopian troop commander in Somalia, was the key person responsible for undermining the collective effort of the Somali government and the Western countries supporting Somalia to stand on its feet. He was responsible for implementing Ethiopia's hidden agenda against Somalia. Ethiopia portrayed itself as a friend to the TFG, committed to democracy and promoting rule of law; however, he was arrogant and threatened government officials, including senior military officers, politicians, and even traditional leaders.

He developed strong relationships with Al-Shabaab and ordered massive bombardment of Mogadishu city and other towns in central Somalia. He issued arrest orders for the Mogadishu governor and mayor without even informing the government. He acted as if he were the sole authority in the country. Whenever government officials raised concerns about the colonel's behavior and extreme lack of collaboration with the government, he would remind them that Ethiopian forces had saved the

---

157. Dahir, A. (2015, December). Who's afraid of General Gabre? Hiiraan Online. Retrieved from https://www.hiiraan.com/op4/2015/dec/102847/who_s_afraid_of_general_gabre.aspx

government and that without ENDF, Al-Shabaab would overthrow the TFG. Since the Ethiopian forces entered Somalia, whether they came through a request made by the TFG or not, the commander never listened to suggestions made by the TFG leaders, including the president.

It is noteworthy that when Ethiopia withdrew its forces from Somalia in January 2009, in his remarks at the ceremony held in Villa Somalia, he said, "It is time Somalia stands on its own feet," said Ethiopian commander General. Gabre Yohannes Abate, as he handed over security operations during a ceremony at the presidential palace in Mogadishu. "So we are saying goodbye to all Somalis and their dignitaries." However, Gabre Yoannes Abate kept calling Somali officials asking whether they were being attacked by AS or not. He was directly asking if the TFG could survive from Al-Shabaab attacks after their withdrawal. Somalis overwhelmingly welcomed the Ethiopians' withdrawal from their country for several reasons. These include people who fled their houses in Mogadishu due to the indiscriminate bombardment by the Ethiopian forces who were taking orders from General Gabre Yohannes Abate.

Although many media outlets reported that the Ethiopian troops had been propping up Somalia's weak U.N.-backed government for two years amid a ferocious Islamic insurgency that had killed thousands of civilians and prompted the president to resign in December, saying he had lost the country to the Islamists, the truth was that the Ethiopian military and Al-Shabaab militants had been in good collaboration. Al-Shabaab received military ammunition from Ethiopian field commanders who were in turn receiving instructions from General. Gabre Yohannes Abate.

Every Somali citizen knew of the close collaboration between Ethiopian forces and Al-Shabaab. People widely believed the reason SNA was weakened was the massive ammunition Al-Shabaab received from Ethiopia whenever they left a military base. Ethiopian forces withdrew from the battlefield without informing their SNA partners; however, Al-Shabaab had information that the Ethiopian military was withdrawing, and they not only replaced them but also found massive ammunition left behind by ENDF for Al-Shabaab. The pullout received wide support from ordinary Somalis, officials, and diplomats. Many had seen the Ethiopians as occupiers, and their two-year deployment had been a rallying cry for the insurgents to gain recruits even as the militants' strict form of Islam terrified people into submission. However, the then Somali prime minister said, "The Ethiopians have begun withdrawing, there is no need for fighting again. I urge all Somalis to become peace-loving people."

The U.N. envoy to Somalia praised the Ethiopians for honoring their withdrawal commitment made with the power-sharing deal signed the previous year in Djibouti. "The ball is now in the court of the Somalis, particularly those who said they were only fighting against the Ethiopian forces, to stop the senseless killings and violence," Ahmedou Ould-Abdallah said in a statement issued Tuesday in neighboring Kenya. Fadumo Wehliye, who lost three of her eight children during the violence, described the Ethiopian pullout as "great" and said she would go back home to Mogadishu.

"For the last two years... I have been living in a makeshift house in the outskirts of the capital," she said. Now *"I will return to my home."* (Reuters)

However, by design, Somalia is not a stable country, which worries most of us about what's lurking behind its instability and the major forces that foster such instability. For example, unlike other foreign diplomats in the country who tend to barricade themselves in the Halane compound, Col. Gebregzabher Alemseged surprisingly enough travels around the country with no restrictions on who he conducts business with or what the end game is of him participating in the formation of all Somali regional governments.[158] But above all, traveling nonchalantly to some of the most hostile districts controlled by the Al-Shabab terrorist group raises questions about his indirect support or collusion with these extremists who daily target government buildings and major hotels occupied by government officials. As a matter of fact, many Somali officials have indirectly accused him of having suspicious links with the terrorists and other destabilizing groups.[159]

Lately, Kenya seems to be copying the wrong approach from Ethiopia's neo-colonial mission in Somalia by appointing their own emissary, Mohamed Abdi Afey, as the IGAD Special Envoy to Somalia,

---

158. Dahir, A. (2015, December). Who's afraid of General Gabre? Hiiraan Online. Retrieved from https://www.hiiraan.com/op4/2015/dec/102847/who_s_afraid_of_general_gabre.aspx
159. Ibid

whose sole mission is to keep Somalia in a state of perpetual turmoil. Thus, Gabre and Afey have become Somalia's de facto paternalistic neo-colonial African envoys bent on sowing the bitter seeds of animosity among Somalia's weak regional states. In fact, both men have supposedly gained large sums of wealth and influence from the conflict and chaos in Somalia.[160] They both exhibit exceptionally the characteristics of neocolonialists by pretending to sympathize with the Somali cause while undermining the federal government in place, despite its flaws and weaknesses. Nonetheless, it is now common knowledge that both Ethiopia and Kenya have no intentions whatsoever to ever see Somalia regain its power and influence in the Horn of Africa.[161]

The abhorrent tactics used by the likes of Col. Gebregzabher Alemseged and Ambassador Afey open a new window into the hidden and contradictory machinations that regional players like Ethiopia and Kenya use against Somalia for its continued destabilization under the guise of their emissaries' pretense to support a peaceful solution.[162] As history shows, Somalia had a long history of border disputes with both Ethiopia and Kenya and always considered them archenemies; therefore, it is just too contemptuous and disingenuous for these countries now to send "goodwill" ambassadors to Somalia anticipating to pacify relations with the country. I just cannot imagine how many Somali freedom fighters must be rolling over in their graves when they realize how their country fell under the likes of Gabre and Afey, enemies of the State.[163] In the end, Somalia's long quest to find lasting peace will remain elusive and unattainable as long as divisive elements like Col. Gebregzabher Alemseged and Ambassador Afey are allowed to play the paternalistic neo-colonial power to keep Somalia in the status quo of turmoil and political disenfranchisement at the behest of the enemy, while the country's leadership turns a blind eye and acts as though they were honest brokers.[164] Thus, the country's current government, by not honestly acknowledging

---

160. Ibid
161. Dahir, A. (2015, December). Who's afraid of General Gabre? Hiiraan Online. Retrieved from https://www.hiiraan.com/op4/2015/dec/102847/who_s_afraid_of_general_gabre.aspx
162. Ibid
163. Ibid
164. Ibid

and facing up to the deep underlying roots of the country's conflict and how neighboring countries, mainly Ethiopia and Kenya, are major contributing factors, is committing what amounts to national treason.[165]

7.32. About ONLF and the so called *"Jail Ogaden"*

Ethiopia's securitization move of Somalia extended back to Ethiopia's Somali region. The securitization move badly affected the Somali region of Ethiopia. Ethiopia recognized the opposition, primarily the ONLF, as terrorist. This resulted in the formation of what Somali inhabitants in Ogadenia call Jail Ogadenia, a prison created by the Ethiopian regime and the Somali leader who was allied with them. The media and human rights organizations have documented heart-wrenching reports which are difficult to conceive such atrocities could happen in the 21st century. Women, children, elderly people, young people, politicians, and traditional leaders—none of them was spared in the Somali region of Ethiopia. They were arbitrarily detained and tortured in Jail Ogaden until they passed away. Under the administration of President George W. Bush, US policy in the Horn of Africa focused on combating the threat of terrorism and prioritizing strong relations with the Ethiopian government, Washington's only stable and reliable ally in the Horn. This narrow policy framework exacerbated serious human rights problems across the region. Rethinking policy on Somalia means rethinking policy across the wider Horn.[166]

The United States consistently failed to exert significant pressure on the Ethiopian government to improve upon its dire human rights record—even though Washington has considerable leverage as the aid-dependent country's largest bilateral donor and most important political backer.[167] Some high-ranking US officials rejected all evidence of human rights violations to insist that they did not know whether abuses in Ethiopia had taken place at all. In 2007, for example, US Assistant Secretary of State for Africa Jendayi Frazer publicly stated that allegations

---

165. Ibid
166. Human Rights Watch, "So Much to Fear": War Crimes and the Devastation of Somalia, 1-56432-415-X, 8 December 2008, https://www.refworld.org/reference/countryrep/hrw/2008/en/64117 [accessed 26 February 2025]
167. Ibid

of ongoing ENDF war crimes and crimes against humanity in Ethiopia's Somali region were "unsubstantiated," rather than express concern about the abuses to Ethiopian officials.[168]

The same policy framework has driven United States policy in Somalia. As in Ethiopia, Washington has turned a blind eye to ENDF laws of war violations in Somalia. US law forbids the US government from providing assistance to foreign military units involved in serious human rights abuses. But US officials have made no credible effort to investigate and determine whether ENDF units implicated in abuses in Somalia are past or potential beneficiaries of US military training and assistance to Ethiopia.[169]

7.33. General Abdi Qeybdiid Prevents Ethiopian Intelligence from Dismantling Somali Police Force, as done previously done with SNA

General Abdi Qeybdiid was the Commissioner of the Somali Police Force who deterred Ethiopia's effort to destroy the existence of effective Somali Police Forces the same way as they destroyed the Somali Military Force. Ethiopia, using its influence within government branches including parliament and cabinet ministers built over past years, has destroyed

---

168. Ibid
169. Ibid

most of the security apparatus including the military and the national intelligence, and was now committed to uproot the Somali Police Force to their advantage. The Somali Police has been the only security wing that survived from the plight of the civil war. The documents of the Somali Police forces and operating mode remained intact, and archives and other crucial files were not looted. Although the central government collapsed in 1991, the collaboration between Somali Police Forces across the country continued to operate in the absence of required resources and general command. As the prospect of building a new government which could restore rule of law was high, the Somali Police Forces could be the foundation for creation of law enforcement and the judiciary system in the country.

It is noteworthy that despite Western countries' efforts to restore law and order in Somalia and spending millions of dollars on that goal, Ethiopian forces in Somalia, whether under the name of AMISOM or its invasion in December 2006 to fight with the terrorists, have continuously crippled such efforts while simultaneously gaining both financial and diplomatic support. The objectives of the international community, which was to stabilize Somalia, and the Ethiopian one, which was to further ruin Somalia, were quite inconsistent (Help stabilize Somalia vs. create more instability).In view of the above, however, the Ethiopian government had been committed to the realization of their objectives, including weakening the Somali Police forces. Fortunately, the then Somali Police Commissioner was Gen. Abdi Qeydiid, who exerted considerable efforts to prevent Ethiopia's ill-fated mission against Somali Police Forces. However, on the Ethiopian side, they put forth a lot of efforts through all their influence within the government, including elements in parliament, cabinet, and other institutions to place the Somali Police Force under Ethiopian forces, then to further ruin it and ensure all security sectors of the country had been weakened, but it was Abdi Qeybdiid who insisted not to do that.

7.34. How Gen. Abdi Qeybdiid Prevented Ethiopia's Ambition to bring Somali Police Force under Ethiopian control

Ethiopia mobilized all its networks including members of the Somali parliament, ministers, and even regional countries to bring the

Somali Police Forces under its control and dismiss the current Somali police commissioner and deputy commissioner. It wanted Ethiopian officers to manage and control the Somali Police forces; this would enable Ethiopia to get access to the Somali Police Forces systems and files, exploit it, and eventually replace all Somali Police work forces with newly recruited ones instilled with its own doctrine. The office of the President received the news relating to Ethiopia's desire to bring the Somali Police Force under their control and the dismissal of the commissioner. Ethiopia's argument was that there were potential police officers who could play a significant role in the fight against terrorists, so if handed over to them, they could make use of these potential forces for that purpose. However, the true objective was to destroy the police as they did to other branches of the army. President Abdullahi Yusuf Ahmed, who was on overseas official duty, was pressured to convince the Somali Police Commissioner to hand over his responsibility to Ethiopian commanders. But General Abdi Qeybdiid's decision was to maintain his position and responsibility, as well as deterring the Somali Police Forces from being placed under Ethiopian commanders in Mogadishu who would use them for their own agenda.

As the situation became a stalemate, General Abdi Qeybdiid decided to meet with the president who was in Addis Ababa. He traveled secretly to Addis Ababa through Nairobi. He knew the Ethiopian intelligence was monitoring his movement. He misled his office staff by telling them that he was going to Nairobi for medical reasons, but as he arrived at Jomo Kenyatta Airport, he booked the next flight to Addis Ababa and went there to meet with the president in his hotel.

7.35. General Abdi Qeybdiid and President Yusuf

It was evening, I was sitting at the residence of the president. There was no scheduled meeting. However, the president came out from his suit dressed as if there was a fixed scheduled meeting. The president ordered me to go to the hotel reception and usher in General Abdi Qeybdiid. I went to the hotel reception and saw him with an angered face, and ushered him to the president's suite. On our way to the president's suite, the General asked me who was with the president. I told him no one. He felt relief and said okay. I felt something was wrong. As we arrived at the president's suite, the president received him with a question. The president asked him what happened? I realized they had prior communication. And I thought it might be the usual political crisis revolving around the different branches of the government such as the parliament, the executives, and the presidency. There must be a new situation that brought Abdi here in Addis Ababa. However, it was quite the opposite. Ethiopia wanted the Somali Police Force to be placed under their control. General Abdi Qeybdiid provided an exhaustive explanation about Ethiopia's desire to bring the Somali Police Force under their control and eventually destroy it. Being a witness of this case was what motivated me to document all those issues and events as I found them not in alignment with both Somalia's desirable future state and the real intentionality of Western countries who committed to the stabilization of Somalia.

General Abdi Qeybdiid and the president agreed and reached consensus that the Somali Police Force would not be placed under Ethiopia's control. Then Abdi Qeybdiid flew back to Mogadishu the same day through Nairobi. The commissioner's secret meeting for which he traveled from Mogadishu was not known to anyone. Immediately after the president returned back to the country, the Ethiopian intelligence offices and other military commanders organized a meeting between the president and Ethiopian commanders along with politicians loyal to Ethiopia. The aim of the meeting was to convince the president to hand over the Somali Police Force to Ethiopia. General Abdi Qeybdiid was also invited, despite his repeatedly refusing to hand over the Somali Police Force to Ethiopia. Nevertheless, Ethiopian intelligence in Mogadishu, those in Addis Ababa, and in the neighboring countries didn't know about the meeting between the president and the Somali Police Commissioner in Addis Ababa – Hilton Hotel.

As the meeting started, the Ethiopian commanders presented their proposal seeking the Somali Police Force to be placed under the control of Ethiopia in order to further advance their skills and capabilities and use them in the war against the terrorists. Before the president spoke, however, General Abdi Qeybdiid said, "Mr. President, it is unacceptable for the proposal and we are not ready to be under the control of Ethiopia." President Abdullahi Yusuf Ahmed, who had prior discussion with the Commissioner, said the Somali Police Forces will be under the control of General Abdi Qeybdiid. "General Qeybdiid is also responsible for

security of the whole country," he concluded. "The meeting is closed." Therefore, Ethiopia's mission and goal to get the Somali police systems and files to destroy utterly failed. Ethiopian representatives who organized and participated in the meeting were the following:
1. General Youhanis, Commander of the Ethiopia forces in Somalia
2. Col. Tafsay, Commander of the ENDF brigade based at Villa Somalia
3. Con Gabre, Head of intelligence ENDF
4. Ethiopia ambassador to Mogadishu - Fisaha Shawel
5. Secretary of the Ethiopian ambassador - Jamal Hassan

Somalia:
1. President Abdullahi Yusuf Ahmed
2. General Abdi Qeybdiid, Somali Police Commissioner
3. Hussein Ali Saylaan, Chief of Staff of Somali Presidency
4. The author: Presidential security
5. Mohamed Omar Habeeb - Mogadishu Governor and Mayor

7.36. A call from Ethiopian commanders who withdrew from Mogadishu to terrorize TFG

Following the unacceptable Ethiopian cruel objectives grounded on the enmity between the two countries over past decades and the deliberate destructions which were crippling the stabilization, state building, and peacebuilding processes, the TFG leaders decided the Ethiopian Forces should completely withdraw from Somalia. As they withdrew from Mogadishu, they attempted to depict it as a deserted city for fear of Al-Shabaab taking over. They ordered all their supporters to go along with them. Some of their sympathizers went along with them, while others remained in Mogadishu. They left Mogadishu repeatedly saying "Al-Shabaab will take over." General Gabre Yohannes Abate had frequently been calling General Qeybdiid, asking about their survival from Al-Shabaab. But Qeybdiid repeatedly said, there is nothing to fear in Mogadishu. He kept calling Abdi Qeybdiid until they crossed the border, asking whether Al-Shabaab had taken over Mogadishu. Abdi gave him the same answer: "We don't see any threat, leave us alone." That was their end, and the Somali Police Force survived from Ethiopia's crippling hidden agenda.

7.37. Conclusion

Ethiopia invaded Somalia in December 2006 to empower terrorists and weaken the TFG forces. Their intention was to deter the emergence of a strong Somali government forever on one hand and to create a conducive environment for terrorists so that it would always have a clear justification to invade Somalia whenever deemed necessary or to justify its military presence in Somalia to be embraced by Western countries. After 2 years of terrible securitization against TFG and the Somali people, ENDF left Mogadishu and part of South Central Somalia with a totally weakened TFG and powerful terrorists controlling everywhere, including all military bases occupied by ENDF as well as MoD Mogadishu. It was obvious that ENDF had intentionally handed over all those bases and MOD to Al-Shabaab. They were always in close communication and collaboration with Al-Shabaab and, as a result, AS took over and occupied all military bases from ENDF. This outcome reflects their initial intention of invading and applying the securitization move to the Somali people and government.

7.38. On strategic issues, Ethiopia will be the China of Africa from the Western interests perspective

In general, what is really obvious was that Ethiopia flourished through Western support in the war against terrorists in Somalia or even beyond and through being a key Western ally in the Horn of Africa. But this unconscious and unchecked support from Western countries will only drive Ethiopia to become China's Africa and it will deter Western interests in the region and beyond. Ethiopia, by continuing to exploit resources from Western countries under the name of war against terrorists in Somalia, will only ensure increasingly nurtured powerful terrorists in Somalia, as it is always committed to supporting terrorists and weakening the government of Somalia. Ethiopia's goal is to consolidate its strategic positions in the global war against terrorists and achieve its strategic interest, which will never align with Western interests.

Based on that, so long as there are terrorists in Somalia, there will be justification for Ethiopia in getting Western military, economic, and diplomatic support. This has been its goal in Somalia during the securitization move to Somalia from 2006-2009. Despite huge civilian deaths and displacement of millions of Somalis during 2006-2009, when ENDF was withdrawing from Mogadishu and parts of South Central Somalia in 2009, the terrorists maintained the same power as in December 2006 and controlled all territories under their control when Ethiopia invaded the country in December 2006. The securitization move was intended to ruin the TFG-SNA and Somali people and not the terrorist.

It was a well-orchestrated strategy that served the interest of Ethiopia rather than the objectives of the war against terrorists and maintenance of global order. The driving factor was lack of accountability of those who funded or supported the securitization move in December 2006. Ethiopia's strategic options are merely based on its own strategic interest rather than objective criteria regarding Somalia and Western countries' interests. But Ethiopia enjoys Western aid and diplomatic cover until it achieves its final objectives that eventually revolt against the same Western objectives and strategic interests in the region. If it continues in this way, Ethiopia will grow increasingly powerful just like India and China and will view Western countries as a threat to its existence.

For instance, if we look back or map from the past about how Ethiopia has behaved for decades in terms of Western interests, it is not hard to figure out the way things will evolve in the future. For example, Mengistu Haile Mariam turned to Moscow and shifted towards communism while his country was dependent on Western support; Meles Zenawi turned towards China while he was receiving substantial financial and military support from Western countries and eventually ordered USAID to leave the country in 2005 during an election process dispute. Now Abiy Ahmed has preferred China, Turkey, and Russia and even BRICS. They all behaved and showed the same patterns through having strong relationships with China and Russia whenever deemed necessary, while disdaining Western support and interests. .Despite massive financial and political support, they are now on the way to joining BRICS. Furthermore, Ethiopia has recently signed an agreement with Russian nuclear giant Rosatom. According to the Russia Today website, "the agreement the African state signed with Rosatom includes the opening of a Nuclear Science and Technology Center.[170]

Ethiopia's Minister of Innovation and Technology, Belete Molla, expressed optimism about the partnership, highlighting the importance of Rosatom's role in helping Ethiopia advance its nuclear energy and non-energy programs. He believes that the Russian company "will assist Ethiopia in developing national nuclear power and non-energy programs as well as individual projects.[171] It is time for Western countries to review, reassess, and rethink their policy in the region and make a realignment of their Horn of Africa policies before things get out of hand or they are made extinct. Imagine, the recent statement from the Federal Government of Somalia regarding Ethiopia's role in the new peacekeeping mission that will replace the ATMIS mission reflected on the 2006 invasion by Ethiopian National Defense Forces and the implications left on the people in Somalia. The statement accused Ethiopia of supporting terrorists in its role over past peacekeeping operations, including during the securitization move. See attached statement from the Federal Government of Somalia.

It is also worth noting late President Abdullahi Yusuf's book in which he emphasized Ethiopia's never-ending concern about a strong Somalia as a threat to its existence on one hand, and the growing terrorist influence in Somalia on the other hand as being key challenges against country stabilization efforts.[172] A prominent Somali journalist and author of "Inside Al-Shabaab" posted on his X account a press release by the Ministry of Foreign Affairs of Somalia. He wrote, "The Somali government has confirmed it will choose which countries will contribute troops to the upcoming AU stabilization mission known as AUSSOM." In a statement on Wednesday, the Ministry of Foreign Affairs said Somalia will lead the mission's direction "with a clear focus on sovereignty."

---

170. Global Construction Review. (2019, October 24). Rosatom signs agreement for nuclear science centre in Ethiopia. Retrieved from https://www.globalconstructionreview.com/rosatom-signs-agreement-for-nuclear-science-centre-in-ethiopia/
171. Ibid
172. Yuusuf, Cabdullaahi Axmad. *Halgan iyo Hagardaamo: Taariikh Nololeed (Struggle and Conspiracy: A Memoir).* (Sweden: Scansom Publishers, 2012), p.360

Somalia said the agreement that Ethiopia reached with Somaliland violates Somalia's sovereignty.

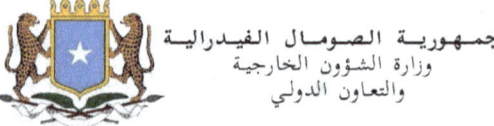

Federal Republic of Somalia
Ministry of Foreign Affairs and International Cooperation

Press Statement: Somalia's Stance on Sovereignty and Ethiopia's Role in the African Union Stabilization Mission (AUSSOM)

Mogadishu, Somalia | October 23, 2024

The Federal Government of Somalia reaffirms its commitment to protecting its sovereignty and ensuring peace for its people. As we transition from ATMIS to the African Union Stabilization Mission in Somalia (AUSSOM), Somalia will lead the mission's direction with a clear focus on sovereignty.

Ethiopia's recent unilateral actions, including an illegal agreement with Somalia's northern region, violate our sovereignty and erode the trust essential for peacekeeping.

Past Ethiopian deployments have led to increased Al-Shabaab activity and little development. This demands a more strategic selection of troop partners to ensure AUSSOM aligns with Somalia's security and development goals.

As we prepare for the next phase of peacekeeping under the upcoming African Union Stabilization Mission in Somalia (AUSSOM), it is essential to reiterate that Somalia, as a sovereign state, holds the authority to decide which Troop Partner Nation (TPNs) will contribute troops to this mission. The decision on troop contributions must align with Somalia's national interests and the preservation of its sovereignty.

We remain committed to working with the African Union, United Nations, and European Union on AUSSOM, with Somalia leading the selection of partners that respect our sovereignty. Somalia will not compromise on decisions affecting its future and security.

We call on all partners to uphold these principles for a peaceful and prosperous Somalia.

--End of Statement--

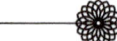

CHAPTER

TRANSITIONING FROM RESISTANCE TO GOVERNMENT AND AL-SHABAAB

CHAPTER 8

TRANSITIONING FROM RESISTANCE TO GOVERNMENT AND AL-SHABAAB

> *Despite Islamist President came to power, terrorist attack continued relentlessly.*

8.1. Sheikh Sharif Election as a President and the Task I Was Assigned

In June 2008, the TFG and the Djibouti-based wing of the ARS, through UN mediation, signed an accord calling for a cease-fire between the two parties, the eventual withdrawal of the ENDF, and the deployment of a UN peacekeeping force. However, the Djibouti-based ARS, a more moderate and conciliatory faction of the party than that based in Asmara, Eritrea, did not have control over critical components of the insurgency, including Al Shabaab, a radical Islamist group that once formed the military arm of the ICU. The diplomatic breakthrough did little to quell the escalation in violence that took place in 2008.

End of Ethiopian Presence? President Sheikh Sharif Sheikh Ahmed was elected as president in Djibouti on January 31, 2009. A few days later, he came to Mogadishu where tension was high, particularly the growing conflict between Ugandan and Ethiopian peacekeeping forces over Villa Somalia control. Ethiopia wanted to dominate Villa Somalia's security control and influence the president as they were key security providers. In parallel to this tension, there was massive misunderstanding among Somalis, particularly between Villa Somalia presidential security guards and the Somali National Army, who were quite disorganized, with each group wanting to protect the president. On the other hand, clan militia who was their close relative to the president had mobilized to provide security to the president. There was also one additional group consisted of the president's insurgent fighters who also tasked themselves with his protection simply because he was one of them.

Villa Somalia became a disorganized and chaotic place full of assault vehicles mounted with heavy guns, including P10, SK43, and other rockets deployed by insurgents and Al-Shabaab who had been in fierce fighting with government forces over the past three years. This pandemonium created more tension between these groups, with each gunman trusting only the group they belonged to. In light of this confusion, the new president Sharif Sheikh Ahmed issued a directive: all varieties of armies were to exit Villa Somalia except the Ugandan peacekeeping forces. This affected the 54th brigade, including the presidential VIP Protection team. The president's directive created confrontation between Ugandan forces and insurgents and Al-Shabaab, who had perceived that they would be the only forces the president trusted.

However, the Ugandan commanders informed the new president that his directive affected the presidential VIP Protection team, particularly that of his predecessor Abdullahi Yusuf Ahmed. As a result, he changed his mind, and we were called for a parade. The new president addressed us at the parade and informed us that we would continue our legal duty as usual. He stated that everyone should remain in his position of duty and that there would be no substitution of one soldier for another. All other military officers were instructed to reunite with their initial units, while unregistered military personnel or civilians would be sent to new training courses. It became possible to distinguish between different groups, predominantly insurgent fighters and a few individuals from

Al-Shabaab who accepted the new directives. Those who accepted the new directive from the president were encamped within Villa Somalia and offered new training courses. Weeks later, they were sent to Sudan for further training. Among the most notable officers were: Liibaan Ali Yarow, Hassan Ali Shuute, and Mohamed Adan Kofi.

General Abdirahman Turyare, a military officer who completed a degree course overseas through the Transitional Federal Government, was tasked with leading the new cadet training. Gen. Abdirahman Tuur was among the first cadets sent overseas for higher education by the Office of the President during the harsh time in Jowhar. He was a young man interested in improving his skills who approached President Abdullahi Yusuf with his ambition, and the president approved his request. Unlike General Turyare, other officers including: Gen. Liibaan Aliyarow, Col. Hassan Nuur Ali Shuute, and Col. Mohamed Adan Koofi went through a long struggle to become visible and eventually achieved prominence. Gen. Liban Aliyarow and Col. Hassan Nur Ali Shute were appointed to become chief magistrate and deputy magistrate of the military court respectively, while Col. Mohamed Adan Kofi became commander of the 60th brigade based at Villa Somalia, the chief intelligence officer of Banadir region, and head of the Somali Immigration Authority.

In his leadership, Col. Mohamed Adan Kofi ensured sufficient service to the people by expanding passport services access to Gedo, Hiiraan, Mudug regions and other border points. As a result of his service delivery, many Somali people appreciated him for making passports available in their locations without requiring to travel to Mogadishu.

The transitioning period from insurgents to Al-Shabaab and the formation of government led by the insurgent leader was the toughest time for Somalia and its people and left severe consequences for the 54th brigade based inside Villa Somalia. A new president, Sharif Sheikh Ahmed, was in charge of the villa. He had been the commander of militia insurgents attacking Villa Somalia and particularly the 54th brigade who were there to defend it from their attacks. Both commanders and lower-ranking officers and soldiers knew their new boss was their recent enemy, and other militia accompanying him were insurgent fighters. Dynamic tension prevailed in the environment; there was no integration process or process enabling a mode of collaboration.

The new president invited a meeting for those groups they used to share the same views and objectives with during the war against the Transitional Federal Government forces and AMISOM forces. He told them the ball was now in their court and they should work on bringing all people together, improve security, carry out the reconciliation process, and demonstrate trustworthy leadership for all. After their meeting, they started the process. However, we, the commanders of the 54th brigade and our VIP Protection team, had assumed there would be no more attacks against us and Villa Somalia, and it was time for peace and stability to prevail, making us much better off. Unfortunately, the fierce fighting that used to happen between us and insurgents was now happening around Villa Somalia; the intensity of the war was an ever-increasing around-the-clock attack. So I asked myself who was now attacking Villa Somalia, as the new president was the leader of insurgents, they were now in power—who else was attacking us and why?

Contrary to our assumption, there was a group of insurgents who had already opposed their boss and his new objectives for bringing people together for reconciliation and the formation of an inclusive government. The insurgents attacking us now were against such ideas and they still saw us as their enemies. The truth was that what we had perceived the situation would be was totally wrong, and we were facing a new challenge, a new beginning of war. We had to prepare for new attacks against us and be ready to bear with the continuous roaring of artillery barrages and relentless bombardment using RPG-7 and other dangerous weapons around the clock.

The insurgent militias' integration with the national army began, as having a unified army that could defend Villa Somalia was highly crucial. However, the process was easier to describe than to achieve, as they could not even agree to pray together during prayer time. We were three officers, including myself, who attempted to join a group from the insurgents, but they broke the prayer and started cursing us. Late Abdullahi Mohamed Ibrahim, who was among the three of us, laughed at them and said, "They are cursing us and insulting us as being pigs," and we left to pray at a different location. We recognized how profound the risk was that we were involved in, both inside and outside the parameters of Villa Somalia. A few days later, someone among the militias living within Villa Somalia carried out a suicide attack at the military canteen, killing a number of

54th army personnel. This undermined the integration process and increased mistrust. In particular, our VIP Protection team quickly developed a new model of protection, which consisted of dual layers: the official one to protect the president and another layer of protection to protect those who were protecting the president.

Again, a few days later, an AMISOM Ugandan forces convoy providing protection to several cabinet ministers entered Villa Somalia. However, at the entrance of the villa, someone jumped up on one of the vehicles and was identified as someone planning to carry out a suicide attack. The convoy became aware that someone wearing a suicide vest was on one of their vehicles. They sped up the vehicles, crossing all the checkpoints of gate one and gate two, and didn't stop until they reached the front of the president's office. Fortunately, they shot him dead before he could set off the suicide vest. This further increased the level of mistrust and ruled out the prospect of achieving an integrated army.

8.2. The TFG after Ethiopia's withdrawal in 2009

On the president's side, he comprehended that the only army that could be trusted with the safety and security of Villa Somalia should be the 64th army, for their experience and required attitude and understanding of responsibilities, as well as being free from terrorist involvement. As a result, he instructed all other armed security personnel to leave Villa Somalia, as it was hard to discern whether someone was an honest insurgent or was planning to carry out a suicide mission against him or other officials. General Indho Ade and Mohamed Mohamud Garabey were tasked to lead all insurgents inside Villa Somalia and fight with those insurgents who opposed their leader.

This led to a good number of insurgents defecting and joining the opposition who named themselves as Al-Shabaab (The Young). They defected with vehicles, weapons, ammunition, and other crucial equipment. The culture of those insurgents who remained as loyal militias to the president affected some of the 54th commanders and soldiers, causing them to leave the army as a result of the attitude, behavior, and even the way newly integrated insurgents dressed, which did not align with the national army code of conduct and operational procedures. A new defense plan was outlined to protect Villa Somalia from defected insurgents and other groups who opposed their former colleagues. From Hareryale to the Junction of Sayid Mohamed Abdulle was assigned to the 54th brigade, whereas from Hararyale to Shangani district flank was assigned to newly reformed insurgents. However, General Indho Ade was monitoring implementation of the outlined defense plans. He was among the newly reformed insurgents and had not adopted the military conduct, terminology, and behavior required, including wearing a military uniform and behaving as a military commander.

Went together with newly reformed soldiers to monitor the 54th flank of defense. Shockingly, they were not in uniform and their behavior and approaches weren't the standard of the 54th brigade. Col. Jama Bashir, who was on duty that day, was monitored by General Indho Ade and his soldiers wearing Pakistan-style clothes which didn't conform with Somali military uniform. After monitoring the defense flank of the 54th brigade, Indho Ade left. However, Col. Bashir, who was aware of the monitoring system, could not believe that those guys with Pakistan way of dressing were monitoring the 54th brigade, and he decided to leave the army for good. As a result, he got a flight ticket for Galkacyo and left early in the morning. The rumors of his decision became the word of mouth, and I called him for confirmation. He confirmed to me that he was already in Galkaio and had left the army for good, following when he saw those monitoring the national army dressed like Pakistan Taliban, and he could no longer stay in the army.

8.3. The Liberation of Mogadishu

Mogadishu Liberation plan was among the most difficult stages that the Somali government ever faced. SNA forces were fighting without receiving any salary, but there was an ambition that a peaceful Mogadishu, where there was law and order, would be an environment that would enable every soldier to get everything and every right they deserved. As such, there was no difference between high-ranking officers and soldiers in terms of ranks, salaries, and other incentives. They all ate the same food and stayed in the same place, except the SNA commander and battlefield commander who were exercising a little immunity.

Upon the SNA commander and his deputy's arrival at the army encampment base, it was possible to sense minimal attention from the regular army, while all other higher-ranking officials paid no attention at all. Because of the unique situation that the SNA found itself in, the code of conduct and the rules of engagement changed. There was a clear hierarchy; they had collective objectives and anticipated outcomes. The situation became complicated and extremely challenging, with the battlefield limited to the perimeter of Villa Somalia. A soldier complained, "Are we fighting terrorists in our own state house? What else shall we fight if not for the liberation of our own government palace?"

Furthermore, the intensity of Al-Shabaab attacks grew increasingly severe, which led to the capture of eastern and northern Mogadishu. As a result, the following districts in Mogadishu fell under their control: Daynile, Huriwaa, and Yaqshid. These areas became their military bases, while adjacent districts became their defensive positions where they built very strong trenches from which they organized offensive operations. In addition to that, they had established an administrative system in Afgooye and Balcad districts, the northern and southern districts of Mogadishu. This limited the movement of the Somali government, and the only road available was the route from the Somali Presidency through Yoobsan, Mogadishu port, and Mogadishu International Airport. Somali government officials could use only that road to travel from Villa Somalia to destinations outside the country and back.

Ethiopia's plan to forever depict Somalia as a threat to Ethiopia and the global order must be understood. Ethiopia's securitization was not meant to stabilize or fight the terrorists but rather to portray Somalia as a threatening country. Thus, they never engaged terrorists in conventional combat, let alone acted on securitization measures. ENDF soldiers were also accused of using indiscriminate small arms fire that resulted in further civilian casualties. In an August 2008 incident, ENDF soldiers responded to the detonation of a roadside bomb with wild gunfire that left approximately 40 Somali civilians dead.[173]

In addition to recorded instances of reckless use of force, human rights groups also claimed that search and seizure operations conducted by the ENDF, like those carried out by the TFG, occasionally resulted in assault,

---

173. Human Rights Watch, "So Much to Fear": War Crimes and the Devastation of Somalia, 1-56432-415-X, 8 December 2008, https://www.refworld.org/reference/countryrep/hrw/2008/en/64117 [accessed 26 February 2025]

rape, looting, and killing of Somali civilians.[174] Ethiopia never came to Somalia to fight terrorists, as most Western countries assumed, but rather to further advance its own strategic interest in conquering Somalia. Thus, during those two years, Ethiopia not only carried out massive killings and displaced millions but even destroyed the SNA reconstitution process, the democratic process that the TFG was implementing, and exerted profound political influence across the country.

---

174. Human Rights Watch, "So Much to Fear": War Crimes and the Devastation of Somalia, 1-56432-415-X, 8 December 2008, https://www.refworld.org/reference/countryrep/hrw/2008/en/64117 [accessed 26 February 2025]

CHAPTER 9

HOW DID OTHER AMISOM FORCES PERFORM IN THE PEACEKEEPING OPERATIONS?

HOW DID OTHER AMISOM FORCES PERFORM

Major Abdirahman O. Warsame "Jeeniqaar"

CHAPTER 9

HOW DID OTHER AMISOM FORCES PERFORM IN THE PEACEKEEPING OPERATIONS?

> *All contributing countries to the peacekeeping mission in Somalia have been accountable for any violation that their forces might commit against civilians in Somalia except Ethiopian forces. As a result, they performed the highest ethical possible.*

[**Fig. 9:** The Contingent Commander of Ugandan troops serving under AMISOM, Brigadier Richard Otto, speaks during an interview in Mogadishu Somalia on 28 July 2020. AMISOM Photo/Steven Candia.]

Amisom contributing countries include Uganda, Ethiopia, Kenya, Djibouti, Burundi, Nigeria and Sieralione. Their total number is estimated around 22,000 soldiers. Despite, they are all peacekeeping forces, Ethiopia is the only country which has a different objective and set goals not in alignment with official peacekeeping objectives. While all other contributing countries have a shared meaning and objective in line with the Amisom mission, Ethiopia had come to Somalia to defend its sovereignty and integrity and deter irredentism. It came to Somalia in December 2006 not as peacekeeping forces but to defend its sovereignty. The defined and agreed objective is what defines the action points and describes the anticipated performance and the type of behavior needed to be exhibited. As a result all other peacekeeping forces were more likely to meet the agreed mission objectives.

Its principal mandate was to reduce threats posed by Al-Shabaab and other armed opposition groups, and to support stabilization efforts in a complex and dangerous environment. As a result of this, the collaboration between Amisom forces was always messy because of Ethiopia's misaligned objectives and goals. Ethiopia benefited the early entrance and attempted yo dominated the ecosystem. Only Uganda could compete with Ethiopia in the landscape. It is noteworthy, that there had never been confrontation between SNA commanders, or other political leaders and all other peacekeeping forces except Ethiopian forces. Unlike the do called SNA/ENDF Operation as from December 2006 to 3NDF withdrawal which ended up utterly failure, SNA Operations to liberate Alshabaab from Mogadishu, with the support from Uganda and Burundi forces was not only successful but also sustainable and large part of the southern part was liberated. However, in such a circumstance, the mission, along with its Somali counterparts and international partners, created a level of stability which allowed local and global actors to implement many political and peace initiatives.

According to the official AMISOM website https://amisom-au.org/, the United Nations Security Council Resolution 2628 has authorized the African Union Peace and Security Council to reconfigure AMISOM and replace it with the African Union Transition Mission in Somalia (ATMIS), effective from April 1, 2022. This was possible only after al-

Shabaab's hold on major population centers across southern and central Somalia was reduced. The country has made significant progress since 2012. At minimum, government structures at federal and state levels have been established. However, how other major AMISOM peacekeeping forces acted and behaved over the years of peacekeeping in Somalia including Uganda, Burundi, Kenya, and Djibouti, the roles they played and the approaches they adopted differed in many ways. What drove the differences between them were experience in peacekeeping operations, level of influence each player had in Somalia's security ecosystem, international community support, and strategic interests.

The key leaders competing for the AMISOM operations leadership were Uganda and Ethiopia. As a result, they took advantage of their positions to exploit every activity tasked and carried out by AMISOM. Ethiopia brought more Ethiopian forces under AMISOM cover. Thus, they had greater troop presence in Somalia as AMISOM but not officially designated as AMISOM.

9.1. Uganda's Role

Ugandan forces had sufficient experience in peacekeeping operations. From 2007 to 2025 Ugandan peacekeeping forces were important players in the field and contributed immensely to stability and peacekeeping processes in Somalia. Later, they adopted the rules of the game and focused on exploiting business opportunities. Uganda peacekeeping forces are the most trusted which protect the residences of the President, Prime Minister, and the speaker. Ugandan forces were seen as fair AMISOM forces, trusted by all Somali stakeholders and politicians. Ugandan forces were permitted to be in the meeting room when the Somali President was meeting with foreign dignitaries. The foreign dignitaries and diplomats held the perception that Ugandan forces were the primary peacekeeping forces in comparison with all other AMISOM peacekeeping forces. Ugandan forces never meddle with Somali politics. They behaved in the most appropriate manner.

Uganda currently has over 5,000 soldiers and officers from the Uganda People's Defence Force (UPDF) serving with the 10,000-strong AMISOM mission, along with troops from Burundi and Djibouti.. The East African country was the first to deploy troops under AMISOM into

Somalia in March 2007. To date, Uganda has provided all four AMISOM Force Commanders, with the recently outgoing Lt. Gen. Andrew Gutti being replaced by Lt. Gen. Silas Ntigurirwa from Burundi.

The Ugandan contingent remains the largest in AMISOM with 6,223 troops based in Sector 1, which comprises Banadir (Mogadishu), Middle and Lower Shabelle regions. They are led by Sector Commander Brig. Dick Olum, who replaced Brig. Michael Ondoga. The current Deputy Force Commander Operations and Planning, Major General Geoffrey Baraba Muheesi, hails from Uganda. Uganda has deployed 12 battle groups into the Mission area. The recently deployed Battle Group 12 joined their Burundian counterparts in Baidoa. Mogadishu, 23 January 2024.

Working jointly with the Somali Security Forces, ATMIS Ugandan soldiers conducted successful operations to disrupt and degrade Al-Shabaab and participated in reconciliation dialogues with local leaders and communities to foster peace in their Area of Responsibility. The troops also cleared and secured Main Supply Routes (MSRs) linking neighboring towns to the capital Mogadishu and provided security to local communities. We acknowledge the exceptional work they executed including countering Improvised Explosive Devices (IEDs), clearing Main Supply Routes (MSRs), conducting joint patrols and ambushes with their Somali counterparts as well as securing population centers," said Sector One Commander Brig. Gen. Anthony Lukwago Mbuusi. Uganda first deployed troops to Somalia in March 2007 and is one of the five Troop Contributing Countries to ATMIS along with Burundi, Ethiopia, Djibouti, and Kenya.

9.2. Burundi's Role

According to the official AMISOM website https://amisom-au.org/, Burundi forces were less experienced in the Somali security ecosystem than Ethiopia, Kenya, and Djibouti. Burundi operations in Jowhar were undermined by Ethiopia. They were subjected to confrontations. Burundi was a key AMISOM force that fought with Al-Shabaab in Mogadishu, suffering severe consequences. How Ethiopia and Uganda Benefited from the AMISOM Operations Burundi never received sufficient logistics support compared to Ethiopia and Uganda. 70%

of Burundi forces never returned to Burundi and they were killed in battlefields with Al-Shabaab. The Burundi contingent is the second largest within AMISOM with 5,432 troops. The country was also the second to deploy troops into Somalia, its first soldiers having arrived in Mogadishu in December 2007. Based in Baidoa and commanded by Col. Jean Luc Habarugira, the contingent is primarily responsible for operations in Sector 3, which covers Bay and Bakool regions but also maintains troops in Sector 1 where they work closely with the Ugandan forces. Burundi has so far sent six battle groups to Somalia and has provided three Deputy Force Commanders. Lt. General Silas Ntigurirwa from Burundi is the AMISOM Force Commander. He recently took command of the mission from Lt. Gen. Andrew Gutti from Uganda.

Early on Tuesday, May 3, 2022, Al-Shabaab forces overran a Burundian African Union (AU) peacekeeper's base in Middle Shabelle, Somalia. Three civilians were killed, as well as 30 soldiers. A further 22 soldiers were injured. The militants deployed two car bombs before storming the base with heavy gunfire. Al-Shabaab sent a suicide car bomber into the base's main gates, allowing the alleged 400 fighters to enter the building. Al-Shabaab claims to have killed 59 soldiers in the first hour, as they took control of the base, but these numbers have not been confirmed. AU forces retaliated with helicopter gunships and drones after the Burundian soldiers retreated to a nearby hillside in Ceel Baraf village.

9.3. Djibouti's Role

According to the official AMISOM website https://amisom-au.org/, deployed in Somalia as part of the African Union forces, Djibouti troops operate in ATMIS Sector Four Area of Responsibility (AoR) together with Ethiopian forces. Djibouti troops play a significant role in degrading Al-Shabaab and restoring peace and stability in the Hiraan and Galgaduud regions. In December 2011, Djibouti became the third country to contribute to AMISOM. The country has deployed a contingent of 960 troops into Somalia, and they are based in Beledweyne, which serves as Sector 4 headquarters covering the Hiiraan region. The contingent is commanded by Colonel Osman Doubad. Djibouti has also contributed several officers to the AMISOM Force Headquarters, including Chief of Staff Major General Osman-Noor Soubagle and Colonel Ali Aden

Houmed, the Force Spokesman. Last year, the contingent came to the aid of civilians in Beledweyne, helping to organize evacuations after heavy rains caused massive flooding in the region. In Hiiraan alone, they married Somali girls in Hiiraan and intermingled with the local community. Djibouti was less active in conducting peacekeeping operations compared to other Uganda and Burundi AMISOM forces. Djibouti was involved in Somali politics, thus, they were having additional goals in Somali politics rather than merely for the stabilization mission along with other peacekeeping forces.

9.4. Kenya's Role

According to the official AMISOM website https://amisom-au.org/, the troops from Kenya were later formally integrated into AMISOM on February 22, 2012, via the United Nations Security Council Resolution 2036 (2012). Kenya launched Operation Linda Nchi and entered Somalia on October 14, 2011. The purpose of this operation was to degrade the Al-Qaeda-affiliated Al-Shabaab Islamist group in Somalia who were posing a security challenge in Kenya, hence threatening Kenya's security and national interest. This decision was reached after a series of incidents of border attacks and incursions by the militia group along the common border with Somalia where Kenyan aid workers in Dadaab, a couple in Kiwayu Safari village in Lamu, and a French tourist lady were abducted. In light of continued threats to the Republic, the Government of Kenya invoked Article 51 of the UN Charter in order to secure the right to self-defense from these unwarranted attacks by the militia group. To sustain the gains made by KDF after a few months in Somalia, the UN and AU invited Kenya to incorporate KDF into AMISOM in November 2011. The troops from Kenya were later formally integrated into AMISOM on February 22, 2012, via the United Nations Security Council Resolution 2036 (2012).

Kenya has played a significant role in AMISOM peacekeeping operations in Somalia. Kenya's peacekeeping forces and leadership have shown a certain level of ethics and operational standards. It is noteworthy that despite the maritime dispute between Kenya and Somalia, which was later resolved at the International Court of Justice, Kenya maintained its commitment.

Resolution 2036 expanded the AMISOM mandate by increasing the manning level from 12,731 to 17,731. Kenya's military intervention in Somalia re-energized regional and international resolve to address the al-Shabaab threat to peace and security. The revised mandate required AMISOM to establish its presence in four sectors, in coordination with local security forces, so as to reduce the al-Shabaab threat and set conditions for restoration of state authority. KDF troops were assigned to Middle Juba and Lower Juba regions that were designated as Sector 2. To mitigate the threat posed by al-Shabaab to the counties of Mandera and Wajir, KDF maintained the prevailing posture in Gedo region that formed part of AMISOM Sector 3. This measure sought to allow time for the deployment of Ethiopian troops who had been assigned to the sector. By 2018, KDF still maintained its presence in Gedo Region due to the threat posed to Mandera County. In addition, Kismayo City and its environs had been carved out of Sector 2 to form Sector 6 that was manned by multinational troops.

Under AMISOM, KDF conducted a complex operation codenamed "Operation Sledge Hammer" that led to the capture of Kismayo City on September 28, 2012. The operation consisted of a two-pronged assault involving an amphibious landing that was synchronized with an advance operation that was conducted by ground troops from Afmadow. The coordinated linkup of amphibious and ground troops, joint fires, and the rapid seizure of enemy strongpoints in Kismayo and its environs affirmed the meticulous planning that preceded the operation. The fall of Kismayo to AMISOM troops was a classic case of deception that surprised Al-Shabaab, thereby leaving the terrorist group with no alternative but to abandon the city so as to avert complete destruction. During the overnight attack that took place at 2:00 am EAT, Kenyan Defence Forces troops used a beach landing approximately six kilometers north of Kismayo, close to the main road to Mogadishu, to start the assault and claimed victory over the final militant stronghold. The attack and the final liberation of the port city dealt a fatal blow to the rebels.

This was a significant accomplishment, considering that Kismayo was by then Al-Shabaab's economic, political, and military nucleus. Notably, "Operation Sledge Hammer" had the potential to dent Kenya's image as well as that of KDF in the event that the desired objective was not realized. However, the operation's overwhelming success was worth the risk. Indeed, the jubilation witnessed upon the announcement of the capture of Kismayo was inspiring and a relief to the residents of the seaport town, which immediately acquired a new lease of life, at least judging from the economic transformation that ensued. To AMISOM and its international partners, the achievement was a crucial milestone in the fight against transnational terrorism. The other objectives captured by KDF troops after their integration into AMISOM include Afmadow in May 2012, Koday Port in March 2015, and Bardhere in July 2015. Overall, the landmark battles fought by Kenyan soldiers against Al-Shabaab comprise the battles of Hoosingo, Fafadun, Miido, and Koday. This was accomplished with the support of Kenya's air and naval forces. For this reason, the Kenya Defence Forces inherently upholds the tenets of joint operations for shared success..

10

HOW AL-SHABAAB CRIPPLED SOMALIA'S STATE BUILDING PROCESS

CHAPTER 10

HOW AL-SHABAAB CRIPPLED SOMALIA'S STATE BUILDING PROCESS

> *The blockade rages on for the 7th year amid the heavy presence of Somali and Ethiopian forces in the region, where millions are on the brink of death from hunger.*

[**Fig. 10:** Seated in the middle: Former Deputy Al Shabab, and from 2022-current Minister of Religious Affairs of Somalia, Sheikh Mukhtar Robow "Abu Mansur".]

Al-Shabaab, Al Qaeda affiliated terrorist group emerged from various Islamist groups including Al-Ittihad Al-Islamiya, Islamic Courts Union, and other independent groups resisting the presence of Ethiopian army on Somali soil. The Islamic Courts Union and other resistance groups formed following Ethiopia's invasion on December 2006, and later approved by AU to be in the country as peacekeeping forces, but began to execute their hidden agenda (securitization move) in which they were deliberately crippling the state-building processes funded and supported by Western countries and the desirable future state for Somali people (a peaceful, prosperous democratic nation). Ethiopia's twisted agendas, including weakening SNA, indiscriminate bombardment of Mogadishu and arbitrary arrest and murdering of individuals such as business people, students, and intellectuals, had been the main drivers of the formation of resistance groups who came from across the eighteen regions and overseas countries.

Nevertheless, Al-Shabaab officially came into play in 2009, immediately after the Djibouti conference was held and its outcomes produced a new unity government led by Sharif Sheikh Ahmed, one of the Islamic Court Union ICU leader, previously fighting with Ethiopia and the Federal Government of Somalia. Then, newly formed group called Al-Shabaab in turn waged a war against the newly formed government led by their own former colleague. It was an eerie move that questioned their integrity and goals. Among key issues agreed on in Djibouti was the withdrawal of the Ethiopian army from Somalia's soil, which was a shared agenda by all groups fighting with the Federal Government and regional peacekeeping forces.

However, what was puzzling was that when Ethiopian forces withdrew, they left behind massive weapons and ammunition for Al-Shabaab as they abandoned unilaterally from all their military bases across Somalia. As a result of this gesture by Ethiopian forces, Al-Shabaab became a powerful player in Somalia and demonstrated gallant efforts to fight SNA forces and other AMISOM peacekeeping forces except Ethiopian army.

Ethiopia's intention of providing massive weapons and ammunition to Al-Shabaab as widely viewed was to undermine the Somali government based on the historical enmity and never worked on thr bases of genuine and honest in its peacekeeping role by Somalia. This revealed that Ethiopia's ultimate goal was to ensure Somalia remained a weak government, incapable of posing any sort of threat to its sovereignty and integrity both in the present and future.

For Ethiopia, it needed the Somali government to remain weak and incapable of defending itself from terrorists, thus dependent on its forces and the continued need for their presence in the country. As a result, they always preferred Al-Shabaab's military superiority to prevail rather than a Somali National Army capable of defeating terrorists. Conversely, the Somali government never viewed Ethiopia's presence in Somalia as a favor or aligned with its interests and objectives. The Somali government believed Ethiopia was in Somalia in pursuit of its own agenda, which in many ways opposed Somali national interests and violated peacekeeping rules and objectives.

The Somali Government was, even without the support of Ethiopian forces, committed to fighting Al-Shabaab and eradicating them with the support of other peacekeeping forces primarily Uganda and Burundi peacekeeping forces. The deployment of Ethiopian forces into Somalia as peacekeepers was widely being viewed not only did Ethiopia cripple Somalia's efforts to fight terrorists but also it enormously undermined the international community's collective efforts in combating terrorism and all state and peace-building processes that had received billions of dollars in investment. Here is where Ethiopia and Al Shabaab converged and generated unified agenda against Somalia and supporting western countries and their strategic interests.

10.1. How Al-Shabaab Took Advantage of the 4.5 Power Sharing System in Somalia

Al-Shabaab effectively uses the 4.5 model of power sharing employed by Somali major clans for representation in the parliament and sharing cabinet ministers' allocation, as well as other higher positions including army ranks, to purge senior commanders with gallant efforts who successfully defeated them in many battlefields. The system limits the number of representatives that each clan has in the government, including the army. Taking advantage of this weak system, they promote a military officer of the same subclan as a powerful officer who defeated them in many battlefields as a candidate and use their influence on elders, politicians, and even use money to lobby for their candidate to be appointed to a higher commander position in the military. This appointment forces the replacement of the targeted brave officer with gallant efforts whom they view as a threat.

10.2. Revenue Collection

They impose predictable taxation on transport and trade, aiming to depict themselves as consistent with a single taxation system across the areas they control, contrary to the federal government's multiple taxation of business and transportation. Despite this projected image, and in many ways contrary to it, Al-Shabaab conducts widespread revenue collections in rural areas which utterly lack credibility and integrity. This has left huge implications for pastoralists and farmers predominantly in the rural areas. In fact, they tax pastoralists in many ways that undermine their livelihood and prospects of life. They blindly impose monthly taxes depending on their budget deficit and yearly zakat taxation of 2.5% on individual family properties. Consequently, they collect massive amounts of livestock from pastoralists and food crops from farmers.

No farmer has the right to cultivate his farm unless imposed tax by Al Shabaab are paid to embark on the farming process. Shockingly, they (Alshabab) never deliver any services to both the pastoralists and farmers from whom they always impose huge taxes. This merciless revenue collection has made them wealthy and capable of corrupting government individuals and military officers. But Alshabaab has also compelled many families as a result of huge tax imposed on them to become IDPs, leaving their livelihood mechanisms and becoming dependent on humanitarian aid.

10.3. Justice and Al-Shabaab

Contrary to the Federal government's justice system, which is overwhelmed by corruption and lack of skills, Al-Shabaab seems to have been taking advantage of weak justice and expedites both criminal and civil cases in their courts in an effective way without the huge payments required by federal government courts. As a result, people have embraced their quick and transparent judiciary system.

10.4. Al-Shabaab's Use of Direct Deals to Compromise Senior Commanders

Very often when there is a massive operation against Al-Shabaab, and Al-Shabaab realizes the scale of the attack, they identify the potential commander leading the operation and directly offer between $200,000 to $400,000, depending on the grit of the commander. This shows Al-Shabaab's flexibility in the battlefield, for they don't only consider their capability and competence but they are also self-aware about themselves and the gallant officers they face in the battlefield. The narrative they use when attempting to compromise the morale of the brave commander is as follows:

"We, Al-Shabaab army, are just fighting with the puppet government formed and supported by the Western countries. This government is representing the interests of the Western countries and not our people. They are the most corrupt government and you are working with such an immoral, meaningless puppet government. We know you well, stay away from the puppeteers and we offer you $400,000 for you and your children. The puppet government and Western countries backing them will never offer you such money." If the gallant commander takes the offer, he will make an excuse that he cannot lead the operation and request someone else to take over the position. But if he refuses the deal, then Al-Shabaab will begin to orchestrate blowing him up through a suicide attack.

10.5. How Al-Shabaab Threatens People to Achieve Its Objectives

Al-Shabaab employs various threatening tactics to achieve its objectives. They systematically intimidate individuals through direct threats, surveillance, and punishment to maintain control and compliance. The group targets anyone perceived as opposing their authority or collaborating with the government. When targeting individuals, Al-Shabaab often begins with phone calls, warning messages, or public announcements in mosques or community gatherings. These threats typically escalate if the initial warnings are ignored. They conduct thorough intelligence gathering about their targets, often knowing personal details about family members, daily routines, and vulnerabilities. Punishment for non-compliance is severe and public, designed to serve as a warning to others. Executions, amputations, and other violent acts are often performed in public spaces to maximize their psychological impact on the community. Additionally, Al-Shabaab maintains networks of informants within communities, creating an atmosphere of constant surveillance where people never know who might be reporting to the group. Through these methods, Al-Shabaab creates a climate of fear that extends beyond the territories they physically control, allowing them to influence behavior and decision-making even in government-controlled areas.

Al-Shabaab effectively uses the 4.5 model of power sharing employed by Somali major clans for representation in the parliament and sharing cabinet ministers' allocation as well as other higher positions including army ranks to purge senior commanders with gallant efforts who successfully defeat them in many battlefields. The system limits the number of representatives that each clan has in the government including the army. Taking advantage of this weak system, they propose a military officer of the same subclan as the powerful officer who defeated them in many battlefields as a candidate and use their influence on elders, politicians, and even use money to lobby for their candidate to be appointed to a higher commander position in the military. This appointment will forfeit and replace the targeted brave officer with gallant efforts whom they view as a threat.

10.6. How Al-Shabaab Crippled Somalia's Election Processes

Al-Shabaab understands Somalia's intention: a free and fair election process that can pave the way for the formation of a legitimate government that enjoys people's trust and support. Al-Shabaab began targeting Somali traditional leaders and selected voters involved in the election processes. A significant number of Somali traditional leaders involved in the election processes were killed by Al-Shabaab due in part to lack of security staff to protect them, as the government neglected their safety after each election. Sometimes, amnesty has been extended to traditional leaders who survived Al-Shabaab assassination attempts by Al-Shabaab commanders, but only if they pledge to cease participating in any form of election processes. As a result, some traditional leaders benefit from this amnesty, visit Al-Shabaab's stronghold areas, and take oaths never again to be involved in any election processes. In addition, Al-Shabaab targeted voters casting their ballots to elect MPs in the parliament. Consequently, many people have abandoned participation in all election processes and lost their democratic right to decide who represents them in parliament.

This is how Al-Shabaab undermined the election processes and the entire democratic processes and values highly invested in by Western countries. Al-Shabaab is dedicated to ruling the country through Sharia Law rather than democracy. Both international communities and the Somali Government devote significant efforts and resources to ensuring greater stability, democratization, and a conducive environment where people can exercise their democratic rights. Al-Shabaab, which frequently receives substantial ammunition from Ethiopia, targets any person who opposes their agenda, whether in the government or other social spheres. People often attempt to resist Al-Shabaab's instructions by mobilizing armed militants, but due to Ethiopia's military aid to Al-Shabaab, they find themselves unable to confront them. In this light, both Ethiopia and Al-Shabaab have deliberately crippled Western efforts in Somalia and undermined the desirable future state that Somalis were pursuing.

10.7. Parallel Traditional Leaders

Although Al-Shabaab controls a large part of south-central Somalia, the biggest challenge they encounter is traditional leaders and other elders who have people's support and influence. Elders and traditional leaders have greater, long-standing influence which deters Al-Shabaab's desire to fully control the people and collect revenue without contempt. However, elders' and traditional leaders' entrenched leadership is difficult to uproot, particularly those who resist Al-Shabaab's demands for collaboration to impose taxation on the people. Al-Shabaab developed a new method to overcome this challenge. The method involves nominating new traditional leaders to replace those who resist Al-Shabaab's agenda and refuse collaboration for taxation and recruitment of militants from the people.

10.8. Empowering Pro-Al-Shabaab Traditional Leaders

Al-Shabaab's policy to undermine genuine traditional leaders includes appointing new parallel traditional leaders. In areas they control, only Al-Shabaab-appointed traditional leaders are allowed to have true power to engage with Al-Shabaab offices, discuss matters related to conflicts between communities, handle criminal cases, and release people on bail. As such, newly appointed traditional leaders became more valuable for the communities. As a result, community members seek assistance from Al-Shabaab-appointed leaders for nearly all cases in the hands of Al-Shabaab judiciary offices rather than genuine traditional leaders who resisted collaboration with Al-Shabaab.

10.9. Potential Cases Undertaken by Mr. Ereg

Ereg said, "Al-Shabaab is not a powerful army that is impossible to defeat; the government forces are more powerful in terms of logistics, skills and capabilities, resources, and global support. However, there is lack of political will to eradicate them, and that is the reason why they still exist in Somalia."

10.10. Factors Contributing to Weakening Government Plans Against AS but Enhancing Al-Shabaab Plans' Success: Job Security

Job security was one of the factors that affected government officers planning and leading the fight against Al-Shabaab to underperform and become disillusioned. This is because of the lack of policy and concerns about commanders' futures. The government, particularly at the highest political level, fires commanders for their interests and ends and means rather than serving public interest. This resulted in many officers taking responsibility to fight against terrorists with caution, which in turn affected the level of performance and created a conducive environment for the terrorists to carry out deadly operations and suicide attacks on the public and government officials. Having realized the increasing job insecurity surrounding the skilled officers capable of not only fighting with terrorists but defeating them to the eradication level, and the easy way the government not only fires them but also neglects them to the extent they became vulnerable to terrorist attacks. What further exacerbated the situation, however, was when Al-Shabaab defectors were appointed to lead key roles in the army, primarily in the fight against Al-Shabaab. Most of the soldiers and commanders found it difficult to cope with the situation as the newly appointed defectors lacked necessary military skills, culture, and behavior (contradicting orientation). As a result of this, both commanders and junior officers became disappointed.

Many senior military officers left the country because they weren't at the decision-making level and the policies adopted by the politicians favored the terrorists, creating a thriving environment for terrorists and stifling or suffocating the creativity, knowledge, and skills of the army. This means the military training offered by the USA and European countries has been undermined by the politicians who are merely focusing on their own interests. So many Al-Shabaab fighters turned out to be members leading police and military institutions, while many other members from Al-Shabaab became members of Parliament. They are in Parliament at both state and federal governments, state presidents, and cabinet ministers at state and federal levels.

10.11. Consequences of AS Intermingled with Government

Muktar Robow, the Minister for Religious Affairs of the FGS, and Ahmed Madobe, who is the Jubaland State President, were among key members from the terrorist group intermingled with the government of Somalia. The increasingly high level of intermingling and influence of the defected members from Al-Shabaab within the government has reached a state where trust within the government has drastically diminished. It has reached the extent that they exchanged rhetorical speeches in which they recounted the Al-Shabaab position commanders they used to hold and their brutal role in the eyes of the president, prime minister, and police and military commanders. Instead of regretting their brutal actions and crimes including suicide and other killings and assassinations against civilians and government officials, they were demonstrating more happiness about their past actions.

More startling was when the president, prime minister, police, and military commanders who were present at the conference hall laughed at hearing such weird speech from former Al-Shabaab defectors. It was shocking when the then Al-Shabaab leader, currently a minister in the cabinet, speaking to the audience mentioned teasingly in his speech that he is happy to see his former leader when they were terrorist leaders. The other notable concern was when the Jubaland leader, who was a defector from Al-Shabaab, said he sustained injury when he was captured by Ethiopian forces and taken as a prisoner to an Ethiopian jail, where he was detained for two years. He confessed before the audience that he received a salary every month from AS during his arrest in Ethiopia. Furthermore, it was not really clear why Ethiopian forces took him outside the jurisdiction of Somalia. What made it possible for him to receive his monthly salary from Al-Shabaab during the two years he was under arrest by Ethiopians in Ethiopia? This salary was sent to him in Ethiopia by AS—why?

The Jubaland president continued his speech and said, when he was released, Al-Shabaab welcomed him in Somalia, offering him leadership of the organization and $10,000. The million-dollar question is how he managed to become a president through an election process managed primarily by IGAD, particularly Ethiopia and Kenya, and supervised by the international community. However, he didn't state who facilitated him to become president of Jubaland in the election process managed by IGAD countries, mainly Ethiopia.

10.12. How Al-Shabaab Treats Population Living in Territories Under Their Full Control

Is it possible for people to resist against Al-Shabaab brutality? No, it is not possible for people to resist Al-Shabaab's gross human rights violations due to the severity of the punishment. The range of punishment is between death sentence to $1,500 or an AK-47 with four magazines. They have established their own courts and persecution system, and they accuse people the way they like and courts make judgments based on the file prepared by untrained Al-Shabaab who very often make tough accusations from the religious perspective rather than a solid criminal case.

10.13. Foreign Fighters and Women Marriage

Every foreign fighter fighting for Al-Shabaab has a right to marry any unmarried woman of his choice regardless of the consent of her parents or guardian and other immediate relatives. As a result of this, foreign fighters, as they move out of their bases through rural areas and villages, look out for beautiful women and mark the location and woman. Then they inform their Somali colleagues who will immediately identify her and inform her parents about the case. Thereafter, parents will be informed their daughter will have a Muslim husband and they will come for her through Islamic practice marriage process. Parents who are familiar with the repercussions they will face should they refuse their daughter to an unknown man stemming from another country and culture will accept the marriage process. The most likely repercussions include 100 lashes on the father. A number of livestock in the family's possession will be taken by force and eventually they take the girl and force her to sleep with foreign fighters. However, it is worth noting that foreign fighters who are high-value targets are even very cautious about girls whom they see as intelligent and likely to understand their true game within Al-Shabaab. As such, one foreign fighter better known as Al-Americi married a deaf girl, and it is believed he made this choice for security reasons; thus, his intention was not to marry her but rather he just wanted her merely for prostitution purposes.

Al-Shabaab very often recruits uneducated youths living in the territory under their control and who also could not have an opportunity for training that would pave the way for employment. During drought is the best time they recruit youth from drought-affected families through radicalization programs set to influence them. However, the most dangerous times are when they force pastoralist families in their territories to bring boys aged between 8 to 12 for education and they take children to a training camp far from the villages. They inform their parents children will be taught basic education when in actuality they train them as fighters. Children will never be returned to their families, while some parents later heard their children were killed in the battlefield between Al-Shabaab and Federal Government forces.

10.14. Al-Shabaab and Forestation Program

Al-Shabaab never allows deforestation of the territories under their control, because they use the forest as a safe haven from potential drone attacks during military operations against them. On the contrary, pastoralists and farmers who rely on rain-fed farms wish to cut the trees to prepare the land for cultivation. Thus, anyone found cutting a tree will be arrested and the judgment is known to all. The detained pastoralists or farmers will be held until an AK-47 with four magazines is brought to the court. This being a prologue for people's displacement and abandonment of their rain-fed farms.

10.15. 14th October Zope Suicide Attack

One of the indelible terrorist car bomb suicide attacks that Al-Shabaab killed 587 in was the one that occurred on 14th October at Zope Junction in Mogadishu. Al-Shabaab orchestrated a deadly attack against civilians in Mogadishu on 14th October 2017. They used two truck bombings and it took place in Mogadishu, the capital of Somalia, killing at least 587 people and injuring 316 others. Nearly all of the casualties were caused by one of the trucks which detonated when the driver was unable to escape from the security forces who wanted to stop it. The driver attempted to escape from security officials, crashed through a traffic jam and exploded, inflicting tremendous casualties and destruction to all hotels and business premises and all vehicles using the road and people. The bodies and flesh of the dead were scattered all along the road. The intended target of the attack is believed to have been a secure compound housing international agencies and troops. The second blast happened close by, killing two people. A third explosives-laden truck was captured by police. Though no organization claimed responsibility, officials stated that a key member of the cell that carried it out had informed them that the Islamist group Al-Shabaab was responsible. The attack was the deadliest in Somalia's history, surpassing the 2011 Mogadishu bombing that killed 100 people. It is widely believed that Al-Shabaab is the only organization with the capability, motive, and experience to pull off anything on this scale. However, Al-Shabaab denied responsibility for the attack. According to multiple sources, the attack at Zoobe Junction involved an aging TM (Bedford) truck – a model formerly used by the Somali army and ubiquitous in the country – converted for civilian use as a cargo transporter and packed with explosives.

10.16. Al-Shabaab and Ethiopian Collaborations

Although Ethiopian forces who are present in Somalia under the name of AMISOM numbered 4,500, there are nearly 40,000 others operating in Somalia to implement Ethiopia's hidden agenda. These non-AMISOM Ethiopian forces are widely believed to have a collaboration with Al-Shabaab fighters, offering training and plenty of ammunition to Al Shabaab militants, clan militia and Federal Members States loyal to them. Some Ethiopian soldiers are in Somalia as part of AMISOM while others are there as a result of a bilateral deal with Somalia's federal government.[175] The Ethiopians serving the AU mission are responsible for securing Bay, Bakool, and Gedo regions in South Western Somalia, but they are also present in Hiran and Galgudud regions, where they have been moving into towns and withdrawing from others at will.[176] The vast majority of non-AMISOM Ethiopian forces were operating in Central regions of Somalia, while the official Ethiopian AMISOM forces were assigned to operate in Gedo, Bay, and Bakool. Ethiopia has more than 4,300 soldiers in Somalia as part of the African Union Mission in Somalia (AMISOM) – a UN Security Council-mandated mission to combat the armed group. The East African country also has thousands of other troops that are not part of AMISOM in Somalia.[177]

10.17. El Bur District

The Ethiopian forces, who are part of AMISOM alongside SNA troops, had captured the town from al-Shabaab in 2014, officials from the

---

175. VOA News. (2017, March 27). Al-Shabab Seizes Key Somali Town After Ethiopians Pull Out. Retrieved from https://www.voanews.com/a/al-shabab-seizes-key-somali-town-after-ethiopians-pull-out/3794065.html
176. Ibid
177. Al Jazeera. (2016, November 11). Al-Shabab regains land as Ethiopia pulls troops. Retrieved from https://www.aljazeera.com/amp/features/2016/11/11/al-shabab-regains-land-as-ethiopia-pulls-troops

area said.[178] El Bur was once the commercial hub and main stronghold of al-Shabaab in central Somalia, but the group lost the town to Ethiopian troops serving under the African Union peacekeeping mission known as AMISOM three years ago.[179] One of the biggest challenges that people face is severe harassment and torture by the Ethiopian forces and al-Shabaab forces whenever they capture a city in central Somalia. The federal government officials and senior military leading SNA accused Ethiopian forces of being in close collaboration with al-Shabaab. They accused them of providing massive ammunition and weapons, and training. They also blamed them for sharing information with al-Shabaab instead of SNA. The accusation came out following Ethiopia's unilateral withdrawal from all its military bases in central Somalia and when al-Shabaab took over all those bases without the knowledge of SNA forces who were committed to collaborating with ENDF in the effort to fight terrorists.

Recently, the Ethiopians have been abandoning their bases in towns in southern Somalia; 10 towns in the last four months, four of them in the past four weeks, without notice or explanation.[180]

Immediately, Ethiopian forces abandoned almost all their military bases without notifying the SNA, and Al-Shabaab took advantage and captured them. Somalia's al-Shabaab Islamist group has taken control of El Bur, a town in the Horn of Africa's semi-autonomous region of Galmudug, after Ethiopian forces left, a government official has said.[181] "Ethiopian troops left the town... thus al-Shabaab captured

---

178. Reuters. *"Somalia's Al Shabaab Takes Town After Ethiopian Troops Leave, Official Says."* April 4, 2017. Accessed March 31, 2025. https://www.reuters.com/article/world/somalias-al-shabaab-takes-town-after-ethiopian-troops-leave-official-says-idUSKBN1760FD/
179. VOA News. (2017, March 27). Al-Shabab Seizes Key Somali Town After Ethiopians Pull Out. Retrieved from https://www.voanews.com/a/al-shabab-seizes-key-somali-town-after-ethiopians-pull-out/3794065.html
180. Al Jazeera. (2016, November 11). Al-Shabab regains land as Ethiopia pulls troops. Retrieved from https://www.aljazeera.com/amp/features/2016/11/11/al-shabab-regains-land-as-ethiopia-pulls-troops
181. Reuters. *"Somalia's Al Shabaab Takes Town After Ethiopian Troops Leave, Official Says."* April 4, 2017. Accessed March 31, 2025. https://www.reuters.com/article/world/somalias-al-shabaab-takes-town-after-ethiopian-troops-leave-official-says-idUSKBN1760FD/

it today," Burhaan Warsame, Galmudug's minister for ports and sea transport, told Reuters late on Monday. The reason for the Ethiopian troops' withdrawal was not clear, and their military officials were not immediately available for comment.[182] Analysts have warned the town was vulnerable to reoccupation by the militants because al-Shabaab blocked all roads leading in and out, forcing almost all of the residents to leave.[183] Al-Shabaab is seeking to drive the African Union-mandated peacekeeping force, AMISOM, out of Somalia and topple the country's Western-backed central government.[184] The Islamist militants also want to rule the country according to a harsh version of sharia, or Islamic law.[185] Residents fled into nearby bushland with the arrival of al-Shabaab forces in El Bur, Warsame said. He said the town was deserted when al-Shabaab fighters entered.[186]

10.18. Moqokori, Another Crucial Town

As Aljazeera media reported on 11th November 2016, Al-Shabaab regained land as Ethiopia pulled troops from Moqokori, in the Hiiraan region of Somalia.[187] Ethiopian forces in Central Somalia were not part of AMISOM forces with clear UNSC mandate as mentioned above. Contrary to this, their main goal and objectives were to destroy the nascent Somali government and empower the terrorists in order to legitimize

---

182. VOA News. (2017, March 27). Al-Shabaab Seizes Key Somali Town After Ethiopians Pull Out. Retrieved from https://www.voanews.com/a/al-shabab-seizes-key-somali-town-after-ethiopians-pull-out/3794065.html
183. Ibid
184. Reuters. "*Somalia's Al Shabaab Takes Town After Ethiopian Troops Leave, Official Says.*" April 4, 2017. Accessed March 31, 2025. https://www.reuters.com/article/world/somalias-al-shabaab-takes-town-after-ethiopian-troops-leave-official-says-idUSKBN1760FD/
185. Reuters. "*Somalia's Al Shabaab Takes Town After Ethiopian Troops Leave, Official Says.*" April 4, 2017. Accessed March 31, 2025. https://www.reuters.com/article/world/somalias-al-shabaab-takes-town-after-ethiopian-troops-leave-official-says-idUSKBN1760FD/
186. Ibid
187. Al Jazeera. (2016, November 11). Al-Shabab regains land as Ethiopia pulls troops. Retrieved from https://www.aljazeera.com/amp/features/2016/11/11/al-shabab-regains-land-as-ethiopia-pulls-troops

their presence in Somalia. This is because Ethiopia's invasion in Somalia was purely to increasingly weaken Somalia's nascent government, and for them to claim they were there to support the TFG and fight against terrorists was just a fig leaf. Many people who were deluded into thinking Ethiopia had been in Somalia to support the TFG assumed the reason Ethiopia withdrew its forces from all military bases in South Central Somalia was related to its domestic problems. However, the armed group's fortunes appear to be changing in central Somalia this year. Since January, Ethiopia has faced deadly street protests at home. With no sign of the wave of unprecedented violent protests stopping or slowing down, Ethiopia declared a state of emergency this month in an effort to halt the demonstrations from spreading across Africa's second most populous country.[188]

Al-Shabaab Regains Moqokori from Ethiopian NDF – As the clock ticked past 11 a.m. and birds nestled on the short dry shrub trees chirped away, a large group of young men in camouflage uniforms and black face-wraps appeared suddenly and marched toward an open clearing in the bush. Their feet kicked up dust in the soft, sun-baked brown soil beneath. Totaling more than 150 men with only their eyes visible, they made no eye contact or engaged in small talk as they lined up..[189] The men are part of al-Shabaab's Special Forces gathered in this rebel base in southern Somalia to undergo final training before dispatching to nearby towns in preparation for taking them over from African Union (AU) and Somali government troops.[190] The training base is approximately 10 km outside the strategic town of Moqokori in the Hiiraan region, a town the al-Qaeda-linked group retook after Ethiopian troops withdrew last month.[191]

---

188. Al Jazeera. (2016, November 11). Al-Shabab regains land as Ethiopia pulls troops. Retrieved from https://www.aljazeera.com/amp/features/2016/11/11/al-shabab-regains-land-as-ethiopia-pulls-troops
189. Al Jazeera. (2016, November 11). Al-Shabab regains land as Ethiopia pulls troops. Retrieved from https://www.aljazeera.com/amp/features/2016/11/11/al-shabab-regains-land-as-ethiopia-pulls-troops
190. Ibid
191. Ibid

10.19. Ethiopia's unilateral withdrawal and handover of the military bases has been a pattern repeated many times recently across Somalia.

After regaining Moqokori, "Jihad," shouts the group's commander under the watchful eyes of two of al-Shabaab's most senior and well-known figures. "Strength, honor," the fighters shout back, drawing admiring looks from their leaders. This group of fighters – which includes medics, mechanics, explosives experts and suicide bombers – has been handpicked from al-Shabaab's many battalions as the group seeks to retake territories it lost to Somalia's internationally recognized government and AMISOM.[192] Although it is widely believed by Somalis across sectors that there had been collaboration between the ENDF and al-Shabaab militants, yet al-Shabaab justified Ethiopia's withdrawal in their own terms and depicted as if they are enemies to each other. This is how al-Shabaab described Ethiopia's withdrawal: "The reason they [Ethiopia] invaded our country, the reason they came to Moqokori, was to harm the Muslim population," Sheikh Ali Mohamud Raage, the group's spokesman, a tall, bulky figure with red eyes and a greying beard, told the gathered fighters who were now sitting on the hot sand.[193] "They came here to mistreat and degrade our people and to stop them from worshipping Allah. But God chose you to defend His religion and the honor of the Muslim people," Raage said, as shouts of "God is great" from the fighters filled the midday air.[194]

10.20. Changing Fortunes

Ever since the rebel group was pushed out of the Somali capital, Mogadishu, in 2011 by Somali and AU troops, they have been on the back foot, losing major towns and cities across the Horn of African country. The group has also lost several senior leaders in recent years.[195]

---

192. Ibid
193. Ibid
194. Ibid
195. Ibid

10.21. What Al-Shabaab Said About Ethiopia's Withdrawal

"They ran away in the middle of the night because they were too scared. They did not tell even the non-believers that used to work with them. Their country is falling apart. Their people are protesting because they do not want their government. But we will hunt them down until they leave all of our country," Sheikh Hassan Yakub, al-Shabaab's governor of the Galgaduud region, told the assembled fighters outside Moqokori.[196] However, the armed group's fortunes appear to be changing in central Somalia this year. Since January, Ethiopia has faced deadly street protests at home. With no sign of the wave of unprecedented violent protests stopping or slowing down, Ethiopia declared a state of emergency this month in an effort to halt the demonstrations from spreading across Africa's second most populous country.[197]

10.22. What Addis Ababa Said About Its Withdrawal from 10 Military Bases in Central Somalia

Horn of Africa observers believe events back in Ethiopia are the reason why Addis Ababa is cutting down its troop numbers in Somalia. "Ethiopia said it was in Somalia to preserve and protect its country from external threat," Abdullahi Boru, a Horn of Africa expert, told Al Jazeera. "But Ethiopia is facing a domestic threat now – the largest threat since the overthrow of the Derg regime.[198] "For the government, there is a change of priority. Ethiopia is a large country, and every boot is needed in Ethiopia to stem the domestic threat. The Oromo and Amhara protests are a bigger threat to the government than al-Shabaab.[199] The protests in Ethiopia and the unexplained troop withdrawals have come as a timely

---

196. Ibid
197. Ibid
198. Al Jazeera. (2016, November 11). Al-Shabab regains land as Ethiopia pulls troops. Retrieved from https://www.aljazeera.com/amp/features/2016/11/11/al-shabab-regains-land-as-ethiopia-pulls-troops
199. Al Jazeera. (2016, November 11). Al-Shabab regains land as Ethiopia pulls troops. Retrieved from https://www.aljazeera.com/amp/features/2016/11/11/al-shabab-regains-land-as-ethiopia-pulls-troops

boost for al-Shabaab, and the group's leaders are trumpeting it as a victory.[200] Ethiopia's justification for its invasion of Somalia in December 2006 and its recent justification for its unilateral withdrawal from so many military bases to the enemy it claimed was a threat to its sovereignty and existence are inconsistent and suggest it had a hidden agenda. This has really undermined the collective efforts of Western countries and the Somali people to achieve normalcy and greater stability. Addis Ababa denies the latest troops' withdrawal has anything to do with events back home. "We are pulling out because for a long time our country has shouldered a heavy financial burden having troops in Somalia and it is time the international community took over," Getachew Reda, Ethiopia's communications affairs minister until earlier this month, told Al Jazeera.[201]

"We do not need our army to deal with any domestic issue. Our troops leaving towns in Somalia is not related to anything happening domestically in our country.[202] It is purely an economic decision. We have done a lot to help our Somali brothers stabilize our country, but we cannot continue taking the financial burden. And I expect our troops to pull out of other towns," Reda said.[203] The minister also denied the troops that had been withdrawn were part of the African Union mission.[204] "The troops are not part of AMISOM. We have a significant number of troops in Somalia as part of an agreement signed with the Somali government," Reda added.

10.23. What AMISOM Said About Ethiopia's Withdrawal from Its Bases in Central Somalia

It is noteworthy that Ethiopian forces in South-central Somalia were not in collaboration with SNA as many assumed, but also not with all other AMISOM peacekeeping forces in Somalia. The African Union mission said Ethiopia's move would not make its operation in Somalia

---

200. Ibid
201. Ibid
202. Al Jazeera. (2016, November 11). Al-Shabab regains land as Ethiopia pulls troops. Retrieved from https://www.aljazeera.com/amp/features/2016/11/11/al-shabab-regains-land-as-ethiopia-pulls-troops
203. Ibid
204. Ibid

any easier.[205] "The withdrawal of troops will, of course, bear more responsibilities on our troops and how we carry out our mandate. It is not an ideal situation, but we can manage with our current troop numbers," Joe Kibet, the spokesman for AMISOM, told Al Jazeera. As the troops made their way through the town and Ethiopia continued to threaten to pull its troops out of more towns, the locals were left to wonder whether their own, which changed hands more than twice in the past month, will experience a lasting peace.[206]

10.24. How al-Shabaab Blockades Exacerbates Humanaitarian Crisis in Somalia

In Hudur town, which has been under siege for 7 years and falls under the Ethiopian sector, both Al-Shabaab (AS) and Ethiopian National Defense Force (ENDF) are in sight of each other, yet Ethiopian forces never take action against the siege taking place at their presence. ENDF has been complicit in the Al-Shabaab siege. An ongoing blockade by al-Shabaab insurgents in parts of Somalia is worsening the humanitarian situation in the Horn of Africa country. Bakool region in Southwest Somalia is one of the worst drought-affected regions. It has been under an al-Shabaab blockade for more than a decade, with the only means of reaching people in need of humanitarian assistance being by air or using donkey carts to transport food. As such, the people in the region are in dire condition. The blockade is worsening and families have been suffering under a devastating drought for the past four years, said Ali, adding that the drought is the worst he has ever seen. "I have a lot of family there, was born and raised there, and I know the situation. The people in the region are facing a double-edged sword – the drought and the al-Shabaab blockade," he said. "If the government in Mogadishu and the state government continue to ignore how bad the humanitarian restrictions and blockade are, a lot of people will die of hunger or drought-related illnesses and malnutrition," he added. Omar Atu, mayor of Bakool's provincial capital Hudur, told Anadolu Agency that al-Shabaab terrorists last week torched more than four donkey carts carrying much-needed

---

205. Ibid
206. Ibid

food supplies to the region. The neighboring region of Gedo has also been affected by the al-Shabaab blockade and humanitarian restrictions.

Ali Yussuf Abdullahi, spokesperson for Gedo's regional administration, told Anadolu Agency that although the situation there is different, they have seen al-Shabaab terrorists restricting humanitarian activities. The terrorists also killed several engineers who were digging a water well in the region, he said. He said the terror group's main aim is to pressure the local population into abandoning their support for the government. "The terrorist group is hurting people by stopping humanitarian aid from reaching the areas they control and imposing a blockade on government-controlled areas," he said. "Two months ago, the group killed 11 people who were engineers, including foreigners, just because they were building and digging a water well," he added. The Hiran region, which has seen an uprising after al-Shabaab terrorists destroyed water wells and burned vehicles carrying food supplies, has also been affected, although the government said it had liberated large parts of the region from the group. Mahas District Commissioner Mumin Mohamed Halane told Anadolu Agency that Somalis are fed up with the al-Shabaab blockade and extortion tactics. "We have liberated our areas, and wherever they are, people are getting the humanitarian assistance they need. We will continue fighting because we are fighting to save lives," he said.

10.25. Millions Facing Starvation as a result of Al Shabaab blockade

Currently, there are over 6.7 million people on the brink of starvation in the country, said Ishaku Mshelia, deputy emergency coordinator for the UN Food and Agriculture Organization (FAO) office in Somalia. He said counterinsurgency operations, sieges by non-state actors around some towns, reprisal attacks, and threats of attacks are limiting humanitarian access in hard-to-reach areas. "Although some areas such as Ceelbuur, Jamaame, Hudur, and Dinsoor are classified as hard-to-reach, the FAO was able to reach some vulnerable households with critically needed cash transfers in some of these districts," he said. He added that the worst drought in the last 40 years and elevated global food prices have pushed more than 6.7 million Somalis to the brink of starvation. Humanitarian assistance has been scaled up in the past few months, but the number of people in need continues to outpace the level of assistance, he added. Mshelia said the presence of non-state armed groups makes aid delivery a lot more challenging. "Add to that the war in Ukraine, which caused a skyrocketing of global food prices. We face an unprecedented challenge in meeting the needs of Somalis at this critical moment," he added. Somalia declared the current drought a "national humanitarian emergency" in late 2021.

The UN also raised the alarm and said that famine will likely occur in parts of Somalia as the drought continues to worsen. HUDUR, Somalia – The decades-long armed conflict in Somalia continues to take a heavy toll on civilians in much of the south-central part of the Horn of Africa nation. The leader of Southwest State Abdulaziz Hassan Mohamed alias "Lafta-Garen" arrived in Hudur, the regional capital of Bakool on Saturday by plane from Baidoa city to assess the humanitarian situation. Speaking to the local media, Lafta-Garen called for immediate aid to the people in the region who faced food shortages caused by years of al-Shabaab blockade on the government-controlled towns. "Today I visited Hudur, and I appeal to the Federal Government of Somalia, UN Agencies, Humanitarian Partners, and Donors, for an urgent humanitarian intervention to save lives. Bakool faces serious food security as a result of the al-Shabaab blockade," he said.

Combat troops from the Somali government and African Union mission freed Hudur near the Ethiopian border from al-Shabaab militants in March 2014 following a joint offensive. *The blockade rages on for the 7th year amid the heavy presence of Somali and Ethiopian forces in the region, where millions are on the brink of death from hunger,* according to a regional official, who spoke to KON by phone. The official who asked not to be named accused the Farmajo administration of failing to reopen roads and dislodge the militants from the small areas between the big towns in the province. "It doesn't make any sense of liberating these towns from al-Shabaab if the exit and entry points are still besieged and people can't receive food aid," he added. Al-Shabaab, the al-Qaeda's East Africa ally, controls main supply routes and imposes blockades on towns held by AU and Somali government forces, notably Wajid, Bulo-Burte, and Hudur, all in the Bakool region. The terror group has severely restricted the movement of commercial goods and humanitarian aid with reports that 17 trucks were burnt and drivers killed for breaking the blockade. Somalia has millions of internally displaced people [IDPs], mostly extremely vulnerable women and children reliant on aid agencies that have faced challenges accessing needy populations due to insecurity and restrictions imposed by al-Shabaab.

10.26. ETHIOPIA'S CONNECTION WITH AL-SHABAAB
Hilton Hotel – Addis Ababa

Ahmed Madobe was accompanied by Ethiopian intelligence and a few elders. They met with President Abdullahi Yusuf to appoint Ahmed Madobe as governor of the Lower Jubba region. President Abdullahi Yusuf Ahmed, who was not willing to appoint him, acknowledging the Ethiopian intelligence with him, responded to the request in a democratic fashion by raising the involvement of all stakeholders in Lower Jubba as a prerequisite for him to be appointed to that position. Abdullahi knew that Ahmed Madobe could not get support from all stakeholders in the Jubba region. Ahmed was still a member of the leadership of al-Shabaab. He didn't change his position as a member of al-Shabaab. He was assigned to fight in Mogadishu and in particular, to attack Villa Somalia. Col. Beder, who was the bodyguard of Ahmed Madobe, told me more. The 54th brigade and Ahmed Madobe's al-Shabaab militia fought in Mogadishu, and he was defeated in the battlefield badly. He was expecting backup from other al-Shabaab commanders in Mogadishu but in vain. As a result, he decided to leave Mogadishu with the remaining militia loyal to him for Kismaayo. Then, conflict emerged between Ahmed Madobe and al-Shabaab as a result of his decision to leave Mogadishu for Kismaayo. Al-Shabaab waged fierce fighting against Ahmed Madobe and weakened him more and more, forcing him to flee into the forest.

Later, Ahmed Madobe was given support by IGAD, dominated by Ethiopia, and reinforced with newly trained forces from Kenya to elevate his strategic position against other warlords and powerful players. He eventually became a presidential candidate for the newly formed Jubaland election. The election was managed by IGAD, which facilitated him in becoming president.

CHAPTER 11

EUTM SOMALIA

CHAPTER 11

EUTM SOMALIA

> EUTM Somalia is a key driver to support development of a sustainable Somali-owned training system that provides the Somali National Army with the policies, procedures, expertise, and experience to manage their own force generation.

[**Fig. 11:** European Union Training Mission Somalia Logo.]

As I said, both Ethiopian forces and Al-Shabaab had been crippling the Western efforts in Somalia, including the European Union Training Mission, which was established in 2010 and operated in Bihanga training camp in Uganda due to security reasons to provide the military pillar of the European Union's (EU) efforts to help stabilize Somalia, but later moved to Somalia in 2014. EUTM aims to strengthen the Somali federal defence institutions by providing training, mentoring, and advice through activities tailored to the best interests of the Somali defence institutions, eventually increasing the proficiency, effectiveness, credibility, and accountability of the Somali defence sector to enable Somali authorities to progressively take over security responsibilities. In addition to the above, the key to this will be EUTM Somalia's drive to support development of a sustainable Somali-owned training system that provides the Somali National Army with the policies, procedures, expertise, and experience to manage their own force generation.

EUTM Somalia also supports the development of the Ministry of Defence and continues to deliver tactical training. In addition to light infantry, engineering, and specialized training, development increasingly focuses on Train the Trainer programs and mentoring that will provide the Somali National Army with the capability to manage their own training. Established in 2010, EUTM Somalia's early mandate focused on delivering tactical training support to the newly reconstituted Somali National Army (SNA) working for the Transitional Federal Government (TFG). Strategic advising was added in 2013 during the mission's third mandate renewal. EUTM Somalia is now part of the Comprehensive Approach to Security (CAS) plan, adopted in 2017 by the Federal Government of Somalia (FGS) and international partners as part of a security pact. EUTM Somalia's objectives are to increase "the proficiency, effectiveness, credibility, and accountability of the Somali defence sector to enable Somali authorities to take over security responsibilities progressively."

The strategic advising and mentoring of SNA General Staff and Ministry of Defence (MOD) personnel includes drafting keystone documents and policies and encouraging civilian oversight of the SNA. As I mentioned in previous chapters, the Ethiopian Defence Force had been crippling the Western efforts. The objectives of the key international partners of the security sector of Somalia, including the EUTM, was to help stabilize the country. For instance, according to the assessment report on EUTM by Paul D. Williams and Hussein Yusuf Ali in December 2020, the EUTM was established in 2010 to provide the military pillar of the European Union's efforts to help stabilize the country. As mentioned in the report, EUTM Somalia's early mandate focused merely on delivering tactical training support to the newly reconstituted SNA working for the Transitional Federal Government. Strategic advising was added in 2013 during the mission's third mandate renewal. At that stage, SNA leaders faced a lack of ownership of the processes, the critical infrastructure, and the role they wanted to play in shaping their own future within the ecosystem, primarily because the EDF dominated the landscape. The key players competing within the security ecosystem and landscape were Ethiopia, the first entrant, and Uganda Defence Force, the second player in the ecosystem but, unlike Ethiopia, an honest player.

The ENDF role was deeper than any other players, and it had its own rules of the game to the extent it could create conflict with any political figure or warlord who attempted to stand out in the interest of SNA in line with the EU and other international partners' objectives and goals. Uganda followed peacekeeping policies and laws, and its operational objectives, unlike Ethiopia's, were in line with the coherent vision of Western countries and Somalia, while it also remained neutral between competing Somali politicians. That was a unique capability that Ethiopia had in the ecosystem and used as leverage whenever it deemed necessary, particularly when Uganda proposed that the newly trained SNA be placed in the system according to the skills and positions they were trained for. Ethiopia was using the newly trained SNA forces—both those it trained itself and those from Uganda—for its own agenda. EDF dominated the ecosystem because of its profound influence at all levels in Somalia, which it had built over past decades, and the cynical fig leaf it used that Ethiopia was supporting the SNA that ousted the Union of Islamic Courts and brought the TFG to Mogadishu.

A good example to illustrate the case more clearly could be the following. In 2008, I was among 171 trainees in Bihanga training camp, trained by Uganda People's Defence Force for different disciplines. Some of us were trained as VIP Protection, Snipers, Public Relations, and

Medical personnel. Immediately we returned to Mogadishu, we heard news spreading that Ethiopia had proposed the newly trained 171 SNA personnel be incorporated into its newly trained forces from Ethiopian camps. This was against the reason we were trained, and its intentions were merely to counteract the potential skilled SNA that could pave the way for the attainment of a stabilized country. On the other hand, Ugandan commanders in Mogadishu were planning to place the newly trained 171 professionals in their corresponding areas and levels. However, we knew the huge influence Ethiopia had on both the political and security landscape in Somalia. We decided to meet with President Abdullahi Yusuf Ahmed and present our case to him. The president, who was also fed up with Ethiopia's sinister intentions, concurred with our view and instructed Ugandan commanders to place all newly trained forces in their relevant departments, and he ruled out Ethiopia's request. We were saved from Ethiopia's destruction and disbandment strategy and today work as SNA officers who use the skills we gained. On the other hand, Ugandan government officials came with a file to confirm the 9 people returning to Uganda to be trained as ToT. This was also approved by the president.

11.1. Misalignment

However, the EUTM had been training recruits and releasing them in the absence of Ministry of Defence leadership and infrastructure to lead and manage the newly recruited SNA forces. Thus, from 2010 to 2014, all SNA trained by the EU in Bihanga training camp had been used as fuel by Ethiopia to deter the possibility of emerging potential SNA. The train and release method by EUTM was not serving the interest of the Somali people but just squandering EU funds and crippling its efforts as a result of Ethiopia's hidden agenda. Ethiopia, which was dominating AMISOM, astonishingly placed newly trained forces in line with its sinister intention rather than according to what they were trained for. These challenges weren't limited to EUTM during the time between 2010 and 2014 but extended to Uganda-trained SNA in Bihanga training camp. EUTM Somalia: European Union Training Mission in Somalia – Military Mission

The first five years that EUTM Somalia had been operating in the Uganda training academy were important but not generating the anticipated value for SNA. Ethiopia, which was dominating AMISOM operations, never wanted a strong SNA to be nurtured. Ethiopia's sinister intention was for Somalia not to have a strong SNA. Although it has been widely reported by global media that Ethiopia came to Somalia in December 2006 to support SNA in ousting Islamic Courts Union forces, the reality was quite different. For Ethiopia, this operation had been a cynical fig leaf concealing its own ill-fated hidden agenda. It only wanted to be part of the task to ensure a weak SNA against the powerful Al-Shabaab terrorists, which was inconsistent with the EUTM Somalia Mission in Somalia. The AU Mission in Somalia (AMISOM) was duly deployed to Mogadishu in March 2007, paving the way for Ethiopia's withdrawal in January 2009.

The EUTM Somalia assessment report by Paul D. Williams and Hussein Yusuf Ali mentioned, "One of the major problems was the lack of an effective national Somali army. It was this capability gap that EUTM Somalia was designed to help fill." EUTM Somalia stepped in on time as SNA was suffering due to Ethiopia's continuous negative hidden agenda in which they had been depicting as if they were in support of formulation of a credible Somali National Army when in actuality they were destroying it. In 2010, following the intervention of a coalition of neighboring African countries to secure the national capital and establish a Transitional Government, the EU launched the European Training Mission – Somalia to support the creation of a new Somali National Army to assist with the provision of security. As mentioned in the report by Paul D. Williams and Hussein Yusuf Ali regarding assessments on EUTM Somalia in December 2020, I quote, "One of the major problems was the lack of an effective national Somali army. It was this capability gap that EUTM Somalia was designed to help fill." The question is, given continuous training by EU, Ethiopia, and Uganda provided to SNA from 2007 to 2015, why was SNA not effective? What went wrong with the efforts devoted to SNA by all these players including the EU and USA?

The EUTM Somalia was established on 15 February 2010 and deployed to Uganda on 7 April 2010 because the situation in Somalia was considered too dangerous. The need for such a mission can be traced to December 2006 when Somalia's TFG was brought to Mogadishu with the help of over 10,000 Ethiopian soldiers. In the process, the TFG and Ethiopian forces ousted the Union of Islamic Courts, which had controlled Mogadishu since June of the same year. In response to what it saw as the installation of an illegitimate Somali government and an Ethiopian invasion, the Islamist group Harakat al-Shabab al-Mujahideen (Mujahedin Youth Movement, or Al-Shabab) led an armed resistance.

As battles ensued, Al-Shabab's recruits increased dramatically, and so too did Ethiopia's casualties and financial costs. Within months, Ethiopia's then Prime Minister, Meles Zenawi, was looking for a way out of Mogadishu by pushing the AU to take over the job of protecting the TFG. The AU Mission in Somalia (AMISOM) was duly deployed to Mogadishu in March 2007, paving the way for Ethiopia's withdrawal in January 2009. From 2007 to 2015, a good number of SNA was trained by all players in the Somali security ecosystem. But due to the lack of coherent vision among key stakeholders and conflicting interests, it was not possible to create an effective and efficient SNA in Somalia. The EU training programs in Uganda were in some ways uninformed, not well positioned in the environment, and not aligned with objectives helping SNA but were ending in vain. Because trainees returning to Somalia were falling into the hands of the Ethiopian army, which dominated the ecosystem, and they were placing them where they would perish.

When EUTM Somalia efforts for SNA created value was the time that EUTM moved to Somalia and incorporated into its mandate strategic advice and institution building. Somalis had been facing an extreme lack of ownership of the processes and felt completely marginalized in the security ecosystem. What is worth noting was when EDF was leaving Somalia, Ethiopia refused to hand over the MOD to the FGS and, particularly, SNA leadership. Instead, they handed over the MOD facilities to AS. It was not only MOD, but also all their other bases in Mogadishu. The Ethiopian command moved to Halane.

CHAPTER 12

DANAB SPECIAL FORCES & U.S ROLE

DANAB SPECIAL FORCES & U.S ROLE *Major Abdirahman O. Warsame "Jeeniqaar"*

CHAPTER 12

DANAB SPECIAL FORCES & U.S ROLE

> *Danab is the most competent and powerful organ of SNA. All other stakeholders in the war against terrorists rely on Danab for crucial capabilities. Thanks to the USA, who devoted huge efforts and resources in reestablishing Danab.*

[**Fig. 12:** United States of America National Flag.]

12.1. Reestablishment of Danab Special Force: US Army Role

Whenever you hear Danab, the next thing to come to your mind is USA special force. Furthermore, it is widely reported that all military operations conducted by Danab to contain terrorists across the country have been successful.

The US elite are not only powerful but also highly effective in every aspect of their mission of reestablishing and preparing Somali Special Force. They train members of the Somali Danab Brigade, or "Lightning Force," an elite special operations force within the Somali National Army that specializes in carrying out both symmetric and asymmetric warfare. The Danab Brigade was reestablished in October 2013 with just 150 recruits and has grown to a several thousand-person brigade.[207] Once recruited, brigade members typically underwent three months of basic training by the U.S. Navy SEALs, followed by a month of special courses, such as shooting, navigating dense savannahs, raiding enemy camps, helicopter insertions, and close-quarters combat.[208] Now the Somalis have grown more self-reliant and conduct up to 70% of the brigade's basic training duties.[209] After basic training, recruits go home for a month-long breather before returning to Baledogle Air Base, about 100 kilometers northwest of Mogadishu, where the SEALs gave them crash courses in rappelling from helicopters and securing landing zones, Foreign Policy magazine reported.[210] Through expanded medical training, the brigade now saves more of its wounded Soldiers, with the ratio of dead to wounded falling by more than half over a recent 18-month period, Capt. Hassan Mohamed Mohamud, the physician who heads Danab's medical corps, told The Washington Post.

The brigade constantly seeks about 350 new recruits at a time for training as fighters grow battle-weary. After receiving their diplomas and getting their pictures taken with Somali military leaders, brigade members are sent to fight the notoriously violent, skilled, and battle-ready al-Shabaab militants, who have controlled large swaths of Somalia

---

207. Support Our Troops. "Somalia." Accessed March 31, 2025. https://supportourtroops.org/news/2610-somalia
208. Ibid
209. Ibid
210. Ibid

since many in the brigade were children.²¹¹ The formidable extremist group often hides in the savannah before launching surprise attacks. It employs complex improvised explosive devices, large truck bombs, rocket-propelled grenades and waves of suicide bombers in its attacks. But the Danab Brigade has "grown to around battalion size and has been the only [Somali National Army] unit consistently able to perform offensive operations," Paul Williams, an associate professor at George Washington University and author of several books on war in Africa, told Army Times.²¹²

The Danab unit has been a key pillar of U.S.-backed efforts to combat the Al Qaeda-linked militant group Al Shabaab. Over the years, the unit has regularly conducted strikes that have crippled the Al Shabaab leadership and capabilities. The force has been particularly successful in recapturing territory previously held by the terrorist group who are responsible for a reign of terror that has resulted in a famine that has killed millions. These include: Sabiib, Anole, Aw-dhegegle (more about Aw-dhegele will be presented in the following pages). Many of these operations are undertaken with the direct involvement of U.S. forces in a variety of support roles. U.S. troops have functioned as joint terminal attack controllers directing artillery or calling in air strikes. American assistance has been critical to providing close air support for Danab forces as they engage these terrorist groups while helping avoid civilian casualties.

12.2. About Infrastructure Development

The U.S. Defense Department awarded a more than $12 million contract for "emergency runway repairs" at Camp Baledogle, Somalia, in 2018.²¹³ Camp Baledogle was a training base for Somali Army

---

211. Ibid
212. Africa Defense Forum. "Somalia's Quick Strike Danab Forces Wage Fierce Battle Against al-Shabaab." September 2023. Accessed March 31, 2025. https://adf-magazine.com/2023/09/somalias-quick-strike-danab-forces-wage-fierce-battle-against-al-shabaa/
213. Myers, Meghann. "Secret US Base in Somalia is Getting Some Emergency Runway Repairs." Air Force Times, October 4, 2018. Accessed March 31, 2025.

commandos. The trainers were reported to be U.S. contractors working for Bancroft Global Development. Bancroft Global Development had done pretty much a sustainable training program for Somali SNA Danab. The skill and knowledge offered by the trainers were highly effective. Without them, Danab could never have made the achievements accomplished over the past decades. "These repairs are needed due to years of wear and degradation due to inadequate maintenance," said Mike Andrews, the public affairs director for Naval Facilities Engineering Command Atlantic, which executed the military construction contract for Camp Baledogle.[214] He also provided the specifications for Camp Baledogle's runway: 10,092 feet by 140 feet and made of asphaLt. "Our strategy in East Africa is to enhance partner capability to ensure that violent extremist organizations, who wish harm in the region, are contained," Weist said.[215]

12.3. United States Increases Security Assistance through Construction of SNA Bases

On February 15, 2024, a new project valued at over $100 million aimed at construction of up to five military bases for Somali National Army (SNA) Danab Brigade was approved by the USA.[216] According to Assistant Secretary Phee, U.S. support to the Danab Brigade is "a centerpiece of our ongoing security cooperation with Somalia" and the construction of the new bases "reflects our recognition of the success of our joint efforts to build a capable, professional, and accountable force." In 2017, the United States and Somalia reached an agreement to recruit, train, equip, and mentor 3,000 men and women from across Somalia to build an enduring light infantry capability within the larger SNA. Since its creation, the Danab Brigade has demonstrated its capacity to engage al-Shabaab as a quick reaction strike force in battle and has maintained

---

https://www.airforcetimes.com/news/your-air-force/2018/10/04/secret-us-base-in-somalia-is-getting-some-emergency-runway-repairs/
214. Ibid
215. Ibid
216. Ibid

a clan-neutral character.[217] Over the past 12 years, the Somali special force Danab has been effectively countering al-Shabaab attacks and destroying the terrorist bases across the country, resulting in not only winning but also higher reputation.

Danab Composition:
1. Danab Special Forces (Balidoogle M. A) HQ
2. Danab Mechanized MU. (Mogadishu)
3. Danab infantry across (Somalia).

The Somali Danab is a special operations unit within the Somali National Army, playing a crucial role in the nation's ongoing efforts to combat terrorism and stabilize the region. Trained by U.S. and international military advisors, the Danab is recognized for its agility, precision and effectiveness in counterterrorism operations. Danab soldiers undergo rigorous training and receive specialized instruction in areas such as marksmanship, close-quarters combat and intelligence gathering.

US-trained Somali Special Forces "Danab" and US elite forces carried out an unparalleled operation in Somalia to fight terrorism in the country and beyond, creating significant value in this effort in the security ecosystem. During this operation, what we coined "terrorist White flag downed" occurred following extraordinary military operations with unprecedented challenges carried out by Danab and US elite forces against terrorists in Somalia. In this operation, both sides employed sophisticated skills, intelligent actions, tactics, and technologies. Both sides refused submission, instead utilizing all available means to secure victory. Notably, both sides defined victory according to their own terms and perspectives. They demonstrated unique behaviors, skills, and goals while employing all available equipment and resources to accomplish their missions. The Al-Shabaab White Flag waving over Awdheegle, a 2,700-person Al-Shabaab headquarters that had been a zone free from external threats, was captured by Danab and US elite

---

217. U.S. Embassy in Somalia. "United States Increases Security Assistance Through Construction of SNA Bases." Accessed March 31, 2025.
https://so.usembassy.gov/united-states-increases-security-assistance-through-construction-of-sna-bases/

forces through successful penetration of fortified defense systems and brigades of fighters prepared to die.

In this operation, Al-Shabaab employed unprecedented intelligent actions and tactics to defend the White Flag flying over Awdheegle district, which was ultimately captured by Danab and US elite forces. This account presents military action unlike anything portrayed even in Hollywood films. Unforgettable lessons were taught to Al-Shabaab, with consequences difficult to express in words, along with the impressive capacity they exhibited. More remarkably, Danab forces and US elite units quickly and creatively self-organized to respond to new skills and unexpected tactics used by Al-Shabaab during the offensive operation.

12.4. Awdheegle District

Awdheegle district is a safe haven territory for Al-Shabaab terrorists - affiliated with Al-Qaeda - a global terrorist organization. It is under their control, a military base, a headquarters, and a command, communication, and coordination center (for them, their main base and safe zone) where kill and destroy missions are planned and assigned to their fighters to target government institutions, civilians across many parts of the country, and foreign diplomatic missions. However, the most pressing issue was Awdheegle's notorious excessive rape and torture that Al-Shabaab imposed and inflicted on civilians living in Awdheegle in particular and the Lower Shabelle region in general. Despite being an Al-Shabaab stronghold region notorious with the white flag waving 24/7, people are treated in horrific ways, subjected to huge taxation under the name of Zakah, and taxed on every activity carried out daily to generate income for basic needs and livelihoods. In Awdheegle and its surroundings, women are the primary victims of Al-Shabaab rule as they are raped and deprived of their rights to sexual decision-making.

According to Al-Shabaab, the rules set in Awdheegle district and its surroundings include but are not limited to the following: No woman can refuse or resist if a Mujahideen individual chooses her as his sexual partner, and no parent or relative has any say against this decision. Anyone who fails to pay any amount of tax imposed by Al-Shabaab shall be beheaded immediately. Their goal is to ensure that when people are taxed, they rush to make timely payment without further consideration.

12.5. Complaint Filed Unprecedented Scale of Rape and Extortion of Money Reported

Unprecedented violations occurred in Awdheegle district, committed by Al-Shabaab leaders and their militias. Women were raped, millions extorted, and many people who attempted to resist were beheaded. Concern mounted to the extent that all stakeholders in the security sector felt the need to intervene. It has been recognized that Awdheegle was a safe haven for Al-Qaeda affiliated terrorists better known as Al-Shabaab. For them, Awdheegle district is the most protected zone, which they consider impossible for enemies to infiltrate, let alone capture. They invite those who invest in them, particularly foreign elements who fund them. A white flag waves over the Al-Shabaab base in Awdheegle; this white flag represents the headquarters of Al-Shabaab, a well-protected zone that no other force can seize. The office where the white flag waves is a no-go zone, accessible only to Al-Shabaab commanders and high-level foreign funders. In light of this, it became incumbent upon Danab, US-trained special forces, to fight terrorists across Somalia, to liberate oppressed people in Awdheegle district and the Lower Shabelle region generally, and to ensure people regain their freedom and democratic rights.

It is incumbent upon Danab to secure the safety of women who have been raped and to completely ensure women's rights are well protected, as well as to end the extortion of money from the people. As such, the responsibility for liberation operations falls on the shoulders of Danab, despite the support of other players after operations. In this light, to make an informed decision on the strategy and direction of the operation and to secure a successful outcome, Danab's intelligence unit has already been tasked with gathering all necessary information about the region, particularly Awdheegle district where the Al-Shabaab white flag waves 24/7. Jama Gabayre, who is Danab's chief of intelligence, has presented a detailed intelligence report about Awdheegle district, Al-Shabaab's plans and thinking, and the defense model developed to prevent an impending attack from Danab forces. The key points of the Danab intelligence report include:

1. Al-Shabaab defense plan: Al-Shabaab held the perception that Danab would attack Awdheegle from the east, which is the Mogadishu and Balidoogle direction. As such, their strategy focused on the eastern direction, and all efforts and thinking were directed toward the east. They deployed about one thousand militants in trenches and a number of vehicle-borne improvised explosive devices (VBIED).
2. 35 improvised explosive devices planted in all roads coming from the east which Danab might use when attacking Awdheegle.
3. Flooding river water toward the east covering up to 8 km distance.
4. The number of militants and variety of weapons they were planning to use in the event a Danab attack occurred.
5. Awdheegle bridge planted with IEDs on both sides.
6. The weaknesses and strengths, and whether there were foreign fighters present.
7. The opportunities and the threats.

As pressure regarding the ongoing violations mounted, an urgent meeting of all stakeholders was convened for three days in the Halane area of Mogadishu.

12.6. Awdheegle Operation Meeting Convened

Key players who participated in the meeting included SNA, USA, EU, Bancroft Global Development, AMISOM, Danab, Türkiye, and officers from Somali Police Force and National Intelligence Service Agency. The objective of the meeting was to discuss Awdheegle liberation operations. It is noteworthy that for the Federal Government of Somalia, the issue had political importance, and it was putting significant pressure for quick implementation of the operation to ensure people were liberated from the terrorists. Danab had generated, based on its intelligence report, a data-driven plan entirely reflecting the outcome of the intelligence report. With this plan in hand, we attended the three-day stakeholders meeting in Halane. As it is the responsibility of Danab to carry out the operation and pave the way for other SNA forces to take over after liberation, we needed to have a reliable intelligence report and successful implementation plan. However, before Danab presented its operation direction and core strategy to be followed (which emerged from the intelligence report), the head of joint operations presented a plan not aligned with ours in many aspects, for instance in operation and direction, but confirming that Danab had the responsibility to liberate Awdheegle and enable other SNA and AMISOM forces to take over after liberation.

12.7. As the Danab Commander, I responded:

Unlike the plan presented by SNA and other stakeholders, Danab's plan is quite different and in many ways opposite to the way they planned this operation; according to the intelligence information, Danab planned to attack Awdheegle from the west rather than east. As such, Danab will make a movement covering about 200 km distance to attack from the west. Based on intelligence sources, it is impossible to attack Awdheegle from the east. Opting for the eastern direction will result in a longer duration of operation, as the challenges developed by Al-Shabaab are as numerous as they will involve more risk and multiple suicide attacks. Al-Shabaab invested heavily in the east side as they considered it the likely option for Somalia and allied countries to attack Awdheegle. Danab decided to employ the most intelligent tactics against Al-Shabaab. This resulted in two contradicting military plans, particularly regarding the direction of attack: west versus east. Danab's operation plan chose to approach from the west, while other stakeholders preferred the east—a direction Al-Shabaab perceived and devoted more efforts and preparations toward, which would lead to severe consequences.

12.8. Awdheegle Operation Planning Meeting Held in Halane – Mogadishu: Halane Stakeholders Meeting

Day 1, 2, and 3 meetings were participated in by USA, EU, Bancroft, AMISOM Sector One, SNA, Somali Police officers, Somali Intelligence officers, Danab commanders, and Türkiye, this being Türkiye's first operation participated in. **USA** special forces representative **Col Nelson** said: Danab over past months liberated Bareere, Sabeeb-Anole, and El-

Salini and has handed them over to SNA, with defense fortifications and sandbags. Col Nelson continued his opening remarks and said: Today we came together to discuss ***Badbaado Operation*** to liberate Awdheegle. As such, we need to hear each player's presentation of their role in the operation and preparation model to achieve coherence.

12.9. EU Presentation

The first presentation was made by EU: EU said: We are ready to play a humanitarian role, as USA did in the last three liberated areas. This includes food distribution, medicine, and nutrition to enable displaced families to access food and return to their houses, and then schools and hospitals to reopen. EU also presented a well-equipped platoon, named Combat Engineering or Pioneer, composed of AMISOM contributing countries to participate in the operation, and requested clarification on whom it would accompany.

12.10. AMISOM Sector One Presented

As Sector One, we cannot afford to contribute to the subject matter operation. This is because all our forces are now operating in recently liberated areas and some other areas under Sector One control. The only option we have is to withdraw some Sector One Battalion forces from Qoryoley district to join the Awdheegle operation, which would make Qoryoley vulnerable to AS takeover. We don't have any other way to participate in this operation. **USA:** It is unacceptable for AMISOM, which spends huge funds, to say that they don't participate. It is unacceptable, and you need to come up with a reasonable presentation of the way you contribute to this operation. Go back and come up with a way in which you can contribute to this vital operation. **SNA**: In the face of AMISOM's slap, **General Madoobe** said: shedding light on the operation plan as a map on the screen, contrary to Danab operation strategy map. This is because SNA developed the operation plan without consultation with Danab.

Their map exhibited:
1. Danab forces to launch offensive from east of Awdheegle.

2. AMISOM will follow Danab forces. Then a new Somali brigade who will remain in control of Awdheegle after liberation will follow.
3. Then combat engineering or pioneer battalion of AMISOM supported by EU is following.
4. Infantry commander, the governor, media and logistics SNA are following, culminating in over 150 vehicles, excluding Danab.
5. Two Turkish battalions named Eagle are following to protect logistics from potential attack from behind, and an SNA battalion named 27. Except for Danab, apparently all other players have had conducted meetings and they are in agreement with SNA presentation plan over Awdheegle liberation operations.

General Odowaa, SNA infantry commander emphasized SNA plan to be followed and the role of different participating operations led by Danab.

12.11. Danab Presented

I said, as a Danab commander: Danab has three different forces who will carry out the operation. These are Danab special forces, Danab 2, and Danab mechanisms or technicians. Danab special force will take control of the Awdheegle bridge, which is very crucial for AS, and they use it as a weapon.

Danab operation commander: Abdinasir said: presented Danab operation plan. The Danab operation direction and how it will be implemented, the duration it will take, accomplishment and hand over plan to SNA, and eventually how to reinforce one another.

Lt Jama Gabeyre - Danab intelligence chief: briefed on the intelligence report about Al-Shabaab preparation and their defense plan, including 35 road bombs planted, and AS plan to weaponize river water as flood to the east front. Thus, he recommended the operation to be carried out from west of Awdheegle to minimize casualties and ensure the operation liberation would be successful. He also stated other platoon setups and sequences of different forces and operation procedures.

Turkey Military general said: Türkiye wishes Danab to join the SNA plan, as Turkey was part of that plan, and it also recognized Danab had more facilities that other forces didn't have.

Gabayre: This is quite unrealistic to assume it will succeed. Based on today's intelligence information, AS had already weaponized the river water and made an 8 kilometer flooded area, which is the direction SNA is suggesting. As a result of this, the east direction will fail the operation and empower Al-Shabaab to overrun all operation participants' forces and take all equipment. As such, Danab will never go to the flooded area, with over 35 roadside bombs planted. The Awdheegle bridge is planted with 4 IEDs by Al-Shabaab.

Tension heightened. There was a change of mind created by Danab intelligence report. Most of the participants got a different impression than before. EU, Türkiye, SNA infantry commander vs Danab and US commander.

12.12. Conclusion

US commander: Based on the intelligence report presented by Danab, we need to reduce the risk, ensure safety of the bridge, and shorten operation timeline. SNA commander General Dahir Elmi "Indhoqarsho," who was not present in the meeting, sent his view supporting the Danab plan to avoid the flooded area. Other Danab and AS perspectives and strategic significance of this operation:

Despite the goal being to liberate the oppressed communities in Awdheegle and Lower Shabelle region from the evil terrorists, the operation has strategic significance for both sides. **For Danab** special forces, who are the most reliable and powerful brigade trained by US military elites, failure of the operation and defeat will represent not only that the capabilities and competence of Somali special forces are lower than AS, but also it will have implications for the US elite who trained Danab. Moreover, it will provide Al-Shabaab more confidence militarily and they will exploit the defeat to radicalize more youth domestically and globally and for political purposes to gain more domestic support. Whereas if other ally stakeholders who recommended a different operation strategy and direction witness any failure, they will blame us and see us differently. **For Al-Shabaab**, the defeat has several severe consequences for them.

This is because Awdheegle is their stronghold in Lower Shabelle where they collect all revenue and a safe haven which they depict as their power base, where the white flag waves 24/7, and their command center. Losing such a location to Danab and the white flag zone, and the seizure of the flag itself, is their death, and they will lose more local and international support. It will have negative strategic consequences on their political and social influence. They cannot accept defeat, and they prefer huge casualties and material loss to maintain Awdheegle and the white flag zone. Both sides should consider many issues while the operation fighting is going on. Living in this reality, we need to accomplish our mission successfully.

12.13. El-Saliin Operation

However, before we proceed, I would like to present the lessons learned from the recent El-Saliin operation from which the Awdheegle operation stemmed or was built on. The unique feature of the El-Saliin operation was the roadside bombs planted by Al-Shabaab's sophisticated experts and how Danab IED experts encountered these highly developed IEDs planted on the road by AS. IEDs are one of the main causes of casualties among troops and take a heavy toll on local populations. In many ways, mine experts from the two sides are determinants of winning or losing the operation. The two forces (Danab and AS) heavily rely on mine experts as IEDs are a key strategy that terrorists frequently use to weaken the competence of their offensive enemy before attacking to defeat them. For Al-Shabaab, Improvised Explosive Devices planted on the roads that offensive Danab special forces use is a crucial part of their defense plan. There must be serious IED traps on the road, and to some extent, AS experts attempt to challenge Danab Counter IED experts and aim to kill them. This means the devices have been prepared and planted on the road with sophistication. Thus, when experts from the Danab side attempt to dismantle them, they may fail and be killed. As a result, the offensive Danab should stop there and experience unforeseen attacks on all flanks from Al-Shabaab.

In this operation, the mission was to destroy the El-Salin (Al-Shabaab base), before the Awdheegle operation. Danab left from Jazeera base in Mogadishu to destroy Al-Shabaab base in El-Salin. Danab brigade was the lead of the operation but other SNA are just following them to take over after destroying the terrorist base. A unit from Danab Bali-Dogle Military Base was placed at Km 50 to defend from potential attack from behind. This is because the location is their stronghold. Now, as Danab special forces along with US military elite moved to El-Salin, they took coastline road. They went through Jilib-Mark village, then Gendershe, and then Dhanaane. However, when they reached Dhanaane which is xx km to El-Salim a massive variety of roadside bombs was identified by Danab Counter IED. Danab counter IED is now at forefront of the Danab special forces and other SNA in the operation. The Danab Commander Maj Jeeniqaar (author of the book) and other SNA commanders rely on Danab Counter IED and understand his role is determinant of mission success and failure.

While on the other hand, Al-Shabaab's success depends on the IED experts' skills and knowledge. As Danab C-IED was spearheading the army, he communicated with Danab Commander and informed not to budge an inch, and he continued and said the situation is terrible as some of the implanted IEDs are highly sophisticated ones and it requires time and extra skills. He said after dismantling and removing several IEDs, the next one is triple traps one on another. He said AS IED experts planned not only to explode Danab special forces but to also eliminate Danab Counter IEDs. This shocked all commanders and raised increasing concern and stress regarding whether their Counter IED expert would be able to dismantle the sophisticated IED. For them they understand if he fails and is killed, they will face a horrific situation from Al-Shabaab.

On the Al-Shabaab side, their hope to survive is a function of their IED experts' skills. Their commanders are monitoring the effectiveness of the IEDs planted. Furthermore, should their IED experts fail, they will have a blow and hope to survive from Danab attack is very limited. In such cases, Al-Shabaab very often retreats from the battlefield knowing the ferocity of the Danab war. That being the situation, Danab Counter IED expert understood the three layers of the IED planted and he decided not only to dismantle it but to again modify the three traps and make alteration to kill Al-Shabaab IED experts. First of all, he dismantled the whole three layers and facilitated Danab to proceed and after proceeding, he put the three layers as it was with little alteration to eliminate AS IED expert. It took three hours to dismantle all IEDs except one detonated that killed one SNA soldier. It was at sunset, thus, Danab and SNA has made a base close to the area and created a defense trench. For Danab and SNA commanders, it was their relief that their Counter IED not only survived from Al-Shabaab IED triple trap and ensured Danab success rate of the war but put the ball in AS court.

For Al-Shabaab IED expert and commanders managed all planted IEDs. However, their expert was concerned about the triple IED device and several hours later at around 2:00am he went to check his triple trap and didn't figure out the alteration made by Danab Counter IED and as a result it detonated and killed him. Then Danab waged an attack at 6:00 am and captured El-Salin base. The Al-Shabaab IEDs have drastically reduced as key expert on IED was killed through his own traps. The Danab IED expert was then promoted to a higher rank in the army. Based on those lessons learned by both sides, it is expected for Awdheegle operations the bar to be raised to another level.

12.14. One more perception for Danab

One perception that Danab hold is that the white flagged zone is more protected than zones where the black flag is waving; thus, we foresee more tactics and unforeseen challenges will be encountered during the operation. And this has happened. In such a situation, despite Danab having already mobilized all available equipment and required training, we need to come up with a high-level set of change plans and contingencies created within the unforeseen circumstances by conceiving new insights to respond to the situation; this has equally happened during the operation.

12.15. On my way to Balidoogle base

SNA commander General Indho-Qarsho, on my way back to the BMA, called me and said:

SNA commander: You have chosen a very well thought out plan and direction that is more robust. You have my go ahead. You need to prepare in the most effective way, using the most robust options. You should immediately start operation preparations and keep me posted. Danab commander: Copy that commander.

The next day, I communicated with both Danab officers and USA support team, informing them of the final plan approval by the SNA commander and that we needed to meet to define more on the direction and required training and rehearsal. I convened the meeting, and all key players were present.

Participants: All special forces of Danab force commanders. On the USA side: USA commander Captain Dylan Sharrock, US Officer based in Bali Doogle, and other officers attended the meeting including air strike operation officer, USA topography and mapping officer, USA infantry commander, and other officers. **Danab Commander:** presented the plan, and informed of SNA commander approval and commitment. We need to review the plan, identify challenges and changes in the environment.

Dylan Sharrock: We shared with US government about this operation in order to get all kinds of additional support and logistics.

Dylan Sharrock: We urgently need to start the planning process, identify key players, discuss coordination, and determine what needs to be done and what we need to improve. We need to bring all commanders from across the two sides to establish the operation path and develop a shared model of operation and coherence strategy. The next day we brought senior officer commanders to achieve the above shared meaning, goals, and objectives. In the meantime, we the two commanders agreed to engage USA and Somalia respectively to solicit further support and coordination.

12.16. Operation Preparation Started (15/07/2019 to 02/08/2019)

The following preparation was decided to be conducted within two weeks:
1. Joint training on operation model (Danab and USA forces)
2. Medical Unit Training
3. Logistics and other facilities
4. Weapons required
5. Command, Communication, and Coordination
6. Information about enemy and geography of the region

12.17. 7 days later

Sharrock alone came to see me, while I was in a meeting with other Danab officials in the Danab operation office. He got in the room, sat next to me, and said: We are being offered three well-equipped drones, of which two of them will be specifically assigned to work for Danab and the commander, while the third one will guide other forces such as the EU supported platoon, SNA, and the like. **Danab commander**: This is amazing; this will enhance the potential for the operation's success. Finally, rehearsal was made, simulation and gaming were carried out.

12.18. Fully prepared to start operations: Awdheegle Operation Take Off

It was on 05/08/2019 at 6:00 am in Bali Doogle Airport Military Base. The Danab base. Four companies of well-equipped Danab special forces and one company of US elite are ready to embark on and execute Awdheegle liberation operations. They are all in parade. Every soldier is prepared for the operation in every aspect of the operation design and is well equipped to achieve the set goal "liberate Awdheegle from the terrorists." However, we all recognize that this operation is quite complex compared to past operations in many ways and requires consideration of a more coherent approach and skills.

The four Danab special forces and one company of US elite forces were to move from Balidoogle to Awdheegle and reach there 8 hours later. The specific location they needed to reach was a location between Torotorow and Awdheegle from the west side and 15 km to Awdheegle. We moved from BMA from 4:30 am and safely arrived 8 hours later to the location which was 15 km to Awdheegle without the knowledge of Al-Shabaab. Using our own technology, we disabled all communication networks to deprive them of getting any leak of our plan and arrival at 25 km west of Awdheegle.

Al-Shabaab leaders were still holding the perception that Danab would attack from the east, and all their efforts and militants were on the east side of Awdheegle district. It was now 2 pm, the date was 5th August 2019. We stationed and established a defense there. We were constantly communicating with the command center. On 6th August 2019, Danab moved to Awdheegle and stationed as close as 1 km to Awdheegle. However, Al-Shabaab had already learned that Danab was coming from the west, and knowing that time would not permit them to change the direction, they quickly moved from the east defense and from Awdheegle and shifted to Mubaarak and Janaale to re-strategize and avoid massive losses. Yes, it was good for them. Danab didn't immediately move to town and capture offices and houses built in a fashion covered with trees to prevent being seen by US drones. This is a white flagged zone, and their withdrawal doesn't necessarily mean they left and are defeated, but a well-orchestrated attack is coming.

Danab forces carried out searches across Awdheegle district. It was a very strong safe haven for Al-Shabaab, for they never thought Danab would easily take over. It was a well-forested district planned to be a safe haven and a base where they could fight using the environment effectively and where drones wouldn't work. Some offices are under trees, while houses were covered by the branches and leaves of trees. Revenue collection office and court were among properties seized by Danab. Here is where Danab seized the white flag waving over these offices.

12.19. Oppressed Civilians and Their Feelings After Liberation

People celebrated Al-Shabaab's defeat, and were excited with triumph and happiness. They shared with Danab officers the harsh situation and huge oppression they underwent during the terrorist rule. They complained of huge money extortion as taxation, violation of women's rights, rape, and many other forms of oppression. However, a number of people who were loyal to them remained in the city, and Danab considered the potential threat of those few individuals.

12.20. Al-Shabaab Attacked Us on 06/08/2019 at 12:00 PM

The same hours after their withdrawal, they attacked Danab from the east and fierce fighting occurred.

On 07/08/2019 at 12:00 PM, Al-Shabaab attacked us from the west side, and it ended up being unsuccessful.

On 07/08/2019 at 12:30 PM

Al-Shabaab waged an attack from east of Awdheegle and were defeated by Danab.

12.21. Awdheegle Bridge Operation

Danab special forces were tasked to capture the bridge and ensure the bridge was not destroyed by AS and to dismantle all planted IEDs. However, Al-Shabaab had both a very strong defense unit and planted numerous IEDs which were hard to dismantle, so when Danab special forces attempted to dismantle them, the Al-Shabaab unit carried out an extensive attack from all corners and **exploded the bridge**.

12.22. Drawing Scenarios

For Al-Shabaab, it is very strategic that Danab and SNA taking over the bridge is a horrific defeat, and they are supposed to maintain control of the Awdheegle bridge or to destroy it when deemed necessary. As such, they planted four IEDs on the two sides of the bridge, two IEDs on each side. Furthermore, they planted two more explosive devices on the barrier so that when attempts to remove the barrier are made, a huge explosion that destroys the whole bridge happens. On the sides of the bridge are two groups well armed with RPGs and PKMs and grenades, and four sentries at the barriers of the sides of the bridge. The goal is to ensure Danab never crosses towards Awdheegle from the east. However, Danab's plan is different and is coming from the west. Danab forces moved from Balidoogle Military Airport Base to Awdheegle district, making an 80km distance more than the normal route to come from the west side. However, Al-Shabaab didn't devote much attention to the possibilities of Danab coming from the west, but they placed a small unit to patrol this direction.

12.23. Al-Shabaab Revenge Attack

Al-Shabaab carried out successive attacks against the Danab commander and senior commanders. Alshabaab often carry out an ambush on the road that connects Mogadishu and Bali-Dogle Military Base. One of the attacks carried out by Alshabaab they targeted my vehicle as commander of Danab and killed Danab head of intelligence Lt. Jama **Gabeyre**, who was in the vehicle with me (author) on our way to Balidoogle from Mogadishu. Al-Shabaab killed in that revenge operation Jama Gabeyre and 6 other Danab officers; and also Lt. Mohamed Yarisow, who was Company Commander in Danab force. He carried two wounded soldiers and the bodies of six soldiers who had been killed in an ambush, killing himself and two other soldiers. However, I remained unhurt. Their target vehicle was the commander's vehicle in which they were traveling together.

12.24. Drawing Scenarios: Mission Accomplished

On 25th August, 2019 at 6:00 AM, Danab divided into two groups: a group who went back to Bali-Doogle base and a group who went to Mogadishu.

The group that went to Bali Doogle reached there at 10 PM, while the Mogadishu group, which I was part of, encountered some small ambushes on the road between Afgoi and Mogadishu, but no one was hurt. About Danab and US Efforts to Formulate a Special Force for Somalia to Fight Terrorists.

12.25. USA Efforts Devoted to the War Against Terrorism in Somalia

In the wake of the September 11 terrorist attack on the twin towers in the USA, what became obvious was that failed states such as Somalia, Afghanistan, and the like should not be abandoned with the responsibility to protect terrorists in their countries to make a safe haven, and it is incumbent upon the international community to ensure strong states are in place to deter terrorists from taking advantage of the vacuum. Those countries should not be places where terrorists operate to wage attacks against global interests and destroy world order. Another crucial challenge, as Francis Fukuyama mentioned in his book "State Building," was the growing concern about the potential for terrorists to access knowledge of chemicals for weapons of mass destruction due to technology abundance and use it to destroy global interests and security. Having this concern in mind, US leaders focused on Somalia and reinstituted the Danab special forces to play that role and invested, along with other EU countries, in a state-building process, starting from the Somali National Reconciliation Conference in Kenya in October 2012. Somalia has unique geopolitical interest due to its location in the Horn of Africa and proximity to the Gulf of Aden and Indian Ocean, which are global routes for trade and transport.

Despite the devastating destruction and implications that civil war left on the country and consequently on the people, the US government made several attempts to quickly restore a functioning government. In 1992, during the devastating drought that hit the country, in the absence of government and in the middle of clan fighting, the US government didn't watch children and women dying of thirst and hunger and mobilized necessary resources and US army to deliver aid and save the lives of millions of people. This was Operation Restore Hope in 1992 when US Rangers arrived in Mogadishu to deliver food and water to the people affected by the famine. As a result of this, then-US President George H.W. Bush visited Somalia, particularly Baidoa city, which was a center for the famine, to see people affected by the famine. Top US leaders visited Somalia at several points in time in solidarity with the Somali people at critical times and, at other times, in the effort to fight against terrorism and deter terrorists from making Somalia a safe haven. However, our focus on the topic is not to cover all this history, but merely on the US role in the fight against terrorism in Somalia and the unique effort exerted in building the Danab forces to enable state building, peace building, good governance, democratic values, rule of law, and promotion of human rights.

12.26. Danab: US-trained Somali Special Forces

The US government dispatched military experts and elite forces to reinstitute Somali Special Forces "Danab" (which means "lightning") and provided training for newly recruited young generations to enable the Somali government to fight terrorists inside Somalia. Furthermore, the US government provides Somalia with millions in military hardware and ammunition and a support team who remain in Somalia to participate in efforts to combat terrorists and to create a conducive environment in which people in Somalia can exercise their democratic rights. Given past propaganda about Black Hawk Down issues, one could perceive the probability that the US would make a decision to help Somalia as very slim; however, due to its greatness and farsightedness and proud, self-perfecting attitude and characteristics on one hand, and civilization and political stability on the other hand, the US decision on rebuilding Somali Special Forces "Danab" is proof of American values and its stance on global issues. The US goal for rebuilding Somali Special Forces is to protect people's lives and right to freedom of speech, justice, and promotion of human rights and humanitarian laws and rule of law and justice across Somalia, and to combat terrorists and those who radicalize, to enable Somalia to achieve its intentionality as a peaceful, prosperous, stable democratic nation.

12.27. US Military Expertise

US deployed military experts who trained Somali Special Forces in an unforeseen way with capabilities and competences to create the desirable future state that Somalis are in pursuit. Among indelible trainers in my mind include:
1. US Army Col. Nelson
2. U.S. Army Col. Eric L. Hefner
3. Col. Jay B.
4. Captain Dylan Sharrock
5. Captain Ryan

12.28. About Danab Special Forces

Contrary to what many people including the president and other individuals in positions of authority believe as being merely a branch of SNA, Danab is uniquely trained special forces to carry out special operations in and around the country. The purpose is to protect the national interest and the nation from enemies both inside and outside. This unique purpose has led them to be very limited in number and joining has become increasingly restricted. As a result of the purpose and objectives formed, unlike other national army branches, Danab undergoes very limited changes in terms of its structure and its leadership. Danab has remained a strong institution competent to carry out key operations aimed at combating terrorists across Somalia. It is noteworthy that changes have remained limited even when international partners provide substantial funding and technical support.

12.29. Reinstitution of Danab Special Force

The new Danab was reinstituted by the US as part of its efforts to combat terrorism in Somalia and enable Somalia to achieve its desirable future state, which is "a peaceful, prosperous, stable democratic nation." The US government reinstituted Danab in 2013, and its initial units and platoons were drawn from the Somali National Army. Newly recruited Danab members, selected through a tough selection process, were given new training in Somalia and overseas. The new headquarters or Danab base has been selected as Balidoogle Airport Military Base and the former Kaba-hirig base during the Said Barre regime, which is not far from the new base. However, new bases have been created to fill the gap as the scope was to combat terrorists across the country. The government relies on Danab for combating terrorists and ensuring the safety of the people. The need for strong Special Forces Danab has been ever-increasing with respect to new technology and chemicals and other hazardous materials likely getting into the hands of terrorists who must be stopped.

12.30. About the Name Danab "Lightning"

As we mentioned above, the purpose that formed Danab was to carry out unusual, tricky operations which require extensive knowledge and skills, intelligence, and experience that can deal with well-trained and prepared enemies in a complex, turbulent, and dynamic environment with very compressed time. Such kinds of operations can't be entrusted to the ordinary national army. They come back to their camps with "mission successfully accomplished." The compressed timeframe in which they successfully carry out assigned missions is the reason they are named "lightning." The objective is to establish well-trusted special forces who possess extensive military knowledge and skills, intelligence with the required requisite variety to protect the people and defend against enemies domestic and foreign.

12.31. Decision Latitude

Unlike any other officer among SNA, Danab officers have greater latitude in decision making, without consultation with their leaders. However, officers' decisions will be evaluated later, and they may be rewarded or punished depending on evaluation results. It is very rare for Danab officers who took a different decision than initially agreed upon to fail when evaluated, because of the unique capabilities developed and the strong requirements to be enrolled as a Danab officer.

12.32. Danab Population is Very Limited

Due to the requirements in terms of personal ability to overcome hard situations, knowledge and skills, and capabilities to improvise to respond to changes, very few people are recruited for Danab.

12.33. Combating Terrorists

Following the civil war that broke out in 1991 in Somalia, terrorists taking advantage of failed states increased, particularly in Muslim countries. As a result, this brought about a change in global view and led the world community to reconsider its role in preserving global security and global interests. The emerging terrorist challenge was not part of the SNA responsibility and didn't fall under their category. This further necessitated the reinstitution of special forces Danab by the USA. As such, both the international community and the government of Somalia count on Danab for issues relating to terrorism.

12.34. Symmetric and Asymmetric Warfare

Danab has been trained to carry out both asymmetric and symmetric warfare and to deal with terrorists in every form and shape they deploy. The key task is to terminate enemies wherever they are located.

12.35. Joint Military Exercise (US and Danab)

Despite joint military exercises between Danab special forces and US elite platoons, reports from pre-civil war US elites and the current

US trainers remained unchanged. Both reported that Somali elite forces demonstrated a higher level ability to respond to emerging or unplanned challenges in comparison to other countries.

[**Fig. 13:** From left to right: SNA Officer (unknown), Abdulqadir Fuushane, Maryan Shariif (Maryan Danab), the author, Jama Furuh Logistic Commander, Jamal Abdinasir Danab Battalion Commander, Badda Ase MU Commander, Abdulaahi Bidhi, and SNA Officer (unknown),.]

12.36. The First Time Danab Was Badly Defeated in the Battlefield

Danab are being undermined by politicians who interfered in the command and decision of military strategy, and this eventually led to the defeat of Danab by Al-Shabaab. Although it had been widely reported that Danab had success in all battlefields with Al-Shabaab and Daacish due to the unique skills and

[**Fig. 14:** Late Hassan Tuur, Danab Deputy Commander killed in Galcad by Alshabaab]

knowledge offered by the US trainers, it is worth noting that when the command, communication, and control was hijacked by politicians, Danab was badly defeated and all its commanders killed by Al-Shabaab. When command, control, and communication of the army are interfered with by unprofessional politicians, it will only empower the enemy and seriously weaken Danab. Recent offensive against Al-Shabaab in Central regions (Galcad battlefield), spearheaded by the Somali President Hassan Sheikh Mohamud, posed huge challenges to both SNA and Danab special forces in having latitude decisions and deploying unique skills and knowledge in the battlefields. The President's intermingling clan militia known as Ma'awisley and SNA model undermined both SNA and Danab special forces' unique skills and capabilities developed over the past years. Furthermore, there had been politicians, clan elders, and ministers involved in the offensive, particularly in the decision making processes. This challenge weakened Danab's ability to make informed decisions to defeat Al-Shabaab. Power abuse further hindered Danab commanders from making the right decisions and defying the uninformed and unprofessional orders from those individuals.

In the event Danab commanders reject those commands and instructions from politicians and the involvement of clan militia in the operations, they will likely face severe punishment (firing from the army). Hassan Tuure was a leading operation officer for the offensive war against Al-Shabab in Galguduud, Galcad. Hassan Tuure was the second Danab special forces commander and was killed in the operation together with all Danab Army. This was a blow to Danab forces as all its troops and commanders were killed by Al-Shabaab by waging an overwhelming attack that lasted days.RetryClaude can make mistakes.

12.37. Mission (Jowhar to Beledweyne)

His mission was to open the road that connects Jowhar to Beledweyne which is 245km, and after opening the road, he proceeded to Galcad in Galguduud where offensive was going on. Galcad was Al-Shabaab stronghold territory. The Danab commander Hassan Tuure assessed the situation and made a conclusion that they should not make a base within Al-Shabaab's stronghold as suggested by the politicians and clan elders. He insisted the only option was to keep moving to avoid orchestrated and well-planned attacks by Al-Shabaab. However, Danab commanders were forced to make a base within Al-Shabaab stronghold areas of Galcad while the nearest backup was located 85 km away and could reach them 5 hours later.

12.38. Tuure's justification

If he could keep moving around in the four days in the area which AS was dominating, they could never defeat him. The nearest backup was 85 km which made it impossible for Danab to receive any backup in the course of an Al-Shabaab attack. It was out of the norms of Danab special forces to be used as infantry rather than for specific operations. However, he was forced to stay there for four days. Together with a battalion of SNA by politicians such as the defense minister, MPs from the area, and officials at Villa Somalia. Al-Shabaab took advantage of the situation and orchestrated an attack to overrun Danab and other SNA forces. At 4:30am Al-Shabaab attacked Danab using 2,000 army personnel, three vehicles loaded with improvised explosive devices, and 20 mortars. After 1:10 minutes the Danab and SNA battalion was badly defeated and overwhelmingly overrun, killing everyone of Danab and SNA. Al-Shabaab defeated not only the second commander but also key individuals of Danab were killed that day.

12.39. Danab at Justified Accord 2024

Although the Somali Danab Special Force was nascent as it was established in 2013, it has made history in the recent Justified Accord 2024. As reported by army.mil, Danab forces made history at Justified Accord 2024, participated in by 1000 persons from 24 countries. Recently, Danab commandos participated in Justified Accord

[Fig. 15: Lieutenant Abdirahim Muse Mohamed, Company Commander Danab]

2024, a joint military exercise sponsored by the Southern European Task Force–Africa.[218]

Somali soldiers from the Danab unit, dubbed the "Lightning Brigade," joined platoon-sized elements from Kenya, Tanzania, and Djibouti at the Counter Insurgency Terrorism and Stability Operations Training Centre in Nanyuki, Kenya. Throughout the two-week exercise, the Danab consistently demonstrated their professionalism, but also learned valuable lessons from fellow participants.[219] "The Somali Danab is very excited to participate in Justified Accord," said Somali 2nd Lt. Abdirahim Muse Mohamed, platoon commander, Somali Danab Special Forces. "We appreciate all the training from the U.S., but now we can also train together here with other African countries." [2nd Lt. Abdirahim Muse Mohamed, platoon commander]. Overall, the Danab commandos have proven to be a highly capable force.

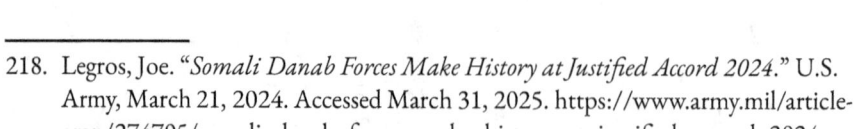

---

218. Legros, Joe. "*Somali Danab Forces Make History at Justified Accord 2024.*" U.S. Army, March 21, 2024. Accessed March 31, 2025. https://www.army.mil/article-amp/274705/somali_danab_forces_make_history_at_justified_accord_2024
219. Ibid

CHAPTER 13

SOMALI NATIONAL ARMY

CHAPTER 13

SOMALI NATIONAL ARMY

> SNA exhibited greater resilience against Ethiopia's fig leaf agenda aimed at ruining them.

[Fig. 16: General Dahir Aden Elmi "indhaqarsho". Former Somali National Army Commander.]

Somali National Army Force was established in April 12, 1960 to protect the territory and sovereignty of Somalia from domestic and foreign enemies. However, Somalia, being located at the Horn of Africa, has the longest coast and largest airspace frequently used by international flights moving across the world. It is strategically important both for global maritime trade and security purposes. In this light, Somalia, instead of focusing on marine and air forces, invested in land forces. The military regime that seized power through a bloodless coup devoted a substantial budget to building a powerful army compared to the preceding civilian government. The military regime initially began building up the Somali marine force. However, due to its ambitious vision of a greater Somalia, they converted all marine forces into land forces to develop the required capability to liberate the Somali French protectorate and Ogadenia, a Somali region under Ethiopian control, as well as the North Frontier District, a Somali region under Kenyan administration.

Somalia built a very powerful army in close collaboration with the USSR and acquired all military hardware and weapons from the USSR. Such capabilities resulted in the liberation of the Somali French protectorate, currently known as the Republic of Djibouti. For the Ogadenia region, Somalia waged what is well known as the '77 war, in which Somalia liberated the target region. Unfortunately, the Warsaw alliance led by the USSR immediately deployed over 15,000 Cuban troops, massive military tanks, and army units in support of Ethiopia. This intervention drove Somalia out of the territory captured in the '77 war between Somalia and Ethiopia.

SNA after the collapse of Central government. SNA reconstitution and Ethiopia's sinister intention TFG POST ETHIOPIAN SECURITIZATION MOVE GENERAL GORDAN APPOINTED TO LIBERATE AL.SHABAAB FROM MOGADISHU WITHOUT THE SUPPORT OF ENDF.

Nevertheless, for SNA, it was beneficial that MOD was now in the hands of AS. This was because they knew they could dislodge them and occupy the facilities rather than leaving them in the hands of Ethiopian forces. General Gordon developed a military strategy to seize all military bases and MOD from AS. It was a highly successful strategy. He himself died during one of those operations. As a result of his experience and courage, one of the current military bases in Mogadishu was named after him: General Gordon Military Base.

13.1. Gen Gordon strategy

Gordon's plan deterred Ethiopia's sinister motive against SNA, allowing it to become more effective in managing its own forces and implementing strategic initiatives to achieve the vision of a strong SNA capable of controlling the country's security and providing protection to Somali citizens. The Ethiopian military easily routed the ICU's militias. For a few days, it appeared that they had won an easy victory and that the TFG had ridden Ethiopia's coattails into power in Mogadishu. But the first insurgent attacks against Ethiopian and TFG forces began almost immediately and rapidly escalated toward a protracted conflict that has since grown worse with every passing month.[220]

13.2. Somali Soldier

It was 13th July 2020, when together with SNA commander General Odowaa Yusuf Raghe and I set out from the Ministry of Defense for Turkish SOM Military Academy to participate in the graduation ceremony for SNA officers completing a one-year course, and he signed the graduation book. We were traveling through the road that passes Military Hospital and Tarbunka Military Parade space. We were a convoy of four vehicles: three were security staff escorting us and a bulletproof vehicle that the commander and I were using. We were sitting at the back and discussing normal issues. I spotted the security vehicle ahead speeding up, and our driver accelerated too. I sensed something might be wrong and looked at the front mirror, noticing we were approaching a black Toyota Surf vehicle. As we came parallel to the Toyota Surf, it exploded instantly, and I lost sight of everything. The whole environment turned black as smoke filled the air. I could hear the roar of the exploded vehicles

---

220. Human Rights Watch, "So Much to Fear": War Crimes and the Devastation of Somalia, 1-56432-415-X, 8 December 2008, https://www.refworld.org/reference/countryrep/hrw/2008/en/64117 [accessed 26 February 2025]

and pieces of metal hitting our vehicle, along with white materials (the airbag) inside our vehicle, which was also badly damaged. I opened the left window and closed it immediately. A few minutes later, the driver, with extensive bleeding on his face, spoke to us, asking, "Are you okay?" Odawa, the SNA commander, said, "Yes, we are okay," and asked about his aide-de-camp who was in the front seat with the driver. The aide-de-camp was seriously injured and unconscious.

Then our driver stepped out and managed to stop a truck to transport us away from the scene, and we exited from the only functioning door in our bulletproof car. It was an extremely complicated situation. At the scene of the incident, people in the surrounding area attempted to find safe positions before assessing the situation. They didn't immediately offer assistance for fear of a subsequent attack. Similarly, we victims tried after a few minutes to identify what had happened, the direction of the attack, and its implications. As military officers, we understood what could happen prior to an attack, but we were now concerned about a potential subsequent attack in the form of gunshots or another suicide bombing. However, another challenge arose when the surrounding community realized the SNA commander was among the suicide bombing targets or victims and sought information about his condition.

Our escort forces were concerned about a potential subsequent attack and didn't allow people to approach us. A mother was among those who wanted information, and she repeatedly asked, "Is the commander okay?" A soldier responded, "Yes, he is fine. Get back, get back, get back." Yet the mother remained standing there, and the commander himself confirmed to her that he was okay and said, "I am okay. Please get back from here; another suicide attack is possible." She replied, "If you are okay, we are all okay." She then left and informed other people about the commander. We felt relieved and were able to extend help for the injured and recover the dead bodies. The implications of the suicide attack were severe, destroying the vehicles behind ours and killing a significant number of security staff. These included a recently graduated officer who was ordered to accompany us, along with many injured persons. The bodies of the dead and injured were scattered across a large area, to the extent that you could see body parts in different locations. The commander ordered documentation of the deceased soldiers, collection of their bodies, and rapid transportation of the injured to the hospital. A team from Danab special forces and the

SNA battlefield commander arrived at the scene and evacuated us to our destination. On our way to TurkishSom, one of the Danab special forces members told me that he had encountered a shocking sentiment from a soldier who had lost his leg. He said the injured soldier, uncertain about his survival, requested to keep his severed leg with him and wanted to maintain his duty. Instead of focusing on his own health, he preferred to stay on duty, but the paramedics team took him to the hospital.

In the light of growing insecurity and uncertainty, the following commanders were appointed as Somali National Army commanders:
1. Gen Abdikadir Sheikh Ali Dini
2. Gen Abdikarim Yusuf Adan (Dhaga-Badan)

The appointment of these two senior military officers was aimed at restoring the lost prospects in Mogadishu security and stability of Somalia as well as Villa Somalia. The appointment of Gen Diini and Gen Dhagabadan was crucial as the terrorists had become more offensive toward the Presidential Palace, thus endangering the safety and security of the president. Areas close to the perimeter of Villa Somalia had become the battlefield between Alshabab and government forces. Alshabab was increasingly offensive. As a result of this, several defensive positions of the government had been breached and captured by Alshabab. The two Generals were well-known to the government forces and engendered Army trust in leadership through their extensive military knowledge. They were also recognized for their willingness to remain in the battlefield alongside Army soldiers, which provided greater encouragement to government fighters to exert more effort and display the required behavior for success.

On the other hand, President Sharif Sheikh Ahmed made commitments in terms of logistics support and guidance, which led him to wear a military uniform for the next three months. In this effort, although the Alshabab fighters were being pushed back in all defense positions around Villa Somalia, their continuous shelling intensified. RPG-7 attacks occurred regularly at every sunset and sunrise. Due to the need for more military experts to defeat the strong defense of Al-Shabab, the president was contacted by General Mohamed Ali Samatar, former Minister of Defense of Siyaad Barre's government, who informed him about a military general named Gordon who was then living in Hargeisa and recommended calling him to lead the operations. President Sharif Sheikh Ahmed called General Gordon and requested him to come to Mogadishu. Upon his arrival in

Mogadishu, General Gordon was appointed as brigade commander. He set out to assess the battlefield situation, the different military strategies deployed by both sides, the SNA forces' capacity and capabilities, as well as logistics. He then developed a new military strategy to liberate Mogadishu, Middle and Lower Shabelle regions. He established a strategy combining both defense and offense. As a defensive measure, he positioned strong defenses from km-4 all the way to Abdiaziz district, while launching offensives toward the western and eastern flanks where Alshabab typically orchestrated attacks against the government.

In Mogadishu, main roads from west to east were highways, while main roads from south to north were single lanes with no crossroads connecting to them. Part of the strategy focused on utilizing main roads and preventing Alshabab from infiltrating army movements and disrupting logistics support transport. General Gordon's strategy enabled SNA to move rapidly across Mogadishu and attack Alshabab from multiple flanks. He encircled Alshabab in their defensive position at Bakara Market zone where they had blocked several roads. He launched an offensive from the industrial road, which was beyond Alshabab's defense line, and the two main roads entering Bakara Market, forcing them to flee from Mogadishu to the Middle and Lower Shabelle regions. The SNA forces continued to pursue them. Unfortunately, General Gordon was killed during the operation, which succeeded despite his absence. It was an unprecedented success for SNA and an unparalleled loss of a hero, General Gordon.

13.3. General Salah Jama Hassan (Salah liif) SNA commander 2007 – 2008

General Salah Jama Hassan (aka Salah-liif) was Somalia National Army commander during President Abdullahi Yusuf's term of office, 2007-2008. This was a period when both the international community and Somalia's newly formed government were fully

[**Fig. 17:** General Salah Hassan Jama (Salah Liif), Somali National Army Commander.]

engaged in forming the Somalia National Army, as there was a huge need for well-trained forces to contain expanding terrorist fighters across the country, except in Somaliland. Despite Somali Generals being extensively busy working on re-establishing the national army while facing resource challenges, they recognized that among the major obstacles in achieving this goal were AU peacekeeping countries, especially Ethiopian peacekeeping forces and intelligence agents who were dedicated to undermining the process. Ethiopia and Somalia had contradicting goals: Somalia wanted to have a strong national army to defeat the terrorists, while Ethiopia's goal was to see a Somalia with a very weak army. Somalia with a strong army was perceived as a threat to Ethiopia; this was how Ethiopia viewed the situation.

Ethiopia's position on Somalia having a weak government favored the terrorists, who also viewed a strong Somali army as a threat to their existence. Here, Ethiopia and the terrorists shared a common perspective against the Somali government. What was further striking was the position of the international community, primarily the USA and EU, who were major donors to Somalia and countries committed to supporting Somalia's recovery. They trusted Ethiopia significantly. Ethiopia never respected the interests of its allies but worked hard to undermine the entire peace and state-building processes as well as the war against terrorists. Somali National Army commanders met with Ethiopia's peacekeeping forces commanders and intelligence officers in Mogadishu. In that meeting, Colonel Gebregziabher Alemseged Abraha, Tesfay, and General Gabre Yohanes criticized the Somali commanders of the divisions and battalions, labeling them as key challenges against the establishment of an effective Somali National Army. Gabre told General Salah, the Somalia army commander, that "Somalia could have an effective army without the current higher rank commanders," by which he meant the commanders of the army divisions and units. General Salah delivered a shocking response, telling him, "Somalia's newly trained armies are good, equally important are the professional division commanders who are also very good, but the truth is that the key challenges against the formation of an effective Somalia National Army are definitely you three Ethiopian high-ranking officers and not Somali division commanders." This was a blow to them; they never expected any Somali commander would challenge them in such a blatant way. For them, it was a shock.

They left the meeting talking arrogantly to the commander of the SNA. However, General Salah Jama disdainfully said, "They are junior officers who are attempting to delude us about what we know better than them." However, the three Ethiopian Generals, leveraging Ethiopia's powerful influence on Somalia's political and security ecosystem and their impunity and blind backing from Western allies, fought tooth and nail to remove General Salah Jama from his position as Somalia National Army commander. As a result, General Salah Jama was asked to submit his resignation, and he resigned from the leadership position. It is worth noting that no one could speak to the Ethiopian Generals the way General Salah did. Everyone who heard about it was shocked and knew the repercussions would be severely negative. General Salah's courage became word-of-mouth across Somalia's security sector during those days. Somalia's political and security leaders failed to report the unhealthy security environment in Somalia and how Ethiopia had mercilessly undermined the re-establishment of the Somalia National Army and the war against terrorists, while all their activities were effectively supporting the terrorists. The Western powers might have changed their perspective if the Federal Government of Somalia had informed Western-friendly countries about how Ethiopia was working against Western efforts and strategic interests in Somalia.

The Ethiopian military easily routed the ICU's militias. For a few days, it appeared that they had won an easy victory and that the TFG had ridden Ethiopia's coattails into power in Mogadishu. But the first insurgent attacks against Ethiopian and TFG forces began almost immediately and rapidly escalated toward a protracted conflict that has since grown worse with every passing month.[221]

SNA HUMAN RESOURCE MANAGEMENT SYSTEM BY PRESIDENT FARMAJO AND GENERAL INDHO QARSHE. AND ORCHESTRATED IMPEACHMENT AGAINST PRESIDENT FARMAJO OVER THE MoD HUMAN RESOURCE MNGT SYSTEM BY ETHIOPIA

---

221. Human Rights Watch, "So Much to Fear": War Crimes and the Devastation of Somalia, 1-56432-415-X, 8 December 2008, https://www.refworld.org/reference/countryrep/hrw/2008/en/64117 [accessed 26 February 2025]

One of the most crucial achievements ever made in the course of Somalia's state building process was the creation and enforcement of Somali National Army database system. The overall objectives of the President and his commander General Indho Qarshe include the following:
- Uprooting existing entrenched corruption and changing the status quo to establish strong, effective and accountable MoD institution
- Fighting the entrenched corruption in the SNA
- SNA soldier rights
- SNA soldier performance appraisal
- General accountability and greater responsibility.

13.4. Ethiopia's Unwillingness to See Effective SNA System and Performance

President's impeachment over establishment of SNA HRM and database system development and application and enforcement was viewed as a threat by Ethiopia government, who instead claimed its mission was to support Somalia's peace and stability efforts.

ORCHESTRATED IMPEACHMENT AGAINST PRESIDENT FARMAJO OVER THE MoD HUMAN RESOURCE MANAGEMENT SYSTEM BY ETHIOPIA

The then Somalia parliament influenced by Ethiopia's intelligence officer tabled a motion against the Somalia president over his effort to create Human Resource Management Office within MoD responsible to develop SNA Database system and collect each and every soldier's biometric data. Despite Ethiopia's relentless efforts against the establishment of SNA data system, the orchestrated impeachment motion by Ethiopia failed to materialize. President's intention was to build effective, fully functional SNA to fight with the growing terrorist activities across the country and restore law and order. He furthermore wanted to put in place a mechanism protecting SNA soldiers' rights and holding accountability through performance appraisal measurement system. President sat down those days in the Ministry of Defense to encourage the speed of the processes and ensure entrenched corruption is uprooted. No one could believe given the extent that the entrenched corruption within the Ministry of Defence has reached, it will be easily uprooted and a HRM system will be put in place and as a result, the SNA database system will be developed and all data collected, analysed and applied for accountability within MoD and for higher performance purposes.

APPENDIX

APPENDIX: ARTICLE HIGHEST COMMENDATION TO DANAB BRIGADE THE SPECIAL FORCE OF SNA.[222]

A published article by Puntland post. By Maj Abdirahman O. Warsame. (2 May 2021)

I am delighted to commend Danab Brigade, the special force of SNA for not siding with none of the opposing sides in confrontation in Mogadishu over the dispute of election model (This was in May 2, 2021) Unlike other SNA forces who recently experienced divisions and then sided with parties in dispute of election model in Mogadishu, Danab Brigade, the special force of SNA showed a great responsibility, professionalism, integrity, requisite discipline, behavior and moral obligation to remain stick to its lawful mandate in combating with AL.Shabab and ISIS terrorists across the country in order to enable Somalia achieves its long term strategic goal "one person one vote, and a peaceful, stable democratic nation. Since 2013, when Danab Brigade, was re-established, all its activities, operation decisions have been consistently in line with its strategic intent and vision serving on the national objectives set out above paragraph.

Its is noteworthy, that leadership style, culture and values and appropriate management processes shaped the way current knowledge is generated, codified and diffused within Danab Brigade through underlying support of US military genius expertise, which ensured a large part of the country are now free from terrorist, where human rights, rule of law and democracy thrived and succeeded. Over past decade, Danab Brigade made a tremendous achievement in this front by weakening and destroying AL.Shabab and Daish terrorists across Somalia. In addition to the above, Danab Brigade, in order to expand its operation across the

---

222. Sheikh Omar, Maj. Jeeniqaar. Puntlandes. *"Highest Commendation to Danab Brigade the special force of SNA."* Accessed March 31, 2025. https://www.puntlandes.com/?p=78703

country, it trained more especial forces and camped them on new bases in each territory of the five member state of Somali. Such tremendous success could never have been achieved without the support of US government and the immense effort and expertise and skills provided by US genius military officers.

We recognize the significant knowledge and skills provided by US trainers to Danab Brigade has been/ is what determined the notorious high performance and clarity in Danab's strategic direction as well as requisite core competencies and capabilities developed during the past decade. I thank US government not only in providing a well thought out relevant skill training and knowledge but also powerful equipment such as MU, that enabled Danab Brigade Forces to act timely in destroying the enemy and provide secure protection to the citizens. In the light of the above, I am delighted once again, to commend Danab Brigade for sticking appropriately to the objectives, responsibility, disciplines, values and moral obligation that was created for, as well as maintaining and advancing its operations aimed at eradicating terrorists across Somalia and supporting Somalia achieves its strategic goal towards peaceful, inclusive, stable democratic nation.

I wish you a law abiding, honest, adaptive, responsible and successful Special Force that brings about the desirable future state of Somalia (Inclusive, peaceful and stable prosperous democratic nation).

By Former Danab Commander. Maj. Jeeniqaar Sheikh Omar"

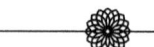

APPENDIX: PICTURES

[**Fig. 18:** President Hassan Sheikh Mohamud and Author.

[**Fig. 19:** From right to left: Prime Minister Abdiwali M. Ali Gaas, President Sheikh Sharif Sheikh Ahmed, Speaker of the Parliament Sharif Hasan Sheikh Adan, Minister of Defense Hussein Arab Issa. Backrow from right to left: author of the book, Colonel Mohamed Ali Abiikar Dalab ADC of President and Door chief protocol prime minster office.

[Fig. 20: From right to left: Secretary of State Hillary Rodham Clinton, President Sheikh Shariif Sheikh Ahmed.
SOURCE: http://2009-2017.state.gov/secretary/20092013clinton/rm/2009a/08/126956.htm

[Fig. 21: From right to left: President of Jubaland State Ahmad Mohamed Islaan, Prime Minister Omar Abdirashid Ali Sharmarke, President Hassan Sheikh Mohamud, Secretary of State John Kerry, Southwest President Sharif Hasan Sheikh Adan, President of Puntland Abdiweli Ali Gas.
SOURCE: https://commons.wikimedia.org/wiki/File:Secretary_Kerry_Stands_with_President_Hassan_Sheikh_Mohamud,_Prime_Minister_Omar_Abdirashid_Ali_Sharmarke,_and_Three_Regional_Leaders_in_Somalia_%2817354857586%29.jpg

[Fig. 22: From right to left: Lifty U.N. special envoy to Somalia Francois F, President Abdulahi Yusuf Ahmed. Back Left: President Abdulahi Farabadan, author of the book. (Photo credit should read STRINGER/AFP via Getty Images)

[Fig. 23: From Right to Left: President Abdiqasim Salad Hassan, President Abdulahi Yusuf Ahmed. In the back: author of the Book.

BIBLIOGRAPHY

BOOKS:

Yuusuf, Cabdullaahi Axmad. *Halgan iyo Hagardaamo: Taariikh Nololeed (Struggle and Conspiracy: A Memoir)*. (Sweden: Scansom Publishers, 2012)

Aimé, Elsa González. "*The Security Issues Behind the Ethiopian Intervention in Somalia (2006-2009)*". State and Societal Challenges in the Horn of Africa, edited by Alexandra Magnólia Dias, Centro de Estudos Internacionais, 2013,

Civins, Braden. *Ethiopia's Intervention in Somalia, 2006-2009*. (Seoul, South Korea: Yonsei University, 2010)

WEBSITE:

Human Rights Watch, "So Much to Fear: War Crimes and the Devastation of Somalia," December 8, 2008, https://www.hrw.org/report/2008/12/08/so-much-fear/war-crimes-and-devastation-somalia

News 22 June 2005 IRIN News https://www.thenewhumanitarian.org/report/55029/somalia-tfg-preparing-begin-operating-jowhar

IRIN News, "Somalia: TFG Preparing to Begin Operating from Jowhar," The New Humanitarian, accessed January 25, 2025, https://www.thenewhumanitarian.org/report/55029/somalia-tfg-preparing-begin-operating-jowhar.

Xan Rice and agencies in Nairobi, "*Somali president escapes car bomb suicide attack*," The Guardian, September 19, 2006, https://www.theguardian.com/world/2006/sep/19/mainsection.international

https://www.thenewhumanitarian.org/report/55029/somalia-tfg-preparing-begin-operating-jowhar

U.S. Department of State. 2009. "Remarks from Secretary Clinton." U.S. Department of State Archive (2009-2013). Accessed March 31, 2025. https://2009-2017.state.gov/secretary/20092013clinton/rm/2009a/08/126956.htm

Voice of America. (2017, March 26). "Al-Shabab Seizes Key Somali Town After Ethiopians Pull Out." VOA News. Retrieved from https://www.voanews.com/a/al-shabab-seizes-key-somali-town-after-ethiopians-pull-out/3794065.html

Dahir, A. (2015, December). Who's afraid of General Gabre? Hiiraan Online. Retrieved from https://www.hiiraan.com/op4/2015/dec/102847/who_s_afraid_of_general_gabre.aspx

Global Construction Review. (2019, October 24). Rosatom signs agreement for nuclear science centre in Ethiopia. Retrieved from https://www.globalconstructionreview.com/rosatom-signs-agreement-for-nuclear-science-centre-in-ethiopia/

VOA News. (2017, March 27). Al-Shabab Seizes Key Somali Town After Ethiopians Pull Out. Retrieved from https://www.voanews.com/a/al-shabab-seizes-key-somali-town-after-ethiopians-pull-out/3794065.html

Al Jazeera. (2016, November 11). Al-Shabab regains land as Ethiopia pulls troops. Retrieved from https://www.aljazeera.com/amp/features/2016/11/11/al-shabab-regains-land-as-ethiopia-pulls-troops

Support Our Troops. "Somalia." Accessed March 31, 2025. https://supportourtroops.org/news/2610-somalia

Africa Defense Forum. "Somalia's Quick Strike Danab Forces Wage Fierce Battle Against al-Shabaab." September 2023. Accessed March 31, 2025. https://adf-magazine.com/2023/09/somalias-quick-strike-danab-forces-wage-fierce-battle-against-al-shabaa/

Myers, Meghann. "Secret US Base in Somalia is Getting Some Emergency Runway Repairs." Air Force Times, October 4, 2018. Accessed March 31, 2025.

https://www.airforcetimes.com/news/your-air-force/2018/10/04/secret-us-base-in-somalia-is-getting-some-emergency-runway-repairs/

U.S. Embassy in Somalia. "United States Increases Security Assistance Through Construction of SNA Bases." Accessed March 31, 2025.
https://so.usembassy.gov/united-states-increases-security-assistance-through-construction-of-sna-bases/

Legros, Joe. "Somali Danab Forces Make History at Justified Accord 2024." U.S. Army, March 21, 2024. Accessed March 31, 2025.
https://www.army.mil/article-amp/274705/somali_danab_forces_make_history_at_justified_accord_2024

Sheikh Omar, Maj. Jeeniqaar. Puntlandes. "Highest Commendation to Danab Brigade the special force of SNA." Accessed March 31, 2025.
https://www.puntlandes.com/?p=78703

INDEX

A

Aadan Dhagah · 47
Aadan Isse Hadde · 47
Aan · 62
Abdalla Deerow · 64
    Abdalla Derow Isack · 63
Abdi · vii, xxvii, 46, 62, 98, 136, 186, 187, 188, 189
    Abdi Qeybdiid · vii, 98, 186, 188, 189
AbdiAsiis Farah Mohamed · 82, 84
    AbdiAsis · 62
    Abdiaziz · 135, 285
Abdifatah Mohamed Hassan · 77, 82, 83, 111
Abdikafi · 172, 180
Abdikari Farah · 48
Abdikarim · 46, 53, 60, 61, 284
    Abdikarim Khaliif Abdi Dhala · 46
    Abdikarim Laqanyo · 53
    Abdikarim Omar · 61
Abdikasim Hassan · 113, 124
Abdilatif Farah Istakiin · 79
Abdinasir · 260
Abdiqafaar Yaasiin Farah Yaaquub · 47
    Abdiqafar Yaasiin Farah Yaquub · 78
Abdirahman Farah Gure · 71
    Abdirahman Farah Noor · 83
    Abdirahman Farah Nuur · 77
    Abdirahman Jeeniqaar · xxiii
Abdirashid · 81, 82, 111, 124, 125, 136, 293
    Abdirashid Dheere · 81
    Abdirashid Dhere · 111
    Abdirashid Hersi · 81, 82, 111, 124, 136
    Abdirashid Hersi Mohamed · 81, 82, 111, 124
Abdirizak · v, xxii, 44, 46, 48, 51, 107, 108
    Abdirizak Afguduud · 51
    Abdirizak Diriye · v, xxii
    Abdirizak Durqun · 46
    Abdirizak Mohamud Gaylan · 46
Abdisaed Farah Gur · 79
Abdishakur Ali Jariiban · 46
Abdiwahid Lugey · 110
Abdiweli Abbi Abdille · 77
    Abdiweli Fadhigo · 111
    Abdiweli Osman Warsame · 77, 111
Abdulahi Ahmed Abdi Jubba Koole · 138
    Abdulahi Yusuf · xxvii, xxix, 294
Abdulkadir Ali Yusuf · 46, 81
    Abdulkadir Ali Yusuf Lugey · 46
    Abdulkadir Ali Yuusuf · 63
Abdullahi · 36, 38, 40, 41, 47, 50, 59, 86, 107, 111, 112, 120, 147, 168, 180, 197, 198, 199, 233, 236, 238, 245, 285
    Abdullahi Boru · 233
    Abdullahi Dheere · 47
    Abdullahi Dool · 180
    Abdullahi Farabadane · 47
    Abdullahi Koolo · 112
    Abdullahi Mohamed Abdi · 111, 112
    Abdullahi Yusuf · 38, 40, 41, 50, 59, 86, 107, 120, 147, 168, 197, 198, 238, 245, 285
    Abdullahi Yusuf Ahmed · 50, 59, 197, 238, 245
    Abdullahi Yusuf Ahmedand Mohamed Omar Habeeb · 59
Abdulsalam Yusuf Ahmed · 86
Abduwak · 44, 54, 55, 58
Abesaley · 43
Abgaalow · 51
Abgalow · 51
Abqaale · 47
Abqale · 43
Abudwak · v, 55, 58
Abuja · 49
Abwaan Mohamed Dhagafe Ilmi · 54
Adaado · 98
Addis Ababa · viii, 144, 152, 163, 187, 188, 233, 234, 238
Aden · vii, 46, 70, 71, 210, 270
    Aden Dhagah · 70, 71
    Aden Isse · 70, 71
    Aden Isse Ali Hade · 70
Adolf Hitler · 106
Adow Humey Weheliye · 77, 83, 111
Afdalow · 46, 62, 76, 78, 83

Afghanistan · 149, 269
Afgoi · 269
Afgooye · 111, 202
Afgoye · 110, 111, 112
Afgub · 55
Afmadow · 212, 213
AFP · 294
Africa · 99, 184, 190, 233, 235, 237, 252, 253, 270, 277, 281, 297
  Africa Defense Forum · 252, 297
  Africa Jendayi Frazer · 184
African Union · xi, xxxii, 49, 93, 159, 164, 178, 207, 210, 228, 229, 230, 231, 234, 237
  African Union (AU) · 49, 210, 231
  African Union Mission · xi, xxxii, 228
  African Union Peace · 207
  African Union Transition Mission · xi, 207
Africom Command · xxx
Afweyne · 172
Ahmed · 46, 47, 62, 70, 75, 78, 84, 123, 197, 198, 217, 224, 238, 245, 284, 292, 293, 294
  Ahmed Abdi Guled Yey · 78
  Ahmed Abdulaahi Yusuf Ahmed Yey · 78
  Ahmed Awle · 78, 84
  Ahmed Bow Bowle · 47
  Ahmed Elmi Dhagow · 70
  Ahmed Gurey · 123
  Ahmed Madobe · 224, 238
Aimé · 100, 144, 145, 146, 147, 148, 149, 150, 151, 153, 154, 155, 161, 162, 163, 164, 167, 178, 179, 296
Air Force Times · 252, 297
AK · 64, 78, 83, 84, 128, 136, 175, 225, 227
AL · viii, 194, 196, 214, 216, 238, 281, 290
Al Jazeera · 228, 229, 230, 231, 233, 234, 235, 297
Al Qaeda · 217, 252
Al Shabaab · viii, 159, 196, 218, 219, 228, 229, 230, 236, 252
Al-Americi · 226
Alexandra Magnólia Dias · 100, 144, 145, 146, 147, 148, 149, 150, 151, 153, 154, 155, 161, 162, 163, 164, 167, 178, 179, 296
Ali Duguf · 46
  Ali Farah · 83
  Ali Gaas · 292
  Ali Mohamed Gedi · 100
  Ali Muhammad Gedi · 56
  Ali Muse Gabayre · 83
Ali Qaataa · 83
Ali Waranle · 55
Ali Yussuf Abdullahi · 236
Alitihad Alislam · 53
Al-Ittihad Al-Islami · 107
Al-Qaeda · xxxii, 211, 256
Alshabaab · 161, 167, 207, 219, 268
Al-Shabaab · xvii, xxv, xxxii, 175, 192, 197, 210, 211, 217, 218, 219, 220, 221, 222, 223, 224, 225, 226, 227, 228, 230, 233, 238, 255, 256, 261, 262, 263, 267, 268, 275, 276
  Al-Shabaab Islamist · 211
  Al-Shabaab Revenge Attack · 268
  Al-Shabaab Seizes Key Somali Town After Ethiopians Pull Out · 230
Alshabab · 101, 150, 158, 159, 166, 219, 284, 285
Al-Shabab · 165, 228, 229, 230, 231, 233, 234, 297
  Al-Shabab Seizes Key Somali Town After Ethiopians Pull Out · 165, 228, 229, 297
AMISOM · viii, ix, xi, xxxii, 42, 173, 175, 178, 186, 199, 200, 204, 206, 207, 208, 209, 210, 211, 212, 213, 217, 228, 229, 230, 232, 234, 235, 245, 246, 247, 257, 258, 259, 260
  AMISOM Ethiopian · 228
  AMISOM Force Commander · 209, 210
  AMISOM Force Commanders · 209
  AMISOM Force Headquarters · 210
  AMISOM Operations Burundi · 209
  AMISOM Sector · ix, 212, 258, 259
  AMISOM Sector One · ix, 258, 259
  AMISOM Sector One Presented · ix, 259
  AMISOM Ugandan · 200
Anadolu Agency · 235, 236
Andrew Gutti · 209, 210
Anole · 252, 258
Ansaloti Public Hospital · xxviii
Anthony Lukwago Mbuusi · 209
AoR · 210
Arab League · 39, 159
Arbiska · 110, 111, 121
Area of Responsibility · 209, 210
Army Col. Eric L · 271
  Army Times · 252
  Army Wehrmacht · 106, 107
ARPCT · xi, 91, 92, 93

ARS · 101, 178, 196
Asha Uun Laye · 70
Asho · 65, 124
    Asho Un · 124
    Asho Unlaye · 124
Asiya Mohamed Hassan · 125
    Asiya Mohamud Hassan · 46
Asmara · 196
Assistant Secretary Phee · 253
ATMIS · xi, 192, 207, 209, 210
    ATMIS Sector Four Area of Responsibility · 210
    ATMIS Ugandan · 209
AU · xi, 39, 49, 50, 87, 95, 178, 192, 210, 211, 217, 228, 231, 232, 237, 246, 247, 286
    AU Mission · 50, 246, 247
AUN · 55, 62, 81
AUSSOM · 192
Awdheegle · ix, 254, 255, 256, 257, 258, 259, 260, 261, 262, 264, 266, 267, 268
    Awdheegle Bridge Operation · ix, 268
    Awdheegle District · ix, 255
    Awdheegle Operation · ix, 257, 258, 266
    Awdheegle Operation Meeting Convened · ix, 257
    Awdheegle Operation Planning Meeting Held · ix, 258
Aweis · 137
Awil Abbi Abdille · 83
Awil Dhiig Sokeeye · 75

B

Babafemi Badejo · 38
Badejo · 39
Baidoa · vi, vii, xxxii, 40, 42, 44, 50, 60, 62, 63, 64, 65, 66, 67, 68, 69, 75, 79, 83, 84, 85, 86, 87, 93, 94, 95, 96, 97, 98, 99, 100, 108, 110, 111, 113, 121, 122, 124, 138, 149, 150, 155, 157, 158, 179, 209, 210, 237, 270
    Baidoa Airport · 63
    Baidoa Palace · 121
    Baidoa Presidential Palace · 121
Bakara Market · 285
Bakool · 58, 91, 109, 151, 210, 228, 235, 237
Balanbale · 44
Balcad · 98, 202
Baledogle Air Base · 251

Bali Busle · 134
Bali Doogle · 110, 265, 266, 269
Bali Doogle Airport Military Base · 266
Balibusle · xxix
Balidoogle · ix, 254, 257, 264, 266, 268, 269, 272
Balidoogle Airport Military Base · 272
Balidoogle M · 254, 268
Balidoogle Military Airport Base · 268
Balihigis · 128, 129
Banaadir · 45
Banadir · 65, 198, 209
Bancroft · 253, 257, 258
Bancroft Global Development · 257
Bandiiradley · 91, 98
Bandiradley · 100
Bardaale · 66
Bardhere · 213
Bareere · 258
Bari · 107
Barre · xxix, 92, 97, 272
Bashiir Suuley · xv
Battalion Commander · 76
Battle Group · 209
Battlefield · ix, 274
Bay · 58, 67, 91, 97, 107, 151, 178, 210, 228
Baydhabo · 47, 60
BBC · 85
    BBC Somali · 85
Bedford · 228
Beledweyne · ix, 44, 49, 51, 52, 53, 76, 98, 162, 168, 210, 211, 275
Belet Weyne · 100
Belete Molla · 192
Berhan Hailu · 100
Bethuel Kiplagat · 39
Bihanga · 243, 244, 245
Bihin Valley · 107
Black Hawk Down · 271
BM · 173, 175, 178
    BM Multiple Katyusha · 175
BMA · xi, 264, 266
Boosaaso · 47
    Boosaso · 48
Bosaso · 53, 151, 157
Bosaso of Puntland · 151
Bosaso Puntland · 157
Bossaso · v, 67
Braden · 92, 93, 101, 156, 157, 296

BRICS · 191
Brig · 209
Brigade · vi, xxxii, 75, 78, 79, 84, 107, 108, 109, 110, 251, 252, 253, 277, 290, 291
    Brigade Commander · 110
    Brigade Defense · vi, 107
    Brigades · 98
Buloburte · 55, 63, 98
Burhaan Warsame · 230
Burhakaba · 97
Burhan Nabadoon · 137
Burtinle · xxix
Burukur · 53
Burundi · xxxii, 207, 208, 209, 210, 211, 218
    Burundian · 209, 210
    Burundian African Union (AU) · 210
Bush · 184, 270
Bussul · 59
Buuhoodle · 107
Buur Hakaba · 100

C

Caasi · 111
Cabdullaahi Axmad · 84, 85, 147, 192, 296
Cali Duguf · 77
Camel Herders · v, xxix
Camp Baledogle · 252, 253
Captain · 111, 124, 125, 136, 180, 265, 271
    Captain Abdirashid Hassan Diriye Afgub · 180
    Captain Dylan Sharrock · 265, 271
    Captain Ryan · 271
CCC · 179
Ceel Baraf · 210
Ceelbuur · 236
Central Somalia · viii, 230, 231, 233, 234
Centro · 100, 144, 145, 146, 147, 148, 149, 150, 151, 153, 154, 155, 161, 162, 163, 164, 167, 178, 179, 296
China · viii, 145, 190, 191
    China of Africa · viii, 190
Clapham · 149
Col Hiif Ali Taar · 51
    Col Nelson · 258, 259
    Col Timo · 177
    Col. Abdirisaaq Mohamed Hirsi · 62
    Col. Abdirizak Mohamed Hersi · 136
    Col. Abdirizak Muse Hirsi Indhol · 54

Col. Abdiwahid Mohamud Hassan · 46, 76, 110, 129
Col. Abdiwahid Mohamud Hassan Lugey · 46, 76
Col. Abdiwahid Mohamud Hassan Lugey Chief Protocol · 76
Col. Abdullahi Yusuf · 75, 128
Col. Abudwak · 121
Col. Ali Abdi Guled · 138
Col. Barre Adam Shire · 97
Col. Barre Hiiraale · 97
Col. Bashir · 201
Col. Beder · 238
Col. Bussul · 59
Col. Dahir Mohamed Hersi · 46
Col. Fardaale · 57
Col. Gaalkayo Warsame Olol · 171
Col. Gebregzabher Alemseged · 69, 110, 168, 169, 172, 182, 183
Col. Hassan Gacmeyo · 55
Col. Hassan Hussein Adan · 78
Col. Hassan Nuur Ali Shuute · 198
Col. Hiif Ali Taar · 98
Col. Jama Bashir · 201
Col. Jay B · 271
Col. Jean Luc Habarugira · 210
Col. Jigre Yusuf Ahmed Yey · 62, 84
Col. Med Med Deer · 67
Col. Mohamed Abdulkadir Hersi · 78
Col. Mohamed Adan Bidaar · 48
Col. Mohamed Adan Kofi · 198
Col. Mohamed Adan Koofi · 198
Col. Qase · 54, 58
Col. Tafsay · 189
Col. Tesfay · 171, 173, 176
Colonel Abdiwahid Mohamud Hassan · v, xx
Colonel Mohamed Adan Bidaar · 44
Colonel Mohamed Ali Abiikar Dalab ADC · 292
Colonel Osman Doubad · 210
Combat Engineering · 259
Command · 253, 265
    Commander · vii, xviii, 76, 77, 172, 180, 189, 209, 210, 258, 263, 265, 269, 291
    Commanders · vi, viii, 52, 62, 114, 209, 210, 220
Commissioner · 185, 188, 236
Company Commander · 269
Con Gabre · 189

Coordination of Humanitarian Affairs (OCHA) · 146
Coordination of Humanitarian Affairs Somalia · 156
Counter IED · 262, 263, 264
Counter Insurgency Terrorism · 277
Courts Union · 91, 92, 96, 143, 217, 246
Cpt. Abdirashid Hassan Dirie Aley · 55
Cpt. Ali Mohamed Artan · 55
Critics of ENDF · 167
Cuba · 152
Cuban · 281

D

Daahir Mire Jibriil · 47
Dadaab · 211
Dahir · vii, 46, 61, 63, 169, 172, 174, 180, 182, 183, 261, 297
Dahir Farur · 63
Dahir Faruur · 46
Dahir Mire · 61
Daish · 290
Danab · ix, xxvii, xxx, xxxiii, 171, 251, 252, 253, 254, 255, 256, 257, 258, 259, 260, 261, 262, 263, 264, 265, 266, 267, 268, 269, 270, 271, 272, 273, 274, 275, 276, 277, 283, 284, 290, 291, 297, 298
Danab Army · 275
Danab Brigade · 251, 252, 253, 290, 291, 298
Danab Brigade Forces · 291
Danab Commander · ix, 258, 263, 265, 291
Danab Composition · 254
Danab Counter IED · 262, 263, 264
Danab Counter IEDs · 263
Danab IED · 262, 264
Danab Mechanized MU · 254
Danab Population · ix, 273
Danab Presented · ix, 260
Danab Special Force Commander · xxx
Danab Special Forces · ix, xxvii, 254, 271, 277
Danbacaad · 47
Dayniile District · 61
Daynile · 60, 202
Daynuunaay · 66, 97
Daynuunay · 67

Dayr · 134
DC · 120
Defense Department · 252
Defense Minister · 96, 97, 99
Defense Minister Col. Barre Hiiraale · 99
Department of State · 160, 297
Department of State Archive · 160, 297
Deputy Defense Minister Salad Ali Jeele · 99
Deputy Force Commander Operations · 209
Deputy Force Commanders · 210
Deputy Intelligence Commander · 54
Derg · 233
Development · ix, xi, 49, 57, 93, 159, 252, 253
Development (IGAD) · 49
Development IGAD · 57
Dhagaweyne Kirtan · 78
Dhagax Tur · 123
Dhame Abdulkadir Jama Abbi · 79
Dhanaane · 263
Dhanbacaad · 47
Dharqo · 99
Dhashike · 128
Dhusamareeb · xxvii
Dhusomareeb · 44
Dhuuso Mareeb · 98
Dhuusomareeb · 52
Dick Olum · 209
Diinsoor · 99
Dinsoor · 100, 236
Diraa Hussein Fagaase · 46
Djibouti · xxxii, 49, 56, 57, 61, 101, 127, 145, 159, 178, 182, 196, 197, 207, 208, 209, 210, 211, 217, 277, 281
Doollo · 134
Door Moallim Abdirahman · 111
Dr. Mohamud Yusuf Wayrah · 47
Dr. Omar Abdi Bare · xv
Driver Vehicle · 77
Driver Vehicle No · 77
Dylan Sharrock · 265, 271

E

Eagle · 260
East Africa · 163, 208, 228, 237, 253
East Mogadishu · 98
EAT · 212
EDF · xi, 244, 247

Egypt · 157
El Ali · 63, 65
    El Bur · viii, 165, 166, 228, 229, 230
    El Bur District · viii, 228
    ElAli · 55, 65
Elders · 222
Elgal · 51, 52
Elsa González · 100, 144, 145, 146, 147, 148, 149, 150, 151, 153, 154, 155, 161, 162, 163, 164, 167, 178, 179, 296
El-Saliin · 262
    El-Saliin Operation · 262
    El-Salim · 263
Embassy · 254, 298
ENDF · vi, vii, xi, xvii, xix, 43, 69, 93, 94, 96, 101, 114, 120, 130, 135, 143, 145, 147, 148, 150, 152, 153, 154, 155, 157, 158, 159, 160, 161, 163, 165, 166, 167, 168, 172, 173, 175, 176, 177, 178, 179, 181, 185, 189, 190, 191, 196, 202, 207, 229, 232, 235, 244, 281
    ENDF Emerged · vii, 161
    ENDF Operation · 207
    ENDF Painted · vi, 120
Ereg · 223
Eritrea · 57, 119, 145, 196
    Eritrean · 144, 164
    Eritreans · 101
Estudos Internacionais · 100, 144, 145, 146, 147, 148, 149, 150, 151, 153, 154, 155, 161, 162, 163, 164, 167, 178, 179, 296
Ethiopia · vi-viii, xvii, xix, xxi, xxii, xxv, xxviii, xxix, xxxi, xxxii, 38, 42, 43, 48, 49, 53, 57, 69, 87, 94, 95, 99, 100-102, 112, 113, 119, 120, 127, 129, 130, 143-145, 148, 151, 152, 155, 157, 158, 160-165, 168, 169-171, 178-181, 183-193, 197, 202, 203, 207, 208, 209, 217, 218, 222, 225, 228-235, 238, 244-247, 281, 286, 287, 288, 297
    Ethiopia Denied Violations · vi, 120
    Ethiopia Launches Attack · 100
    Ethiopia Withdrawal · vii, 178
    Ethiopian AMISOM · 228
    Ethiopian Defence Force · xi, xxix, 243
    Ethiopian Defence Forces · xxix
    Ethiopian Defense Forces · 165
    Ethiopian Embassy · 120
    Ethiopian Forces · vii, 165, 175, 177, 189
    Ethiopian Forces Confrontation Over
    Indiscriminate Bombardments · vii, 175
    Ethiopian Forces Over · vii, 177
    Ethiopian Generals · 287
    Ethiopian Government · 158
    Ethiopian Influence · vii, 168
    Ethiopian Intelligence · vii, 173
    Ethiopian Intervention · vi, 95, 100, 144, 145, 146, 147, 148, 149, 150, 151, 153, 154, 155, 161, 162, 163, 164, 167, 178, 179, 296
    Ethiopian Invasion · 153
    Ethiopian Military · 156
    Ethiopian National Defence Force · xi, xvii
    Ethiopian National Defense Force · 50, 68, 120, 162, 192, 235
    Ethiopian National Defense Force (ENDF) · 120, 235
    Ethiopian National Defense Forces · 68, 162, 192
    Ethiopian NDF · 163, 178, 231
    Ethiopian Somali · 144
    Ethiopian State · 144
Ethiopians · 137, 166, 175, 176, 177, 180, 181, 182, 225, 228, 229, 230
EU · ix, xi, 39, 100, 129, 145, 159, 243, 244, 245, 246, 247, 257, 258, 259, 260, 261, 266, 270, 286
    EU Presentation · ix, 259
European · xi, xxxii, 224, 242, 243, 244, 245, 246, 277
    European Training Mission · 246
    European Union Training Mission · xi, xxxii, 242, 245
EUTM · ix, xi, xxxii, 240, 242, 243, 244, 245, 246, 247
    EUTM Somalia · 243, 244, 245, 246, 247
    EUTM Somalia Mission · 246

F

Fadhigo · 77
Fadhiyare · 44, 48, 51, 53, 60, 66
Fadumo Wehliye · 182
Fafadun · 213
Fanah Isse Aley · 46
FAO · 236
Farah Abdikadir Diriye Warfaa · 46
    Farah Ahmed Dari · 62

Farah Caan · 46
Farah Moallim Mohamud · 162
Fareer · 77, 83
Farey Geesood · 46
Farmajo · 237
Federal Government · vi, xi, 97, 107, 148, 192, 198, 199, 217, 226, 237, 243, 244, 257, 287
    Federal Government of Somalia · xi, 148, 192, 217, 237, 243, 257, 287
    Federal Government of Somalia (FGS) · 243
    Federal Members States · 228
feer · 48, 53, 60, 66
Ferocious War Between · vi, 108
FGS · xi, 179, 224, 243, 247
Finnish · xxviii, xxix
Fire · 130
Fisaha Shawel · 189
Force Spokesman · 211
Forces · vi, xxxii, 108, 153, 187, 209, 212, 213, 231, 252, 271, 272, 277, 291, 297, 298
Foreign Fighters · viii, 226
    Foreign Policy · 251
Francis Fukuyama · 269
French · 211, 281

G

Gaalkacyo · 43
Gaandaa · 108
Gabayre · 256, 261
Gabre · 173, 181, 183, 286
    Gabre Yoannes Abate · 181
    Gabre Yohannes Abate · 181
Gacamey · 47
Galcad · 275, 276
Galgaduud · 75, 98, 210, 233
    Galgala Mountains of Bari · 107
    Galgudud · 56, 151, 165, 228
    Galguduud · 158, 275
Galhamur · xxix
Galkacyo · xxx, 201
Galkaio · xxvii, xxix, 43, 44, 45, 48, 57, 165, 201
    Galkayo · 138
    Galkkaio · 151
Galmudug · 229
Garadoxo · 54
Garcad · 46, 62, 76, 77, 110, 172

Garlogubey · 47
Garoowe · 43, 48
    Garowe · xxxii, 40, 41, 45, 50, 68, 69, 95, 107, 125, 126, 134
    Garowe Airport · 40
Gaydho Hassan Hashi · 46
Gedi · 49
Gedo · 58, 95, 98, 158, 178, 198, 212, 228, 236
    Gedo Region · 212
Gen · vii, ix, 54, 55, 179, 186, 198, 209, 210, 282, 284
    Gen Abdikadir Sheikh Ali Dini · 284
    Gen Abdikarim Yusuf Adan · 284
    Gen Diini · 284
    Gen Gordon · vii, ix, 179, 282
    Gen. Mohamed Adan Bidar · 54
    Gen. Omar Dheere · 55
Gendershe · 263
General · v, vii, ix, xv, xviii, 38, 46, 51, 52, 53, 56, 57, 58, 59, 62, 65, 66, 67, 75, 76, 77, 78, 79, 82, 83, 97, 98, 99, 106, 107, 110, 111, 121, 125, 137, 138, 150, 159, 162, 163, 164, 165, 166, 169, 170, 171, 172, 174, 179, 180, 181, 182, 183, 185, 187, 188, 189, 198, 200, 201, 209, 210, 243, 259, 260, 261, 264, 281, 282, 284, 285, 286, 287, 288, 297
    General Abdi Qeybdiid · vii, 185, 187, 188, 189
    General Abdi Qeybdiid Prevents Ethiopian Intelligence · vii, 185
    General Abdirahman Turyare · 198
    General Abdirizak Afgudud · 110
    General Abdirizak Afguduud · 51
    General Ade Muse · 97, 98
    General Ade Muse Hersi · 97
    General Ahmed Addoye · 66
    General Aideed · 53, 125
    General Awil · 51, 75, 76, 77, 111, 121, 137, 138, 165, 170, 171
    General Awil Ahmed Yusuf · 51
    General Awil Dhiig Sokeeye · 138
    General Awil Dhiig-sokeeye · 121, 170
    General Bashir Goobe · 67, 138
    General Bashir Mohamed Jama · 137
    General Dahir Aden Elmi Indho-Qarsho · 171
    General Dahir Elmi · 261

General Daud · 56, 57, 58, 65
General Duty Of State House Abdulahi Daahir · 172
General Friedrich Paulus · 106, 107
General Gabre · vii, 169, 172, 174, 180, 181, 182, 183, 189, 286, 297
General Gabre Yohanes · 286
General Gabre Yohannes Abate · vii, 180, 181, 189
General Gacmoduule · 166
General Gordon · 150, 159, 179, 281, 282, 284, 285
General Gordon Military Base · 179, 282
General Indho Ade · 200, 201
General Indho Qarshe · 288
General Jigre Yusuf Ahmed · 79
General Madoobe · 259
General Mohamed Ali Buh · xv
General Mohamed Ali Samatar · 137, 284
General Mohamed Nor · 79, 82
General Mukhtar · 98, 162, 163, 164, 165
General Mukhtar Hussein Afrah · 98
General Nur Shirbow · 137, 138
General Nur Shirbow Somalia · 137
General Odowaa · 260, 282
General Odowaa Yusuf Raghe · 282
General Osman Hassan Ali · 46, 62, 76, 78, 83
General Qeybdiid · 188, 189
General Saed Dhere · 52, 53
General Saed Mohamed Hersi · 110
General Salah · v, ix, xviii, 285, 286, 287
General Salah Jama · v, ix, xviii, 285, 287
General Salah Jama Hassan · v, ix, xviii, 285
General Tawane · 98
General Timoshenko · 107
General Youhanis · 189
George Washington University · 252
German · 106, 107
Getachew Reda · 234
Getty Images · 294
Ghion Hotel · 144
Gina Gina · 112
Global Construction Review · 192, 297
Global Development · 257
Goldogob · xxvii, xxviii
Goobe Deputy Somalia Police Commander · 137
Gordon · 159, 281, 282, 284, 285

Gorgor · 171
Government · vi, viii, xxxii, 97, 101, 149, 167, 192, 211, 217, 218, 222, 223, 224, 226, 237, 243, 246, 257, 287
Government of Kenya · 211
Governor Mohamed Omar Habeeb · 98
Grad · 155
Greater Somalia · 144
Gu · 134
Gulf of Aden · 270
Gurac Joomo · 55
Gururub · 46
Gutale · 166
Guulwade Jaaweel · 77, 78

H

Haaji Sayn · 138
Habaallo Barbaar · 99
Habeeb · 60, 61
Hagaa · 134
Hagaayo · 134
Haji Sayn · 138
Halane · ix, 179, 182, 236, 247, 257, 258
Halane Stakeholders Meeting · ix, 258
Harakat · 247
Hararyale · 201
Harawe Ali Jiriban · 46
Hargeisa · 158, 284
Hasan Gurey Warsame · 54, 58
Hassan · v, xxv, 46, 54, 58, 78, 83, 109, 198, 233, 237, 251, 275, 285, 292, 293, 294
Hassan Abshir Farah Waraabe · 83
Hassan Ali Shuute · 198
Hassan Dhooye · v, xxv
Hassan Gurey · 54, 58, 78
Hassan Gurey Warsame · 54, 58, 78
Hassan Mohamed Mohamud · 251
Hassan Tuure · 275
Hawadle · 49, 53
Hawo Abdi · 113
Hawo Dirie Gehle · xxviii
Hefner · 271
High-level US · 157, 161
Hiiraan · 48, 49, 51, 52, 53, 56, 75, 98, 151, 162, 163, 169, 172, 174, 178, 180, 182, 183, 198, 210, 211, 230, 231, 297
Hiiraan Online · 169, 172, 174, 180, 182, 183, 297

Hillary Rodham Clinton · 159, 293
Hilton Hotel · viii, 188, 238
Hiraan · 55, 158, 210
Hiran · 228, 236
Hollywood · 255
Honorable · 55, 63, 64, 75, 83
Honorable Abdalla Deerow · 63, 64
Honorable Abdalla Deerow Isack · 63
Honorable Member of Parliament Abaadir · 55
Honorable Sharif Hassan Sheikh Adam · 75
Hoosingo · 213
Hope University · xxx
Horn · xxi, 100, 101, 144, 145, 146, 147, 148, 149, 150, 151, 153, 154, 155, 161, 162, 163, 164, 167, 178, 179, 183, 184, 190, 192, 229, 232, 233, 235, 237, 270, 281, 296
Horn of Africa · xxi, 100, 101, 144, 145, 146, 147, 148, 149, 150, 151, 153, 154, 155, 161, 162, 163, 164, 167, 178, 179, 183, 184, 190, 192, 232, 233, 235, 237, 270, 296
Horn of African · 232
Hotel Lafweyn · 122, 124, 125
Houmed · 211
HQ · 254
Hudur · 65, 85, 98, 165, 235, 236, 237
Human Resource Management Office · 288
Human Rights Watch · 35, 87, 91, 94, 96, 101, 102, 114, 119, 120, 126, 149, 150, 154, 157, 160, 184, 202, 203, 282, 287, 296
Humanitarian Access · vii, 155
Humanitarian Partners · 237
Huriwaa · 202
Hussein Aideed · 124, 125, 127
Hussein Ali Saylaan · 46, 110, 189
Hussein Ali Saylan · 82
Hussein Ali Yalaan · 79
Hussein Farah Aideed · 124
Hussein Huub Sireed · 46
Hussein Jabiri · 56, 57

I

ICU · v, vi, xi, 42, 43, 50, 91, 92, 93, 94, 95, 96, 97, 98, 99, 100, 101, 102, 107, 108, 109, 110, 119, 126, 143, 144, 145, 147, 148, 152, 157, 158, 160, 162, 170, 196, 217
ICU Forces · vi, 107, 148
ICU Forces Melted · vi, 148

Idaale · 98
IDP · 151, 153
   IDPs · xi, 93, 147, 153, 156, 219, 237
IED · xi, 262, 263, 264
   IEDs · 209, 257, 261, 262, 263, 264, 268
IGAD · xi, 49, 50, 87, 127, 145, 159, 164, 182, 225, 238
   IGAD Special Envoy · 182
Iidaale · 99
Iidale · 107
Improvised Explosive Devices · 209, 262
Indho Ade · 200, 201
India · 191
Infantry · 260
Intelligence · xi, xxvii, 54, 110, 114, 172, 257, 258
   Intelligence Chief (AUN) · 110
   Intelligence Commander · 54
Intergovernmental Authority · xi, 49, 93, 159
Internal Displacement Monitoring Centre · 151
International Court of Justice · 211
International Development · 147
International Media · vi, 95
Iraq · 149
IRIN · 37, 38, 39, 49, 50, 56, 61, 296
   IRIN News · 37, 38, 39, 49, 56, 61, 296
Ishaku Mshelia · 236
ISIS · xi, 290
Islam · 181
Islamic · xi, xxxi, xxxii, 66, 67, 75, 90, 91, 92, 96, 100, 107, 108, 109, 110, 111, 113, 119, 130, 143, 149, 159, 168, 181, 217, 226, 230, 244, 246
   Islamic Conference · 159
   Islamic Court Union ICU · 217
   Islamic Court Unions · 67, 75
   Islamic Courts · xi, xxxi, xxxii, 90, 91, 92, 96, 100, 107, 108, 109, 110, 111, 113, 119, 130, 143, 149, 168, 217, 244, 246
   Islamic Courts Union · xi, xxxi, xxxii, 90, 91, 96, 107, 108, 109, 111, 113, 119, 130, 143, 168, 217, 246
   Islamic Courts Union (ICU) · 91, 119, 168
Islamist · 87, 101, 102, 165, 196, 217, 227, 229, 230, 247
   Islamists · 101, 181
Ismail Warsame · 109
Istakiin · 77, 82, 84

Italy · 157

J

Jail Ogadenia · 184
Jama · 77, 78, 123, 201, 256, 260, 269, 285, 287
    Jama Afguduud · 78
    Jama Dhulun · 77
    Jama Gabayre · 256
    Jama Gabeyre · 260, 269
Jamaame · 236
Jamal Hassan Somalia · 189
    Jamal Said Issa Ibad · 54
Jamhad Gaagaale · 82, 111
    Jamhad Gagaale · 62, 77, 83
Jariiban · xxix
Jazeera · 228, 229, 230, 231, 233, 234, 235, 262
Jeeniqaar · iv, xxiii, xxiv, xxv, 263, 290, 291
Jemis · 108, 109
Jihad · 232
Job Security · viii, 223
Joe · 235, 277, 298
    Joe Kibet · 235
Joint Military Exercise · ix, 273
Jomo Kenyatta Airport · 187
Joseph Stalin · 106
Jowhar · vii, ix, 37, 38, 39, 40, 44, 45, 46, 47, 48, 51, 52, 55, 56, 57, 58, 59, 60, 61, 62, 63, 64, 65, 66, 71, 76, 98, 155, 157, 158, 198, 209, 275, 296
Jubaland · 224, 225, 238, 293
    Jubaland State President · 224
Jubba · 238
    Jubbas · 98
Junction of Sayid Mohamed Abdulle · 201
Justice · viii, 211, 219
    Justified Accord · ix, 276, 277, 298

K

Kalabayr · 51, 52
Kamaal A. Ali · xv
    Kamaal Ahmed Ali · xv
    Kamaal Marjaan Ali · v, xxiv
    Kamaal Murjaan · xv
Karkaar · 107

Katyusha · vii, xix, 120, 145, 155, 167, 172, 175
Katyusha PM · 175
    Katyushas · 167
KDF · xi, 211, 212, 213
Kenya · xi, xxxi, xxxii, 37, 38, 39, 57, 66, 67, 68, 71, 78, 86, 91, 127, 149, 159, 160, 182, 183, 184, 207, 208, 209, 211, 213, 225, 238, 270, 277
    Kenya Defence Forces · 213
    Kenyan · 61, 211, 212, 213, 281
    Kenyan Defence Forces · 212
Kerry · 293
Khaddar Ogaadeen · 79
Khadra Dahir Ige · 80
Kismaayo · 97, 238
    Kismaio · 75, 96, 97, 108, 110, 156
    Kismayo · 212, 213
    Kismayo City · 212
Kiwayu Safari · 211
KM · 122
Koday · 213
    Koday Port · 213
KON · 237
Koole · 112
Korean War · 153

L

Labaatan Jiroow · 79
Labibaar · 47, 48
Lamagalaay · 49
Lamu · 211
Laqanyo · 48
Lasanod · 48
Late Abdulahi Mohamed Abdi Jubba Koolle · 111
    Late Abdullahi Mohamed Ibrahim · 199
    Late Amb. Abdikariim Farah Laqanyo · 55
    Late Captain · 46, 76, 77, 111
    Late Captain Abdirashid Hersi Mohamed · 46, 76, 77
    Late Captain Abdirashid Hersi Mohamed Specail Security · 76
    Late Col. Abdirizak Mohamed Hersi · 46, 76, 77, 110
    Late Col. Ali Abdi Guled · 46, 76, 77
    Late Col. Ali Abdi Guled Duguf Specail Security · 76

Late Col. Jigre Yusuf Ahmed Yey · 76, 77
Late Gen · 75, 110
Late Jigre Yusuf Ahmed · 75
Late Mahad Abdullahi Farah Urdan · 46
Late Maj. Farah Ahmed Dari · 46
Late Mohamed Ali Samatar · 76, 77, 111
Late Saed Mohamed Hersi · 77
Legros · 277, 298
Liban Aliyarow · 198
Lifty U · 294
Lightning · ix, xi, 251, 272, 277
   Lightning Brigade · 277
   Lightning Force · 251
Ligle · 107
Liibaan Ali Yarow · 198
   Liibaan Aliyarow · 198
Long Range Mortar · 153
Lower Jubba · 58, 91, 95, 158, 238
   Lower Shabelle · 98, 151, 209, 255, 256, 261, 262, 285
Lt · 46, 55, 62, 209, 210, 260, 269, 277
   Lt Abdisaid Farah Guure · 62
   Lt Jama Gabeyre · 260
   Lt. Abdi Asis Jinni Irale · 46
   Lt. Abdirahim Muse Mohamed · 277
   Lt. Abdisaid Farah Gure · 46
   Lt. Dayah Abdi Abdile · 55
   Lt. Gen · 209, 210
   Lt. General Silas Ntigurirwa · 210
   Lt. Jama Gabeyre · 269
   Lt. Mohamed Yarisow · 269
Lugey Ali · 63, 81
   Lugey Ali Wagaafe · 63

M

Maanyofuulka · 87
   Maayo Fuulka · 85
Madahey Abdulahi Omar Bootaan · 46
Madam Ayaan Dahir Anshur · 127
   Madam Ayan Dahir Anshur · 125
Madina Hospital · 177
Mahad Doorshe · 46
Mahaddaay · 55, 98
Mahas District Commissioner Mumin Mohamed Halane · 236
Main Supply Routes · xi, 209
Maj. Jeeniqaar · 290, 291, 298

Major · xv, xxv, 51, 77, 82, 209, 210
   Major Abdirahman O · xxv
   Major Commander General Saed Dhere · 51
   Major General Geoffrey Baraba Muheesi · 209
   Major Mohamed Abdiwahid Farah · xv
Maka-Mukarama Avenue · 122
Manaas · 66, 79, 85, 86
Mandera County · 212
MAP · 35
Marchal · 149
Martin Military Hospital · xxviii
Martini Hospital · xxviii
May Gate · 135
Mayaani · 66, 78
Mayor · 173, 189
Medical Unit Training · 265
Medina Hospital · 177
Meghann · 252, 297
Meles · 100, 149, 191, 247
Meles Zenawi · 149, 191, 247
Members of Parliament · 75
Mengistu Haile Mariam · 191
Mercedes Benz · 79
Michael Ondoga · 209
Middle Juba · 212
Middle Shabelle · 55, 56, 58, 59, 60, 62, 75, 210
   Middle Shabelle Governor · 58, 60
MIG · 145, 158
Miido · 213
Mike Andrews · 253
Military Bases · viii, 233
   Military Hospital · 282
   Military Medical Doctor · 111
   Military Mission · 245
   Military Police Base · 121
Millions Facing Starvation · viii, 236
Mine Store · 136
Minister · 47, 61, 63, 97, 98, 99, 100, 148, 192, 208, 224, 247, 284, 292, 293
   Minister Haabsade · 63
   Minister of Defense · 99, 284, 292
   Minister of Defense Col. Hiiraale · 99
   Minister of Defense Hussein Arab Issa · 292
   Minister of Finance · 47

Ministers · 63, 170
Ministers Haabsade · 63
Ministry of Agriculture · 64
Ministry of Defence · xi, 243, 245, 289
Ministry of Defense · 171, 288
Ministry of Finance · 171
Ministry of Foreign Affairs · 192
Ministry of Foreign Affairs of Somalia · 192
misom · 207
Mission Accomplished · ix, 269
MOD · xi, 179, 190, 243, 247, 281
    MoD Mogadishu · 190
    MoD Somalia · 177
MoFA · 163
Mogadishu · iii, iv, v, vi, vii, viii, ix, xxviii, xxix, xxx, xxxi, xxxii, 37, 38, 39, 40, 41, 42, 43, 44, 45, 49, 50, 55, 56, 57, 58, 59, 60, 61, 62, 65, 67, 68, 86, 91, 92, 93, 94, 95, 98, 99, 101, 107, 108, 109, 110, 111, 112, 113, 114, 119, 121, 122, 123, 124, 126, 128, 129, 130, 134, 138, 144, 145, 146, 147, 148, 150, 151, 154, 159, 160, 162, 164, 165, 167, 170, 172, 173, 175, 176, 178, 179, 180, 181, 182, 187, 188, 189, 190, 191, 197, 198, 201, 202, 207, 209, 210, 212, 217, 227, 232, 235, 238, 244, 245, 246, 247, 251, 254, 257, 258, 262, 268, 269, 270, 282, 284, 285, 286, 287, 290
    Mogadishu Airport · 123
    Mogadishu Governor · 189
    Mogadishu Hospital · 59
    Mogadishu I · 122, 202
    Mogadishu International Airport · 202
    Mogadishu Liberation · 201
    Mogadishu Mayor · vii, 173
Mohamed Abdi Afey · 182
    Mohamed Abdiasiis Ispariije · xv
    Mohamed Abdirizak · 83
    Mohamed Adan Kofi · 198
    Mohamed Ali Ghedi · 168
    Mohamed Ali Samatar · 111, 137, 284
    Mohamed Bashir Bidaar · 46
    Mohamed Dhere · 60
    Mohamed Farah · 108
    Mohamed Koreye Ilmi · 54
    Mohamed Maare · xv
    Mohamed Omar Habeeb · 58, 60, 173, 174, 189

Mohamed Omar Samriye · 113
Mohamed Qanyare · 128
Mohamed Somali · xxvii
Mohamed Warsame Darwiish · 110
Mohamed Yare · 83
Mohamud · 138, 200, 232, 251, 275, 292, 293
Mohamud Yaasiin Tumey · 138
Mood Moode · 98, 99
Moode Moode · 98
Moqokori · viii, 230, 231, 232, 233
Mortar M · 153
Moscow · 191
Mpagathi · xxxi, 38
MPs · 37, 79, 84, 85, 128, 129, 170, 222, 276
Mr. Abdirizak Diriye · xv
    Mr. Abdulkafar Yacquub · 84
    Mr. Afgub · 180
    Mr. Ali Mohamed Ghedi · 45
    Mr. Ali Muse Gabayre · 83
    Mr. Ereg · viii, 223
    Mr. Habeb · 61
    Mr. Habeeb · 60, 61
    Mr. Hurre · 86
    Mr. Hussein Aideed · 127
    Mr. Major · 84
    Mr. President · 59, 76, 113, 122, 188
    Mr. Said Mohamed Hersi · 84
Mshelia · 236, 237
MSRs · xi, 209
MU · 254, 291
Mubaarak · 267
Mudug · 43, 56, 75, 91, 98, 107, 134, 198
Muhammad Omar Habeb · 61
Mujaahidiin · 97
    Mujahedin Youth Movement · 247
    Mujahideen · 247, 255
Mukhtar · 163, 164
    Muktar Robow · 224
Muslim · 226, 232, 273
Mustahil · 53
    Mustaxiil · 53, 55
    Mustaxil · 55
Myers · 252, 297

N

Nairobi · 36, 37, 38, 39, 40, 41, 46, 56, 57, 60, 61, 68, 71, 86, 95, 102, 155, 159, 187, 188, 296

Name Danab · ix, 272
Nanyuki · 277
National Army · vii, 47, 157, 170, 197, 218, 243, 246, 251, 252, 253, 254, 272, 281, 284, 285, 286, 287, 288
National Army Payment · vii, 170
National Reconciliation Conference · 127, 270
Naval Facilities Engineering Command Atlantic · 253
Navy SEALs · 251
NDF · 231
News · 56, 228, 229, 230, 296
NGO · 156
  NGOs · 151, 155
Nigeria · 49, 207
North Frontier District · 281
North Mogadishu · 166
Now Abiy Ahmed · 191
Nuclear Science · 192
Nugaal · 107
Nur Hassan Gutale · 166

O

OCHA · 147, 156
October Zope Suicide Attack · viii, 227
Odawa · 283
Offensive Strategy · vi, 98
Office · vii, xx, xxix, 121, 146, 156, 172, 198, 288
Officer Abdirizak Garacad · 112
Officer Koole · 112
Ogaden · vii, xi, 144, 152, 184
Ogadenia · 184, 281
Omar · xxvii, 66, 85, 235, 290, 291, 293
  Omar Atu · 235
  Omar Dhegad · 66
  Omar Warsame Adde · xxvii
One Employed · vii, 154
ONLF · vii, xi, 144, 184
Only Uganda · 207
Operation Linda Nchi · 211
Operation Preparation Started · ix, 265
Operation Restore Hope · 270
  Operation Sledge Hammer · 212
Organization · xii, 159, 236
Oromo Liberation Front (OLF) · 144
Other Danab · 261

Our Commanders · 53
Our VIP Protection · 135

P

Pakistan · 201
  Pakistan Taliban · 201
Palace · 64, 75, 81, 83, 121, 284
Parallel Traditional Leaders · viii, 222
Parliament · 67, 75, 77, 80, 121, 135, 161, 169, 224, 292
  Parliament Sharif Hasan Sheikh Adan · 292
Paul D · 244, 246
Paul Williams · 252
Peacekeeping Operations · xxxii
Performance Evaluation System · vii, 179
Permanent Government · 159
Perspective · iii, vi, 94
PhD · xv
Photo · 294
Pioneer · 259
PKM · 51, 64, 135
Players · vii, 152
PM · ix, 113, 267, 269
Police · 79, 186, 187, 188, 257, 258
Police Forces · 186, 187
Power Sharing System · viii
President · v, vii, viii, xx, xxi, xxviii, xxix, xxxii, 37, 38, 39, 40, 41, 43, 45, 47, 49, 51, 52, 54, 56, 57, 58, 61, 62, 65, 69, 75, 76, 77, 84, 97, 107, 110, 114, 121, 125, 127, 128, 130, 136, 137, 150, 159, 164, 168, 172, 180, 184, 187, 188, 189, 192, 196, 197, 198, 208, 224, 238, 245, 270, 275, 284, 285, 288, 292, 293, 294
  President Abdiqasim Hassan · 130
  President Abdiqasim Salad Hassan · 294
  President Abdulahi Farabadan · 294
  President Abdulahi Yusuf Ahmed · 294
  President Abdullahi Yusuf · v, xxi, xxxii, 38, 40, 41, 43, 45, 47, 49, 51, 56, 57, 61, 69, 84, 107, 110, 125, 187, 188, 189, 192, 198, 238, 245, 285
  President Abdullahi Yusuf Ahmed · xxxii, 56, 61, 84, 107, 110, 125, 187, 188, 189, 238, 245
  President Ade Muse · 45, 107
  President Farmajo · 180
  President George · 184, 270

President Hassan Sheikh Mohamud · 275, 292, 293
President Mohamed Siyaad Barre · 58
President Obama · 159
President of Jubaland State Ahmad Mohamed Islaan · 293
President of Puntland Abdiweli Ali Gas · 293
President Sharif Sheikh Ahmed · 284
President Sheikh Sharif · 150, 159, 197, 292
President Sheikh Sharif Sheikh Ahmed · 197, 292
President Sheikh Shariif Sheikh Ahmed · 293
President Siad Barre · xxviii
President Yusuf · vii, 37, 39, 61, 65, 127, 187
Presidential · 60, 66, 75, 80, 81, 83, 84, 109, 113, 121, 124, 172, 189, 284
Presidential Exhibition · 121
Presidential Guard · 172
Presidential Guard Commander Col Abdirizak Mohamed Hirsi · 172
Presidential Palace · 60, 66, 75, 80, 81, 83, 84, 109, 113, 121, 124, 284
Presidents Abdikasim Hassan · 126
Prime Minister · 37, 43, 58, 61, 65, 75, 99, 100, 110, 112, 113, 121, 122, 128, 148, 149, 208, 247, 292, 293
Prime Minister Abdiwali M · 292
Prime Minister Ali Ghedi · 112
Prime Minister Ali Mohamed Geedi · 58
Prime Minister Ali Mohamed Ghedi · 37, 43, 99, 110, 112, 122
Prime Minister Ali Muhammad Gedi · 37, 61
Prime Minister Ghedi · 65, 75, 113
Prime Minister Meles Zenawi · 148, 149
Prime Minister Omar Abdirashid Ali Sharmarke · 293
Protocol Officer · 129
Puntland · v, xxiii, xxix, xxx, 40, 42, 43, 45, 47, 48, 51, 53, 54, 56, 65, 70, 86, 95, 107, 109, 112, 125, 149, 158, 290, 293
Puntland Defense Force · xxx, 43, 47
Puntland Defense Force (PDF) · xxx
Puntland Defense Forces · 43
Puntland President · 43, 45, 51
Puntland President Ade Muse · 51
Puntland President General Ado Muse · 43
Puntland State · 70, 107
Puntland State of Somalia · 107
Puntlandes · 290, 298

Q

Qaeda · 101, 164, 211, 217, 231, 252, 255, 256
Qaida · xxi
Qanyare · 129
Qoryoley · 259
Qurac Gafow · 47
Qurac Joomo · 55
QuraJome · 98

R

Raage · 232
Raaskambooni · 91, 98, 99, 165
Radio Jowhar · 61
Rapid Response Forces Commander · xxx
Red Sea · 152
Reda · 234
Reestablishment of Danab Special Force · ix, 251
Reinstitution of Danab Special Force · ix, 272
Religious Affairs · 224
Republic · 211, 281
Republic of Djibouti · 281
Restoration of Peace · 91, 92, 160
Reuters · 182, 229, 230
Revenue · viii, 219, 267
Revenue Collection · viii, 219
Rosatom · 191, 192, 297
RPG · 51, 64, 121, 135, 136, 137, 199, 284
RPGs · 268
Ruqiyo Omar Warsame · xxviii
Russia · 191
Russia Today · 191
Russian · 106, 191, 192
Russian Red Army · 106
Rwanda · xxx

S

Sabiib · 252
Saed Dhere · 52

Saed Talohun · 175
   Saeed Talohun · 176
   Said Talohun · 176
Safar Nooleys · 99
Said Barre · 272
Said Mohamed Hirsi · 62, 81
Salah · v, ix, xviii, 285, 286, 287
Salary · vii, 170
Saleban Abdille Khalaf · 110
Saliid · 107
Saliinge · 81, 84
Sanaag · 107
Sanwayne Ali Hashi Geele · 46
Sargudud · 136, 137
Sayid Mohamed · 123, 201
Scansom Publishers · 84, 85, 147, 192, 296
SEALs · 251
Second World War · 106
Secret US Base · 252, 297
Secretary · 38, 159, 160, 189, 253, 293, 297
   Secretary of State · 159, 293
   Secretary of State Hillary Rodham Clinton · 293
   Secretary of State John Kerry · 293
   Secretay Cluntin · 159
Sector · 209, 210, 212, 258, 259
   Sector Commander Brig · 209
   Sector One · 209, 258, 259
   Sector One Battalion · 259
   Sector One Commander Brig · 209
Security Council · 165, 207, 211, 228
See Effective SNA System · ix, 288
Seefta Banaanka · 98
Seoul · 92, 93, 101, 156, 157, 296
Serbian Military Technical Institute · 153
Shaaweeye · 113
Shabaab · viii, ix, xi, xvii, xix, xxi, xxv, xxxii, 95, 101, 150, 152, 154, 159, 161, 165, 172, 173, 175, 178, 179, 180, 181, 189, 190, 196, 197, 198, 200, 202, 207, 209, 210, 211, 212, 213, 217, 218, 219, 220, 221, 222, 223, 224, 225, 226, 227, 228, 229, 230, 231, 232, 233, 234, 235, 236, 237, 238, 243, 246, 251, 252, 253, 254, 255, 256, 257, 258, 260, 261, 262, 263, 264, 266, 267, 268, 269, 274, 275, 276, 297
   Shabaab Blockades Exacerbates Humanaitarian Crisis · viii, 235
   SHABAAB Hilton Hotel · 238

Shabaab Islamist · 211, 229
Shabaab Traditional Leaders · viii, 223
Shabab · 165, 166, 182, 228, 229, 230, 231, 233, 234, 247, 275, 284, 290, 297
Shangani · 174, 201
Shanta-jid · 79
Sharia · 92, 222
   Sharia Law · 222
Sharif Hassan Sheikh Adam · 79
Sharif Sheikh Ahmed · 197, 198, 217, 284, 292
Sharmarke · 293
Sharrock · 265, 266
Sheikh · viii, 70, 84, 144, 159, 196, 197, 198, 217, 232, 233, 284, 290, 291, 292, 293, 298
   Sheikh Ali Mohamud Raage · 232
   Sheikh Door Moalim Abdirahman · 84
   Sheikh Hassan Dahir Aweys · 144
   Sheikh Hassan Yakub · 233
   Sheikh Omar · 290, 291, 298
   Sheikh Sharif Election · viii, 196
Shilaabo · 47
Shilabo · 44, 47
Shukri Wayrah · 78
   Shukri Wayrax · 82
Siad · xxiii, xxvii, xxviii, 93
   Siad Barre · xxiii, xxvii, 93
Silas Ntigurirwa · 209, 210
Siliinge · 62, 77
Siraaje · 76, 111, 137
SNA · vii, ix, x, xi, xvii, xix, xxi, xxx, xxxii, xxxiii, 38, 41, 42, 56, 57, 64, 68, 69, 75, 96, 107, 114, 135, 148, 150, 153, 158, 162, 163, 165, 166, 167, 169, 170, 171, 172, 173, 175, 176, 177, 179, 180, 181, 185, 191, 201, 202, 203, 207, 217, 228, 229, 234, 243, 244, 245, 246, 247, 253, 254, 257, 258, 259, 260, 261, 263, 264, 265, 266, 268, 271, 273, 275, 276, 281, 282, 283, 284, 285, 287, 288, 289, 290, 298
   SNA Database · 288
   SNA General Staff · 243
   SNA HRM · 288
   SNA Operations · 207
   SNA TFG · 173
Snipers · 244
Somali · iii, vii, ix, xi, xvii, xviii, xxii, xxiii, xxiv, xxv, xxvii, xxviii, xxix, xxx, xxxi, 36, 38, 39, 42, 44, 47, 48-50, 53, 54, 57, 64, 65, 67, 69, 80, 86, 87, 90, 91, 99-102, 107, 112, 114,

119, 120, 124, 127, 129, 130, 137, 143, 146, 147, 149, 151-156, 159, 160-165, 168-174, 176-178, 180-192, 197, 198, 201-203, 207-209, 211, 217, 218, 221, 222, 226, 228-232, 234, 237, 243-247, 251-254, 257, 258, 260, 261, 270-272, 274-277, 281, 282, 284, 286, 288, 291, 296, 298
Somali Army · xxviii
Somali Civil War · 151
Somali Danab Brigade · 251
Somali Danab Special Force · 277
Somali Danab Special Forces · 277
Somali French · 281
Somali General · 99, 164, 286
Somali Generals · 99, 286
Somali Girl · vii, 177
Somali Government · xxxi, 87, 114, 153, 164, 218, 222
Somali Government Forces · 153
Somali Immigration Authority · 198
Somali Intelligence · 258
Somali Military Force · 185
Somali National Army · xi, xviii, 44, 53, 64, 127, 154, 162, 165, 197, 218, 243, 246, 251, 252, 253, 254, 272, 284, 286, 288
Somali National Army (SNA) · 243, 253
Somali National Army (SNA) Danab Brigade · 253
Somali National Reconciliation Conference · 49, 127, 270
Somali Ogaden National Liberation Front · 119
Somali PM · 100
Somali Police · vii, 67, 185, 186, 187, 188, 189, 257, 258
Somali Police Commissioner · 186, 187, 188, 189
Somali Police Force · vii, 67, 185, 186, 187, 188, 189, 257
Somali Police Force Commissioner General Ali Madobe · 67
Somali Police Forces · 185, 186, 187, 188
Somali Presidency · 162, 189, 202
Somali President · 173, 208, 275
Somali President Hassan Sheikh Mohamud · 275
Somali Prime Minister Ali Mohamed Gedi · 38
Somali Republic · 47

Somali Salvation Democratic Front (SSDF) · xxvii
Somali Security Forces · 209
Somali SNA · 164, 176
Somali Soldier · ix, 282
Somali Special Force · ix, xxx, 251, 254, 270, 271
Somali Special Forces · ix, 254, 270, 271
Somalia · iii, iv, vi-ix, xi, xiii, xvii, xix, xxi, xxii, xxiii, xxv, xxix, xxx, xxxi, xxxii, 35-44, 47-50, 53, 54, 56-64, 68, 69, 76, 77, 79, 81, 86, 87, 91-98, 100-102, 107, 108, 110, 114, 119, 121-124, 126-128, 130, 135, 138, 143-157, 159-171, 173, 176, 17-186, 188-193, 197-200, 202, 203, 207-212, 217, 218, 222-225, 227-238, 242-247, 251-254, 256-258, 265, 269-273, 276, 281, 282, 284-288, 290, 291, 293, 294, 296-298
Somalia (AMISOM) · xxxii, 228, 246, 247
Somalia (ATMIS) · 207
Somalia Francois F · 294
Somalia National Army · xxx, xxxii, 285, 286, 287
Somalia National Army (SNA) · xxxii
Somalia Police Force · 79
Somaliland · 38, 47, 54, 193, 286
Somalis · xxiv, 43, 50, 69, 87, 96, 112, 126, 149, 151, 161, 162, 170, 177, 181, 182, 191, 197, 222, 232, 236, 237, 247, 251, 271
Sool · 43, 107
South Central Somalia · xxx, 50, 91, 190, 191, 231
South Korea · 92, 93, 101, 156, 157, 296
South Western Somalia · 228
Southern European Task Force · 277
Southwest President Sharif Hasan Sheikh Adan · 293
Southwest Somalia · 235
Southwest State Abdulaziz Hassan Mohamed · 237
Soviet Union · xii, 152
Speaker Sharif Hassan Sheikh Aden · 57, 62
Special Force · xi, 231, 251, 254, 269, 270, 271, 272, 291
Special Forces Danab · 272
Special Presidential Guard · xix
Special Security · 76
SSDF · xi, xxvii, xxviii, xxix, 53, 58
Stadium Mogadishu · 130

Stalingrad · 106, 107
State House · 81
Sudan · 49, 57, 150, 198
Support Our Troops · 251, 297
Supreme Islamic Council of Somalia · 87
Sureer · 47, 65, 70
Sureer Abdi Firin · 47
Sureer Abdi Firrin · 70
Surer Abdi Firin · 65
Surrounding Mystery · v, 75
Sweden · 84, 85, 147, 192, 296
SYL · vii, 177
SYL Hotel · vii, 177
Symmetric and Asymmetric Warfare · ix, 273

T

Tactics Employed · vii, 154
Take Off · ix, 266
Tanzania · 277
Terrorist Attack Happened · v, 81
Tesfay · 173, 176, 286
TFG · v, vi, vii, viii, xi, xix, xxi, xxxi, xxxii, 37, 38, 39, 40, 41, 42, 43, 44, 47, 48, 49, 50, 56, 57, 59, 60, 64, 65, 67, 68, 69, 70, 71, 86, 87, 88, 90, 91, 93, 94, 95, 96, 97, 98, 99, 100, 101, 102, 109, 110, 112, 113, 114, 120, 126, 129, 130, 143, 144, 145, 146, 147, 148, 149, 150, 151, 152, 153, 154, 155, 157, 158, 159, 160, 161, 162, 163, 164, 165, 168, 170, 171, 175, 176, 178, 179, 180, 181, 189, 190, 191, 196, 200, 202, 203, 231, 243, 244, 246, 247, 281, 282, 287, 296
TFG Before Ethiopian Invasion · vii, 157
TFG Before Their Fight Against ARPCT · vi, 94
TFG Commanders · vi, 96
TFG Democratic Efforts Vilified · vi, 95
TFG Democratic Process Distorted · vi, 149
TFG During Ethiopian Invasion · vii, 158
TFG Key Financial Resources · v, 70
TFG Preparing · 37, 38, 39, 296
TFG Prime Minister Nur Hassan Hussein and TFG Presiden · 120
TFG SNA · 163
TFG Strategy Deployed · v, 91
Tigrayan · 174

Tiyeeglow · 65, 85, 98
TM · 228
TNG · 127
Tobon Tolaale · 70
Togdheer Nugaal And Sool · 134
Toyota · 79, 83, 128, 282
   Toyota Land Cruiser · 79
Toyota Surf · 282
Transitional Federal Government · xi, xix, xxxi, 37, 38, 61, 86, 96, 97, 111, 120, 159, 198, 199, 243, 244
   Transitional Federal Government (TFG) · xxxi, 61, 120, 243
Transitional Government · 159, 246
Transitional National Government (TNG) · 127
Troop Contributing Countries · 209
Turkey · xxx, 191, 261
   Turkey Military · 261
Turkish SOM Military Academy · 282
TurkishSom · 284
Türkiye · 257, 258, 261

U

Uganda · xii, xxx, xxxii, 49, 57, 121, 207, 208, 209, 210, 211, 218, 243, 244, 245, 246, 247
   Uganda and Burundi · 207, 211, 218
   Uganda and Burundi AMISOM · 211
   Uganda and Ethiopia · 208
   Uganda and Somalia · 57
   Uganda Defence Force · 244
   Uganda House · 121
Ugandan · 173, 197, 200, 208, 209, 210, 245
   Ugandan and Ethiopian · 197
UIC · 144, 145, 162, 164
UK · iv, 145
Ukraine · 237
UN · xii, 38, 40, 86, 93, 95, 144, 147, 153, 155, 156, 196, 211, 228, 236, 237
   UN Agencies · 237
   UN Charter · 211
   UN Food and Agriculture Organization (FAO) · 236
   UN Monitoring Group · 144
   UN Security Council · 153, 228
UNDP · 64

United Nations Security Council · xii, 93, 207, 211
   United Nations Security Council Resolution · xii, 207, 211
United States · ix, xii, 50, 91, 94, 102, 126, 157, 159, 160, 161, 184, 185, 253, 254, 298
   United States and Somalia · 253
   United States Increases Security Assistance · ix, 253, 254, 298
   United States Increases Security Assistance Through Construction of SNA Bases · 254, 298
Unlike General Turyare · 198
UNMEE · 145
UNSC · 230
UNSCR · xii, 42, 93
US · ix, xxxiii, 56, 91, 92, 100, 101, 129, 145, 147, 154, 160, 161, 184, 185, 251, 252, 254, 255, 256, 261, 263, 265, 266, 267, 269, 270, 271, 272, 273, 274, 275, 290, 291
   US Agency · 147
   US Army Col. Nelson · 271
   US Army Role · ix, 251
   US Assistant Secretary of State · 184
   US Military Expertise · ix, 271
   US Officer · 265
   US President George H · 270
   US Rangers · 270
USA · vi, vii, ix, xii, xx, 39, 92, 96, 102, 157, 159, 160, 224, 246, 251, 253, 257, 258, 259, 265, 269, 273, 286
   USA Efforts Devoted · ix, 269
   USA Position · vii, 160
USAID · 191
USC · xxix
USSR · vi, xii, 96, 157, 281
   USSR Military Academies · vi, 96

V

VBID · 82
VBIED · xii, 257
Vietnam · 153
Villa · vi, vii, xix, xxx, xxxii, 42, 50, 54, 58, 60, 85, 110, 121, 122, 123, 124, 125, 126, 127, 128, 129, 135, 138, 162, 164, 167, 170, 172, 173, 176, 177, 178, 180, 181, 189, 197, 198, 199, 200, 202, 238, 276, 284
   Villa Baido · 85, 177

Villa Baidoa · 85
Villa Hargeisa · 121
Villa Somalia · vi, vii, xix, xxx, xxxii, 42, 50, 54, 58, 60, 110, 121, 122, 123, 124, 125, 126, 127, 128, 129, 135, 138, 162, 164, 167, 170, 172, 173, 176, 177, 178, 180, 181, 197, 198, 199, 200, 202, 238, 276, 284
VIP Protection · 129, 180, 197, 199, 200
VOA · 165, 166, 228, 229, 230, 297
   VOA News · 165, 228, 229, 230, 297
   Voice of America · 165, 297
Volgograd · 106

W

Waajid · 65, 66, 98
Wagas · 172
Waharey · 176
Wajed · 85, 108
Wajid · 86, 237
War Crimes · 35, 87, 91, 94, 96, 101, 102, 114, 119, 126, 149, 150, 157, 160, 184, 202, 203, 282, 287, 296
Wardheer · xxviii, 44, 45, 47
Warsame · iv, xxv, xxvii, 78, 98, 230, 290
Warsaw · 152, 281
Washington · 91, 120, 157, 160, 161, 184, 185, 251, 252
Western and Somali · vii, xix, xxxii, 143, 179
Williams and Hussein Yusuf Ali · 244, 246
World War II · 106, 153

X

Xan Rice · 86, 102, 296

Y

Yalahow · 129
Yaqshid · 202
Yassin Khamriile and Dahir Mohamed Hersi · 63
Yemen · xx
Yohanes · 171, 286
Yonsei University · 92, 93, 101, 156, 157, 296
Yoobsan · 202
Yoole · 78, 82
Yoole Abdi Guled · 82

www.ingramcontent.com/pod-product-compliance
Lightning Source LLC
Chambersburg PA
CBHW052013070526
44584CB00016B/1729